CASE STUDIES IN
CULTURAL ANTHROPOLOGY

GENERAL EDITORS
George and Louise Spindler
STANFORD UNIVERSITY

THE PUEBLO INDIANS OF NORTH AMERICA

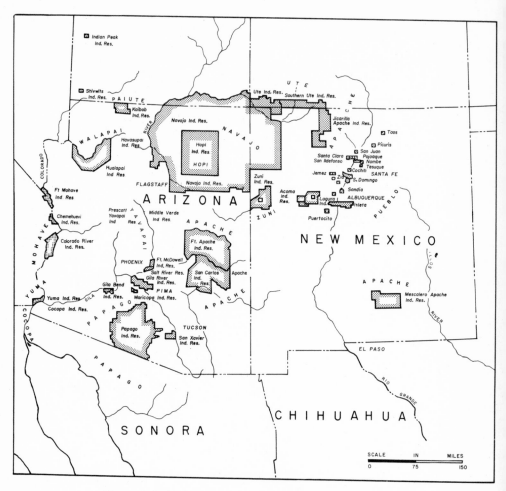

Figure 1. Indian reservations today in the United States Southwest.

THE PUEBLO INDIANS
OF NORTH AMERICA

By
EDWARD P. DOZIER
University of Arizona

HOLT, RINEHART AND WINSTON, INC.
NEW YORK   CHICAGO   SAN FRANCISCO   ATLANTA
DALLAS   MONTREAL   TORONTO   LONDON   SYDNEY

COPYRIGHT ACKNOWLEDGMENTS

Photographs reproduced courtesy of the following: The Smithsonian Office of Anthropology, Bureau of American Ethnology Collection—cover photo (Zuni Pueblo), pp. 11, 12, 15, 20, 51, 74, 111, 123, 135, 136, 146, 162, 163, 173, 180; The Museum of New Mexico, Santa Fe—pp. 13, 48, 66, 126, 142, 143, 149, 161, 164, 166, 168, 175, 183, 200.

The author wishes to thank the following copyright holders for permission to reprint extracts from their listed works:

The University of Chicago Press and the author for *Social Organization of the Western Pueblos*, by Fred Eggan. Copyright © 1950 by the University of Chicago Press.

E. P. Dutton & Co. and Grace V. Collier, Executrix of the Estate of John Collier, Sr., for *Patterns and Ceremonials of the Indians of the Southwest*. Copyright © 1949 by E. P. Dutton & Co.

Harper & Row, Publishers, for *Variations in Value Orientations*, by Florence Kluckhohn and Fred L. Stodtbeck. Copyright © 1961 by Harper & Row, Publishers.

Houghton Mifflin Company and Routledge & Kegan Paul Ltd., for *Patterns of Culture*, by Ruth Benedict. Copyright 1934 by Houghton Mifflin Company.

The University of Oklahoma Press and the author for *Pueblo Warriors*, by Oakah L. Jones. Copyright © 1966 by the University of Oklahoma Press.

The University of Washington Press and the author for "A Tri-ethnic Trap: the Spanish Americans in Taos," by John J. Bodine. The American Ethnological Society. Copyright © 1968 by the University of Washington Press.

for YIYAH and MARIANNE

Foreword

About the Series

These case studies in cultural anthropology are designed to bring to students, in beginning and intermediate courses in the social sciences, insights into the richness and complexity of human life as it is lived in different ways and in different places. They are written by men and women who have lived in the societies they write about and who are professionally trained as observers and interpreters of human behavior. The authors are also teachers, and in writing their books they have kept the students who will read them foremost in their minds. It is our belief that when an understanding of ways of life very different from one's own is gained, abstractions and generalizations about social structure, cultural values, subsistence techniques, and the other universal categories of human social behavior become meaningful.

About the Author

Edward P. Dozier is a native of Santa Clara Pueblo, New Mexico. He was born and spent his early years in the pueblo where he still maintains a home and is an enrolled member.

Dr. Dozier specialized in American Indian studies and the mountain peoples of Northern Luzon, Philippines. He is the author of *The Hopi-Tewa of Arizona* (1954); *Mountain Arbiters—The Changing Life of a Philippine Hill People* (1966); and has contributed to two previous case studies to this series: *Hano: A Tewa Community in Arizona* (1966), and *The Kalinga of Northern Luzon, Philippines* (1967). He has published numerous articles in linguistic and anthropological journals.

Dr. Dozier received his B.A. and M.A. from the University of New Mexico and his Ph.D. from the University of California at Los Angeles. He has taught at the University of Oregon, Northwestern University, and since 1960 has been a professor of anthropology at the University of Arizona. In 1958–1959 he was a Fellow at the Center for Advanced Studies in the Behavioral Sciences at Stanford, California. In his research work he has held a Senior Postdoctoral Fellowship from the National Science Foundation and in his sabbatical year (1967–1968) he was a Guggenheim Fellow. He is vice president of the Association on American Indian Affairs, a Fellow of the American Association for the Advancement of Science, the American Anthropological Association, and the American Sociological Association.

About the Book

This case study on the Pueblo Indians of North America is unique in this series. It is not about a single people and their culture but about a group of related peoples and their adaptation through time to their changing physical, socioeconomic, and political environments. The Pueblo Indian cultures of the Southwest have played a most significant role in the history of their region, and have been of special significance to anthropologists of at least four generations. The space limitations usual to case studies in this series have been lifted so as to allow for an adequate expansion of detail necessary to the analysis of the three periods of time considered in this unusual study.

GEORGE AND LOUISE SPINDLER
General Editors

Phlox, Wisconsin
November 1969

Introduction by Fred Eggan

The peoples and cultures of the American Southwest have a perennial fascination for scholars and laymen alike. In few areas of the world do we find groups who have maintained a distinctive way of life that can be traced for two millennia—and more. During this long period changes have occurred as a result of contacts with Mexico and neighboring regions; later the coming of the Spaniards and the Americans forced the Pueblo Indians and their neighbors to adapt to the pressures of superior force. But the Pueblos have been able to control these changes in considerable measure, in part by erecting a wall around their ceremonial life; and their persistence in the midst of modern America offers us an opportunity to study basic anthropological problems as well as a glimpse into the archaic past.

The Pueblo Indians have been under study for at least a century and there has been an outpouring of literature on the Southwest, both technical and popular, as well as a number of important syntheses: A. V. Kidder's *Introduction to the Study of Southwestern Archaeology* (1924), E. C. Parsons' *Pueblo Indian Religion* (1939), F. Eggan's *Social Organization of the Western Pueblos* (1950), and several others. The reader may well ask what can be said that is new?

First, and perhaps most important, is the fact that the author is himself a Pueblo Indian and can provide us with an "inside" view of native life and culture. Secondly, the data available on the Pueblo Indians and their neighbors has greatly increased during the last two decades. New archeological data have filled in most of the gaps in our chronologies and now provide a firmer foundation for the reconstruction of southwestern culture history and for the study of cultural process. In addition, a large number of new documents on eighteenth and nineteenth century developments has provided the basis for ethno-historical interpretations that go beyond conjectural history and give us a more realistic view of the accommodations of both Spaniards and Indians to one another, as well as their alliance against the Plains Indians and the Navajo and Apache.

Along with the deepening of the historical dimension, there has been a resurgence of interest in the Eastern Pueblos and their culture. Leslie A. White's series of studies on the Keresan-speaking pueblos has recently been supplemented by Charles Lange's detailed account of Cochiti Pueblo and Robin Fox's *The Keresan Bridge* (1967), in which he utilizes insights from modern social anthropology to propose a new interpretation of the position and role of the Keres in relation to the Eastern and Western Pueblos. Our knowledge of the Tanoan-speaking pueblos has also been enlarged, particularly through the researches of

Alfonso Ortiz, a young Tewa-speaking anthropologist from San Juan, whose study of Tewa world view is currently in press. The Tiwa-speaking villages along the Rio Grande are still little known however, and some, such as Sandia, not at all.

These new data and the methods and procedures of modern cultural anthropology and linguistics have provided Dr. Dozier with the materials for a new and more inclusive synthesis and interpretation of the entire Pueblo area. Here it is possible to see rebellion and accommodation, acculturation and continuity, social change and institutional persistence—each occurring in intelligible contexts. What Dr. Dozier's account makes clear is the necessity of viewing the Pueblo area as a whole—even though it is convenient to deal with linguistic or regional groups for certain purposes.

The reader will find this volume the most satisfying and comprehensive account of the Pueblo Indians that has yet appeared. It presents a better balanced view of Pueblo-Spanish relationships and provides a more adequate rationale for the differential accommodation that occurred in the eastern and western regions. Currently new developments are bringing about changes in American Indian communities which may have far-reaching consequences and Indian anthropologists will be in a much better position to record and assess them. We look forward to future contributions from Dr. Dozier and his colleagues.

FRED EGGAN
University of Chicago

Preface

The information contained in this case study is the result of a lifetime spent among the Pueblos. Although I was born and grew up in the pueblo of Santa Clara and still consider it my home, I have lived in or visited every village small and large from the Hopi towns of lower and upper Moencopi in Arizona to the double apartment buildings of Taos Pueblo in northern New Mexico. Language differences among some of the Pueblo groups are extreme, but shared social and ceremonial patterns are many. Such shared characteristics allow for understanding and frequent interaction. The Pueblos are great travelers and they are generous hosts to visitors. There is free exchange of social and cultural information so long as there is no threat to individual or village independence. Pueblo Indians cherish individual freedom and will not surrender it for a unity beyond the single pueblo village. Community life is geared to give each pueblo a highly integrated organization. The survival of the Pueblos as viable, distinct villages is partly the result of such unity. Rigid control mechanisms and equally rigid surveillance procedures have made it possible for the Pueblos to endure in spite of corrosive and divisive pressures, such as droughts, epidemic diseases and Euro-American contact.

My Pueblo work has received the generous assistance of a number of institutions, foundations, and individuals. Over the years I have received a number of summer faculty grants-in-aid from the American Council of Learned Societies, and the Social Science Research Council. During my sabbatical year (1967–68) I was fortunate to receive a John Simon Guggenheim Fellowship, and the National Science Foundation assisted my field studies. Miss Doris Duke and the American Indian Oral History Project have also contributed funds for the collection of oral history materials. During the final stages of organizing and writing this study I received generous support from the Rockefeller Foundation. The faculty and staff of the Department of Anthropology and the Arizona State Museum have provided the use of facilities and extended many other courtesies as well. To all of these foundations and institutions I express my thanks and appreciation.

I also thank the many individuals with whom I have discussed or who have read an initial draft of this study: Drs. Sophie D. Aberle, Fred Eggan, William Longacre, Paul S. Martin, Alfonso Ortiz, Eric Reed, Albert Schroeder, and Frances Swadesh. While I value the comments of these colleagues, none of these people are to be held responsible for the shortcomings of this book. I have profited from their criticisms, but I have not always followed suggestions. A special note of thanks goes to Mrs. Joyce Rehm who drew the maps. The Pueblo Indians who have contributed either directly or indirectly to this study are so many that it would be impossible to single them out individually. My bad temper and moods during the collection and writing of this data have often been vented on my family. They have been patient, understanding, and good-natured. I am grateful that family and home are still intact.

EDWARD P. DOZIER

Contents

Introduction

THIS IS AN ACCOUNT of a people who have preserved a distinctive way of life for many years. Known as the Pueblos in historic times, these Indians stemmed from two great cultural traditions in the past—the Mogollon and the Anasazi. Both of these prehistoric traditions were in turn rooted in an ancient tradition, called the desert culture by the archeologists, which goes back more than 10,000 years. The Pueblos are thus the genetic and cultural descendants of people who settled in the southwestern part of the North American continent many millennia before the time of Christ.

The ancestors of the Pueblos were hunters and gatherers. From 2000 to 3000 years before Christ, they had, however, added domesticated corn (maize) to their diet; by approximately 300 B.C. they were living in sedentary villages in an economy based on the typical New World triumvirate of plants—maize (corn), beans, and squash. Known for the excellence of their basketry products in the early sedentary periods, the Pueblos soon shifted to the manufacture of complex forms of pottery. Architecture became elaborate, with excellent masonry, in building two-, three-, and even four-storied apartmentlike dwellings and large circular and rectangular ceremonial structures. During this period the Pueblos employed flood-farming techniques, and in the larger towns used extensive systems of ditches, dikes, and canals to deflect the waters of small streams into planted fields.

Pueblo culture attained its widest distribution in area during the fourteenth century when it covered vast portions of the southwestern United States. This was the period when the spectacular towns of the Mesa Verde region, in what is now southwestern Colorado, were at their peak. Such towns and sites as Aztec and Chaco Canyon in northwestern New Mexico were developed during this classical Pueblo period. Other impressive sites simultaneously occupied were those of Canyon de Chelley and Kayenta in northeastern Arizona and the Point of Pines area in east central Arizona. To this period also belong the extensive sites of the Mimbres region in west central New Mexico.

In the process of widespread land distribution during the height of their cultural development, the Pueblos enveloped other traditions like the irrigation-based Hohokam culture of the southern Arizona desert region. Then abruptly toward the end of the fourteenth century and the beginning of the fifteenth, there was widespread abandonment of former flourishing towns and villages. The Mesa Verde, Chaco, Hohokam, and other impressive sites were abandoned and the entire

1

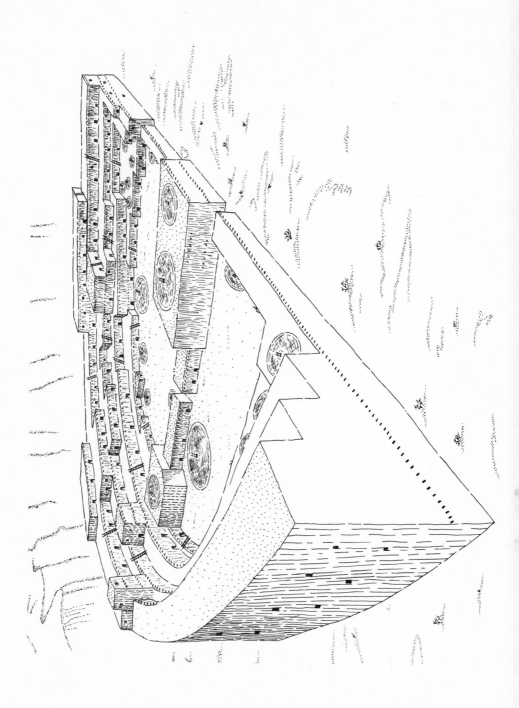

area of Pueblo culture retracted to sites along the Rio Grande and isolated villages in the area of modern Acoma, Zuni, and the Hopi villages.

The reasons for these abandonments are not clear. Explanations based on nomadic enemy raids, intertribal warfare, intratribal social dissensions, severe drought conditions accompanied by deep arroyo cutting that made flood farming and irrigation practices difficult or impossible, have been proposed to account for the abandonments and shrinkage of the Pueblo culture area. Most anthropologists lean toward drought and arroyo cutting as the most suitable explanation.

By the end of the fourteenth century the remaining Pueblos were living in the sites where they were encountered by the first Spanish expeditions in the sixteenth century. The Pueblo villages west of the Rio Grande valley were existing largely by flood-farming techniques like those of the classical Pueblo period a century or two before. Those along the Rio Grande, however, built rather complex canals and diverting ditches, either from the Rio Grande or streams tributary to this big river. Except for the Hohokam in the desert regions of Arizona several centuries before, none of the southwestern prehistoric peoples had really exploited the potential of irrigating from large, permanently flowing rivers. The Rio Grande Pueblos, however, commenced a way of life that promised progression to another cultural peak.

Soon after the establishment of the Pueblos in the sites where they were found by the Spaniards, another people—a group of nomadic wanderers—appeared on the scene. These were ancestors of the Indians known in later times as Apaches and Navahos. They arrived probably no more than a century or two before the Spaniards. As a people without agriculture and without permanent habitations, they began immediately to live in a kind of symbiotic relationship with the Pueblos. When the Spaniards arrived, the Apachean peoples nearest the sedentary pueblos had settled down to an agricultural way of life. This peaceful and symbiotic pattern of sedentary living was to change in the next century or two, however.

The first major expedition into the Pueblo country was that of Francisco Vasquez de Coronado. Two important factors are associated with Coronado's entry: one was the sheer size and impressiveness of the party (five Franciscan missionaries and several hundred mailed and armed horsemen accompanied by Indian servants); the second—an unfortunate omen of things to come—was that the Tiwa pueblos where Coronado established his headquarters had to provide most of the provisions to support the party. When the Pueblos objected to the drain on their food sources, one of Coronado's lieutenants executed several hundred Tiwa Indians. The reputation of the Spaniards as ruthless and brutal rulers had been established. Other exploring expeditions came toward the end of the century and finally the establishment of a permanent colony by Juan de Oñate in 1598.

As Spanish subjects, the Pueblos suffered abuse and were exploited. Spanish authorities, both civil and church, attempted to destroy native religious practices and replace them with Spanish-Catholic beliefs and customs. Seventeenth-century records are replete with instances of attempts to eradicate native ceremonies by force. Pueblo ceremonial structures (*kivas*) were raided periodically and masks and ceremonial paraphernalia burned and destroyed. Religious officials of the indigenous religion were executed or punished in a variety of ways. The *encomienda* system exacted enormous quantities of tribute from the Indians in the form of farm products and handicrafts, while missionaries vied with civil authorities for the services of the Indians. Large mission compounds and massive church structures were constructed—all with Indian labor. To supplant native ceremonial patterns and beliefs, missionaries baptized Indians, forced attendance at Mass and made instruction in Catholic doctrine compulsory. Resistance or laxity in attending church services brought immediate physical punishment meted out by church appointed disciplinarians.

Resentment and hostility toward their oppressors swept the entire Pueblo country and the Indians engaged in a number of minor and local revolts toward the end of the seventeenth century. Finally in 1680 the Pueblos carried out a general revolt under the leadership of the San Juan Tewa Indian, Popé. Popé had been one of forty-seven Pueblo religious leaders given a public whipping in Santa Fe by Spanish authorities in 1675. Smarting under the punishment, Popé planned and successfully carried out the revolt from the headquarters that he established in Taos Pueblo. The rebellion lasted only about three weeks, but for battles fought with the crude firearms of the Spanish settlers and the bows and arrows of the Indians, it was a ferocious and bloody one. At the end of the revolt, 21 missionaries and 375 colonists were dead, while another 2000 settlers had been driven out of the Pueblo country. After the colonists left, the Indians destroyed the mission establishments in all the pueblos and burned church furnishings and records. Attempts were made to erase all vestige of Spanish rule and missionary activity. But in 1693 Don Diego de Vargas with a well-equipped army marched into the Pueblo country and reestablished Spanish control. De Vargas quickly resettled the areas formerly occupied by Spanish and Mexican colonists and again brought under submission the western Pueblos of Acoma, Zuni, and the Hopi.

After the reconquest, the Pueblos compromised by outwardly appearing to have accepted the Spanish-imposed cultural system. They adopted the externals of the new faith and conformed to the demands of labor and tribute, but they continued to practice their own indigenous religion and other customs behind closed doors, heavily guarded against church and civil authorities. In time, with succeeding generations who were brought up completely under the new order, the externally practiced Catholic religion and other Spanish customs also became a part of Pueblo culture. But the two traditions were kept distinct, partly because they had learned them in this manner, but also because of the fear of reprisals.

After the Pueblo revolt, Spanish-Catholic policy changed. The coercive and repressive measures of the previous century were either dropped or relaxed. French, American, and nomadic Indian enemies diverted Spanish interests, while a growing non-Pueblo population turned the attention of the friars to the spiritual needs of the settlers. The Pueblos as auxiliary troops assisted Spanish troops and prevented the frontier settlement from becoming annihilated by nomadic Indian raids. In virtually every campaign against enemy tribes, the Pueblos outnumbered the regular Spanish army and volunteer soldiers recruited from the colonists. As dependable and courageous warriors, the Pueblos received the commendation of almost every Spanish governor-general from De Vargas to the last Spanish civil and military official in the nineteenth century.

With Spanish attention turned to other pressing matters, the Pueblos returned to their native customs and religious ceremonies with renewed fervor. They revived and reorganized ceremonial rites neglected and virtually abandoned as the result of religious suppression. The coming of Anglo-Americans, however, brought a return to earlier conditions. American missionaries and United States Indian Service officials were openly critical of the "obscene" and "immoral" practices of the Indians, and they took steps to stop them. Indian children were forcibly taken and enrolled in boarding schools at considerable distances from reservations. The purpose was to wean Indian youngsters from their traditional culture. In these schools the use of the Indian language and all other "Indian" ways were prohibited. Infractions were dealt with brutally by actual physical punishments. The home base of the children was also infiltrated. During the early 1900s investigators were sent to the pueblos to study the reported immoral and anti-Christian practices of the Indians. These investigators brought back reports of customs that violated Anglo-American standards of decency and morality. Indian Service officials were instructed to stop ceremonial practices that they judged to be contrary to accepted Christian standards. Authority for such action came from regulations contained in a statement on Religious Crimes Code sent to all reservation supervisors. These acts of the missionaries and United States Indian Service officials forced the Pueblos to strengthen their native ceremonial system, and they became again resentful and reticent.

During the second and third decades of the present century, Indians and their Anglo friends rose to resist unfair restraints, not by arms, but by persuasion and by the use of legal methods. After several years of bitter fighting in the courts and the press, a different and more humane policy for Indians was effected in the closing years of the 1920s. The changed policy has not been in existence long enough to indicate changed reactions. The Pueblos are wary, suspicious, and secretive. Information about their sacred religious customs and practices are closely guarded. They fear that knowledge of them by outsiders may bring about, once again, religious persecutions and suppression.

PART ONE

THE PUEBLOS TODAY

Economy

ECONOMIC PURSUITS new to the area have brought about profound changes in the Pueblos' way of life. The changes came about as a result of the establishment of American rule in 1848 and the subsequent development of transportation, markets, and trade. By 1881, railroads linked the Pueblo country with the rest of the United States and brought a steady stream of Anglo-American settlers. The newcomers not only complicated the land problem, but changed the traditional economic system of the region as well. Two economic innovations unknown in the past came into being with the advent of Anglo-Americans: First, a credit system, and later, a cash economy. Pueblo economy until the closing periods of the last century was subsistence farming. Railroads brought trading posts; and soon Hispanos, Pueblos, and Anglos became involved in credit transactions.

Credit operations came into the Pueblo country much later than elsewhere in America. The Pueblos, because of their isolation and well-developed irrigated farming practices, remained out of the credit buying and selling orbit that involved other Indians in their relations with whites. Although the Pueblos were associated rather intimately with a Hispanicized population for almost 300 years, the latter took its cues of livelihood from the Pueblos and hence did not change the basic subsistence pattern. Both groups were subsistence farmers, growing essentially the same kinds of crops, living in similar types of habitations, and producing the basic necessities of life for their own use. There was no specialization either in products of the land or in manufactured items; hence there was no opportunity for the development of complex trading activities. Elsewhere in America Indians quickly came under the domination of the economic practices of the newcomers. The fur trade in the East and Northwest made the Indians in these areas dependent on the white man's goods and tools.

In time, however, the Pueblos and Hispanos also became economically dependent. By the beginning of the twentieth century, the Pueblos were no longer able to meet their own food needs without recourse to a market and a cash nexus. In part, this dependence was due to alienation of land both to Hispanos and Anglos and the decreasing fertility of the increasingly smaller plots of land on which the Pueblos depended for a livelihood. Equally important, however, was the fact that trade became a convenient way to procure food and materials otherwise difficult or impossible to obtain. Some wage work opportunities came for Pueblo Indians as railroads and roads were opened up toward the end of the nineteenth century and during the first and second decades of the twentieth. The final shift from a credit system to a cash economy came about, however, after the 1920s. This was primarily the result of automobile travel which brought hundreds of tourists into the Pueblo area. Pottery and handicrafts brought cash and released many Pueblo families completely from a farming occupation. During the 1930s, the United States Indian Bureau engaged Indians in construction programs that brought the Pueblos into fuller participation with a cash economy (Aberle 1948:22). World War II accelerated this process by providing jobs all over the United States and dependency checks for the families of those in the armed services. After the war, the United States Indian Bureau assisted Indians under the Relocation Program to settle in a number of off-reservation cities. The purpose of the Relocation Program was to lower unemployment and poverty conditions in a number of reservations. Some Pueblo Indian families took advantage of the program and at present virtually all of the larger cities in the western United States have some Pueblo Indian residents. Such families have not broken ties with their home communities, however; they return frequently for long visits, usually timed to take advantage of an important ceremonial event in their pueblo.

While farming is no longer the primary economic occupation of the Pueblos, it is interesting that an indigenous religion and ceremonialism developed around an agricultural society still persists among them. Undoubtedly some reinterpretation in both beliefs and practices has been made by the adherents of Pueblo religion. One obvious function which Pueblo ritualism still affords its members, whether farmers or not, is a recreational outlet and the reiteration of communal identity and unity. Perhaps this is sufficient to keep the religion going and to fill the religious positions needed to maintain the rich religious and ceremonial life. Indeed, all the pueblos from Hopi to Taos appear to be in a period of religious revivalism and ceremonies long dormant have been reenacted in virtually every pueblo in recent years (Ortiz, 1963). At least one study indicates that religion and ritual activities formed and developed in an agricultural context may persist with vigor and vitality in an apparently alien setting. Professor Edward H. Spicer (1940) has documented this seeming anomaly in his study of Pascua, a village of Yaqui Indian refugees in Tucson, Arizona. These Indians, as wage workers in an urban environment, hold fast to a system of beliefs and ceremonies once carried on in agricultural communities along the Yaqui River in southern Sonora, Mexico. The Pueblos appear to be making a similar adjustment in shifting from agricultural subsistence to wage work. These Indians have not migrated; however, finding the land base inadequate for agricultural purposes and attracted by wage work opportunities, they have in recent years shifted almost completely to a wage work economy without giving up cherished religious beliefs and practices. For the most part Pueblo Indians work locally and return to their pueblos in the evening and on weekends.

Changes in Pueblo Life

Most of all, Indians want employment near their homes so that community life may go on. Los Alamos has provided jobs for many in the neighboring Indian communities; but some pueblos are too far from Los Alamos to depend on it for employment. The possible establishment of factories on Pueblo land, offering such lures as tax-free land and a dependable labor pool to prospective companies, is under consideration by a number of the pueblos. Unfortunately there are problems of financing and leasing of land over long periods of time—risks companies are not willing to assume. But much of the opposition comes from the Indians themselves. The Pueblos cherish their isolated pueblos; hence they do not support efforts to establish businesses which will bring incomes. They value the traditional rewards of community life and object to moving too rapidly into the frantic life of modern America. A few pueblos have developed economically helpful recreational facilities —Santa Clara, Jemez, and Acoma are beginning to realize small profits. Nambe and Santa Clara have also begun to hold annual "ceremonial celebrations" to attract the tourist. Such "ceremonials" are held away from their own communities. The Pueblos present authentic Indian dances, but only the secular or recreational type which may be freely observed by outsiders. A number of the pueblos are using the advice of the Indian Bureau, the university, and white friends in establishing money-making businesses. There is, however, a constant clash between old and new ideas. The operation and management of such enterprises is cause for bitter disputes between Pueblo "progressives" and "conservatives." New, unorthodox projects present confusion and bewilderment to a people who are unaccustomed to

Santa Clara Pueblo—Tewa-speaking pueblo, three miles south of San Juan. Rectangular kiva in courtyard.

financing and managing the profits and losses that are inevitable in such businesses (compare Smith 1966:89–92).

Changes wrought by the nontraditional form of economy are evident in every facet of Pueblo life. The village has not disappeared, but it has lost many of its compact characteristics. Pueblo villages are still built predominantly of adobe, but the former apartmentlike family homes are beginning to give way to isolated, single-family dwellings. Multistoried houses are still characteristic of Taos, but in other pueblos only one or two such structures stand as lone remnants from the past. The less conservative villages are beginning new settlement areas where single-family structures have been patterned after American suburban homes, with a garage, yard, lawn, trees, and shrubbery. The interior and exterior walls of an increasing number of houses are finished with hard plaster ranging in color from tans to reds. New houses have three or four spacious rooms and ceilings are of milled lumber beams instead of the traditional round logs or *vigas*. Floors are frequently covered with linoleum, laid either on a packed earth floor or over pine boards. Electricity, as well as running water and plumbing facilities, has been brought into the majority of the pueblos.

Greater affluence is evident in the variety of family possessions. House furnishings have undergone a complete revolution since the turn of the century when furniture and possessions were meagre. The items to be found in a Pueblo home today would not differ substantially from those in middle-class Anglo-American homes in New Mexico, although their arrangement differs considerably. Television antennas resemble a forest of bare trees above Santa Clara. In this pueblo, at least, television programs have replaced the former gathering of the bilateral kin group to listen to old Tewa stories and legends. Pueblo walls are conspicuously cluttered with large pictures of saints, photographs, and snapshots of friends and relatives. Brightly colored Mexican *serapes* are popular coverings for

Pueblo homes—Taos Pueblo.

sofas and chairs. The Pueblos' own handicrafts—pottery, beadwork, and the like—are rarely displayed, however. Instead, purchased items such as glass jars, vases, and bowls are used as containers and as decorative objects. A trunk or chest contains ceremonial and dance paraphernalia and also provides a sitting place along with manufactured chairs and couches. Corn grinding equipment—*metates* and *manos*—common in Pueblo homes only a generation ago is all gone. Conspicuously absent as well are the woven woolen garments of the women and the buckskin apparel of the men. Except among the Western Pueblos, the long pole suspended from the ceiling to hold the family's possessions of clothing and blankets is gone. Modern Pueblo homes have closets and storage rooms where possessions not in daily use are stored. Religious leaders still keep fetishes and sacred paraphernalia in special rooms, but the typical Pueblo food storage room is a thing of the past. Refrigerators and pantries have been substituted for the back rooms where melons were stored and ears of corn stacked. Weekend shopping at the supermarket now takes the place of busy activities at the annual harvest time.

In virtually all pueblos, automobiles have replaced horses and wagons as the mode of travel. Pickup trucks are the most popular of automobile body styles. Horses are in little evidence, although they still perform the bulk of the little farming done in the pueblos. Where farming is still important, at Isleta and Sandia, tractors and other mechanical equipment have been added. Small land-holdings and the custom of planting corn and garden crops rather than multiacre cash crops have tended to make the Pueblo farmer a small operator among profit-minded Anglo farmers. Wage work is now an essential part of the Pueblo way of life; it is unlikely that farming will ever become an important economic venture again. Investment in livestock, land, or farming machinery is alien to Pueblo think-ing; working for wages or selling one's own handicraft is a far less complicated venture and does not entail risks.

Dress and hair styles distinguish Pueblo Indians from their Hispano and Anglo neighbors. The brightly colored shawl is much in evidence among girls and women, and a number of the old women and old men still wear the characteristic hair styles. Indian dress is distinctive, essentially in the array of predominately bright colors in shirts, skirts, and shawls. These are all items of purchase rather than of local manufacture, however. Cash purchases and sales have now completely replaced the former system of bartering. Some villages like San Ildefonso and Santa Clara now derive virtually all of their income from crafts and

Typical Hopi postpubescent hairdo for unmarried girls.

wage work. Even in the few pueblos where farming is important, wages from seasonal employment in nearby towns and cities are an important supplement to income.

Anglo-Americans

Perhaps equally as important to the Pueblos as a new economic system has been contact with the people who brought about the economic revolution. Although there were large numbers of Anglo-Americans in New Mexico by the middle of the last century, the Pueblos' relations with the newcomers were not extensive. Until the end of the nineteenth century, Pueblo contacts with Anglo-Americans were restricted essentially to three sources: (1) Indian agents or "farmers", (2) Protestant missionaries, and (3) United States Indian Bureau boarding school representatives. Only the first group provided direct aid; government farmers taught the Indians better farming techniques and acted as a link between the Pueblos and the Indian agent in Santa Fe.

The early educational efforts of the government and the work of Protestant missionaries are fused in the memory of older Pueblo Indians. In 1881 a boarding school was established in Albuquerque; primary schools had begun to function in many of the Indian pueblos since 1872. The association of Protestant missionaries and government school supervisors is undoubtedly the result of actual close co-operation between the two groups in educating Indians. During this period (the late 1800s), for example, half of the salaries of the teachers in the pueblos was met by the government and half by various Protestant denominations. Bancroft summarizes the efforts made toward the education of Pueblo children between 1870–1885 as follows:

> In education, from about 1873, earnest efforts were made by the Presbyterians aided by the government; and schools were established at several pueblos and with considerable success, especially at Laguna, Zuni, and Jemez. Some 20 children were also sent to Charlisle [sic.] Pennsylvania, to be taught; and in 1881 an Indian boarding-school was founded at Albuquerque, where in later years over 100 pupils from all the tribes were gathered . . . (Bancroft 1889: 741–742).

Some of the Pueblos initially resisted the educational programs of the government; however, in subsequent years they enthusiastically supported such efforts. The forced recruitment of Indian youngsters brought about general Pueblo resentment for educators and government educational representatives. There was no objection to local schooling; indeed, many of the Pueblos employed Hispano teachers to instruct children in the rudiments of writing and reading, prior to American contact. It was the enrollment of Indian youngsters in boarding schools at considerable distances from their homes that the Pueblos opposed, as well as the cultural and linguistic alienation which resulted from such experiences.

Traditional Tanoan Pueblo men's attire—Santa Clara Pueblo.

The United States Indian Bureau

The Bureau of Indian Affairs has undoubtedly affected the Pueblos more profoundly than any other single source of influence from the Anglo-American world. Before the mid-1920s, Indian administration was committed to transforming Indian communities into variants of the dominant American culture as quickly as possible. Anglo-American administrators of Indian affairs during this early period of Indian-white relations accepted without question the superiority of Anglo-American culture. They believed that the solution of the "Indian problem" lay in the complete "Americanization" of the Indian and his assimilation into the American "melting pot." Leo Crane, for many years a goverment Indian agent among the Pueblos, has expressed this philosophy well:

> I had studied with considerable interest the history of the Pueblo Indians, and could look forward to the job of advancing their well-being. It seemed to me that they had a future, whereas it would be generations before the Hopi and the Navajo, as tribes, would advance clearly within the zone of civilization according to our standards. And however one views the Indian, with whatever of sentiment or admiration or affection, he cannot be diverted from laboring toward this proposed destination (Crane 1928:6).

After 1928 the policy of the government toward Indians changed radically, as the result of criticisms culminating in the famous Meriam Report of 1928 (Meriam and Associates). This report was instrumental in bringing about revolutionary changes in American Indian affairs. Indian administrators were instructed to respect Indian ways of life, but assist the Indian to achieve equality with whites in economy, education, and health. Among the Pueblos, the new regime permitted traditional authorities to relax controls that safeguarded Pueblo ceremonial life.

The new philosophy and its implementation was largely the inspiration and the work of John Collier, Commissioner of Indian Affairs from 1933 to 1945. Collier propounded a philosophy of cultural pluralism and worked toward the reestablishment and perpetuation of Indian societies as differentiated cultures in the stream of American life. He believed with almost fanatical zeal that societies like the Pueblos could influence Western cultures to recapture the serenity and meaningfulness of life which he felt the Pueblos possessed.

Collier's vision and plans for change included all Indians; but as he was most familiar with Pueblos, he phrased his program in terms of these Indians:

> The truly deadly peril which the Pueblos face is . . . the acutely multiplied contacts of the Pueblo young people with the white world—the white middle-class world, to which the great realities of Pueblo life are not realities at all, not even existences at all. . . . I believe that with the help of an Indian Service changed in ways difficult but not impossible, they *could* surmount this, their final peril. . . . It would be a service specialized to the Pueblos' problem, just as there should be a service specialized to the Navajos' problem, and the Sioux', the Papagos', and the Eskimos' problems. A true "career service," of men and women sought out and enlisted because they would have the endowment of devotion, attitudes and personality structure to fit them to understand both the Pueblos and the wider world. These men and women would then be trained and retrained through that method of democratic group self-education known as action research.
>
> They would work as advisers to the Pueblos, seeking to help the Pueblos to equip their own young people for every Pueblo task, including all the government's tasks of Pueblo service.
>
> They would presume—accurately—a high, not low, intelligence quotient in the Pueblos, a large, not small, capacity for discriminative and integrative thinking and for social invention, and a great, not petty, destiny as members of mankind.
>
> They would change, gradually and experimentally but radically, the emphases in the government's Pueblo schools: allowing the unexampled aesthetic richness and potency of the Pueblo nature to come into play; building in the young people an awareness of Pueblo values in terms of the whole world's desperate need, and of world time beyond the present extremely unrepresentative and fast-fading hour.
>
> They would help the Pueblo leaders to see the Pueblo in terms of the great world, and world need in terms of pueblo creative power.
>
> Within this sort of help from a possible Indian Service, I deeply believe that the Pueblos could and would surmount the most fateful danger and crises of their thousands of years. Without this sort of help, the Pueblos, not as mere aggregations of human beings, but as citadels of a great, ancient and timeless spirit, may die (Moskowitz and Collier 1949:73–75).

Unfortunately, Commissioner Collier was not able to "sell" his philosophy to the government. Shortly after his retirement from government work, when a return to the pre-Collier regime was imminent in the Indian Bureau, he reported:

In my own twelve years as Indian Commissioner, I was not able decisively to bring about the changed orientation and structure in day-to-day Indian Service . . . and I do not see much progress toward the change now, nor is the general political climate favorable to it. But it remains the hope of the Pueblos, and of all the other tribes and groups of tribes whose creative heritage has not yet died, or whose ecological situation is unique; and of these there are many. And it remains the opportunity of the United States to build a trail far out into that obscure yet world-critical area known as the area of the minorities and dependent peoples . . . (Moskowitz and Collier 1949:75).

For a time in the 1960s, a return to Collier's emphasis on self-government for Indian communities appeared a possibility of United States Indian policy, but it did not take place. Today, the Indian Bureau is treading a path midway between the assimilationists' policies of the past and the "cultural pluralism" position of Collier.

Among the Pueblos, the principle of self-government was applied with earnestness during the Collier regime. This basic philosophy was paramount in the thinking of high ranking Bureau officials. The Pueblos did not fully understand the intentions of the government, interpreting the "new look" of the Indian Bureau as merely "fresh dressing" on old paternalistic and repressive policies of the government. They were not conscious that important or radical changes were anticipated or actually came about in the management of their affairs during Collier's administration. A few communities in trouble, pueblos that had departed from the old *cacique* rule, benefited from the help of Bureau officials. Among these pueblos are Santa Clara, Laguna, Zuni, and Isleta, where community government now operates along secular lines and whose political officials are "elected" by the people. More comprehensible to the Pueblos are the Bureau's changed policies regarding the suppression of Indian customs and ceremonial activities that had characterized the administrations before 1928. The present renaissance in Indian ceremonial life is undoubtedly due to the permissive policies of the Indian Bureau established by John Collier during his long term as Commissioner of Indian Affairs.

Anglo-American neighbors of the Pueblos, whether farmers, business people, or in the professions, have little association with Pueblo Indians and rarely attend the public portions of Pueblo ceremonies. Outside of the pueblos, Pueblo Indians may deal directly with Anglo-Americans in the towns, usually in employer-employee relationships. At home, the Pueblos come in contact most often with Indian Service personnel, local artists, and tourists. The visits of the latter are transient and usually of short duration, but there are numerous instances of a casual first visit developing into an enduring friendship between an individual Pueblo family and a family from a distant part of the country. Such friendships stimulate repeated visits. White friends are often drawn into siding with their Indian friends in petty disputes within the pueblo, a practice which has usually aggravated the trouble rather than helped the Indians. In a few instances, however, friends have helped the Pueblos tremendously in problems that affected them all. For example, in the early twenties, white artists and writers joined the Pueblos in defeating the Bursum Bill which would have divested the Pueblos of most of their land.

Relations with Non-Pueblo Neighbors

Hispanos are the nearest neighbors of the Pueblos. Just prior to American rule, these two populations were coming together in mutual understanding and cooperation. The two groups have much in common. They have shared a common physical environment and engaged in an identical subsistence economy for over 300 years. As we have noted, rather large numbers of Indians, dissatisfied with Pueblo life, moved into Hispano communities. A number of former pueblos, like Cuyamungue and Jacona, became Hispanicized and disappeared entirely as Indian communities. By blood, Hispanos are largely Indian—the result of admixtures in Mexico prior to migration and the absorption of Pueblo Indians and Genizaros (Hispanicized captive Indians of a variety of non-Pueblo tribes). It is understandable, therefore, that the two peoples cooperated and actually participated in two revolts against common grievances in the mid-1900s. The first of these revolts was against the Mexican regime of Governor Albino Perez in 1837 and the second against American occupation in 1847 (Bancroft 1889:317–319; 432–437). In the revolt of 1837, Hispanos and Pueblo Indians killed Governor Perez and replaced him with José Gonzáles, a Hispanicized Indian of Taos and Genizaro parentage (Chavez 1955:193–194). New Mexico's only Indian governor ruled only briefly (he was governor for only about six months). A force of "loyal citizens" under former Governor Manuel Armijo recaptured Santa Fe, and Gonzáles and several of his associates were captured and shot (Bancroft 1889:317–319). In the second revolt, Charles Bent, the first Anglo-American governor of the new territory of New Mexico, was killed by bow and arrow and scalped. While Taos Indian warriors reportedly killed Bent and scalped him, Hispanos of northern New Mexico were in the pact with the Pueblo Indians in attempting to overthrow American control of the country (Bancroft 1889:432–437; Hallenbeck 1950:271–274).

Specialized treatment of Indians by the United States government brought about a rift between Hispanos and Pueblos soon after the American occupation of New Mexico. Initial friction grew out of the establishment of reservations, often at the expense of Hispano landholdings. Other privileges extended to the Pueblos but not to Hispanos, such as government schools and free hospital and medical services, further aggravated relations. This Hispanicization process of Pueblo Indians has stopped; instead, both groups must now accommodate, at least in some areas, the dominant Anglo-American culture.

Relations with Other Indians

Interpueblo relations continue to be friendly and intimate. Pueblo Indians visit one another on annual saint's day celebrations or in the West on the occasion of other ritualistic performances. Intermittent contacts go on the year round, hosts in each pueblo taking pride in their generous hospitality in receiving outsiders (Lange 1952:19–26; Vogt 1955:820–839).

Boarding schools and off-reservation employment provide other opportunities for interpueblo relations and contacts with members of other tribes as well. Los Alamos, the "Atom City," employs large numbers of Indians from virtually every pueblo. Inter-Indian fairs and celebrations, like the Gallup Intertribal Ceremonial and the Flagstaff Powwow, are other occasions on which Pueblos meet other Indians. Pueblo Indians travel constantly, visiting not only other pueblos, but Indian friends in nonreservation locations as well. There is a growing heterogeneous Indian population in places like Denver, Santa Fe, Albuquerque, and Phoenix.

The former endogamous characteristics of the pueblos are changing. There are now an increasing number of interpueblo and intertribal marriages. Thus, new influences are modifying traditional Pueblo life and cementing relations among Indians of diverse backgrounds. Despite these contacts and interactions, however, the Pueblo sense of community has not disappeared. The Pueblo spouse married to an outsider returns frequently with his or her family to renew kinship and community relations. Only the most conservative pueblos, like Taos and Santo Domingo, disapprove of outsiders residing within the old pueblo walls. But marriage with outsiders has taken place even in these tradition-bound pueblos. There is no sign of the disorganization of community integration; and the necessity for greater tolerance of new ideas and practices has resulted in less rigid attitudes than formerly.

Pueblo Government

The tenacity of the Pueblos to survive as a people and as tightly knit communities over many centuries is well-known. Undoubtedly their social, ceremonial, and political organization has been responsible for their survival. While dissension is common, even endemic in every pueblo, disputes have rarely broken up a village completely (Dozier 1966:172). Most of the Pueblo communities occupy the sites in which they were encountered by Spanish explorers and that, indeed, they had occupied for several hundred years prior to white contact.

The persistence of the pueblos may be attributed partly, at least, to the harsh disciplinary measures imposed on deviant behavior and the "skimming off" of malcontents—both discipline and eviction are common practices in all the pueblos (Hawley 1948; Hoebel 1962; Dozier 1966; Leighton and Adair 1966). Such practices would leave the villages oriented along traditional lines with populations restricted to those who valued communal living. Perhaps a more acceptable answer for persistence, however, is the integrative pattern of Pueblo society. Kroeber's characterization of Zuni integration is in general applicable to all of the pueblos:

Four or five different planes of systematization crosscut each other and thus preserve for the whole society an integrity that would speedily be lost if the planes merged and thereby inclined to encourage segregation and fission. The clans [among the Tanoans, extended families and moities], the fraternities, the priesthoods, the kivas, in a measure the gaming parties, are all dividing agencies. If they coincided, the rifts in the social structure would be deep; by countering each other they cause segmentations which produce an almost marvelous complexity, but can never break the national entity apart (Kroeber 1917:183).

Taos Pueblo—A Tiwa-speaking pueblo, the most northern of the New Mexico Pueblo villages.

The Pueblos have thus persisted, despite factional disputes, and appear to be as vigorous and vital today as during any period in their past. The fact is obvious, despite popular notions, that Pueblo communities are highly adaptive social organizations, adjusting to differing ecological conditions, economies, and to differing social environments as well. Although the Pueblos have borrowed heavily from others, the core and the special organization of their society and culture remain uniquely Pueblo. The following statement regarding the present status of Pueblo secular government is relevant:

> The increasing complexity and number of relations with the world outside the pueblo are putting greater and greater strain on their movements. At present there is a wide range from the more conservative pueblos which have retained the old form completely, to those few which have overtly separated church and state. It must be remembered that, though the appearance of power has changed, the influence of the religious hierarchy is still imporatnt and undoubtedly plays a large part in elections, Santo Domingo, San Felipe, Jamez, Cochiti, Taos, and Acoma retain the old system in unchanged form; the smaller pueblos such as Santa Ana, Zia, and Sandia also may be classed as conservative; the Tewa pueblos (Tesuque, Santa Clara, San Ildefonso, San Juan, Nambe, and Pojoaque) have made some modifications and may be called transitional, while Isleta and Laguna have theoretically at least, separated religious and civil leadership. Santa Clara and Isleta are the only two pueblos with written constitutions which provide for the election of village officials, but there is increasing agitation in all but the most conservative pueblos to adopt a constitution. Zuni, this year [1966] for the first time, elected its officers by a majority vote and permitted women to vote (Smith 1966:84–85).

American Indians enjoy limited sovereignty on reservation lands—the result of treaty agreements. Reservations and sovereignty were partial concessions for ceded land. The Pueblos, perhaps more than other Indians, are keenly aware of these rights. Pueblo officials, realizing that they were immune from state or federal intervention, have disciplined their own pueblo members rather harshly at times to bring about conformity to Pueblo mores. Pueblo autonomy and control over internal or tribal affairs goes back to Spanish times. A rather significant case—a dispute over the right of a pueblo to exercise control over its members—was settled in favor of the pueblo in 1815. This is the case of a family by the name of Canjuebes at Santa Clara Pueblo. The Canjuebes had taken residence away from the pueblo and were living a Hispanicized existence; but, nevertheless, they wanted to retain rights to family land in the pueblo. The instructions of Bernardo Bonavia, Commandant General at Durango to the acting governor of New Mexico, underscore the undisputed right of a pueblo over its members. Bonavia directed the acting governor as follows:

> To give the Canjuebes to understand that if they want to hold the lands in dispute, they must go back and become part of the pueblo community, but if they want to retain their Spanish citizenship they must buy the lands they need elsewhere, as do other citizens of the Province (Twitchell 1914:372).

Under United States jurisprudence the rights of an Indian tribe or community over its internal affairs, particularly in law enforcement cases, is contained in Public Law 280. A succinct interpretation of this law is given in "laymen's" language by Oliver La Farge:

> With certain exceptions since the passage of Public Law 280 in 1953, "Indian country," that is land within the exterior boundaries of an Indian reservation or grant, or land allotted in trust to an Indian by the United States, is exempt from state and local jurisdiction so far as the Indians on it are concerned. Law enforcement is divided between the tribe for most matters and the federal courts and police agencies for certain major offenses.
> This is a portion of the home rule which tribes retain as a fragment of their lost sovereignty. The Indians regard it as a vitally important protection against the prejudice and mistreatment they commonly encounter in dealings with local police and local courts. Tribal-federal jurisdiction is constantly under attack by local forces; less so in New Mexico, perhaps, than in most Western states . . . (La Farge 1959:250).

Although Indians have been citizens of the United States since 1924 when they were given the privilege for their services in World War I, they were disenfranchised in New Mexico until 1948 (Trujillo vs. Garley, District Court of New Mexico). The Pueblos have not been eager to flock to the polls, although potentially the Indian vote in New Mexico can be an important one. They now (1968) number about 70,000 in New Mexico and about 200,000 in the Southwest. They are increasing at a faster rate than any other ethnic group in the area (about 3 percent annually). At present there are no clear-cut political issues that the Pueblos can support or reject. They have united on two former occasions: the Pueblo Revolt of 1680, and in the 1920s to defeat a bill which would have given free title to non-Pueblo squatters on their land (Moskowitz and Collier 1949:71–72).

Pueblo land grants were given them by the Spanish crown and subsequently confirmed by the Mexican and American governments.

Education

Until recently Pueblo Indians received all their formal schooling in government operated schools. Such education started in the pueblo "day school" and ended in an off-reservation boarding school. Day schools went from grade one through six, boarding schools through grade twelve. Except for Haskell Institute in Kansas, higher education was not supported by special schools of the Bureau of Indian Affairs. Haskell did offer, however, the equivalent of a two-year college program. In more recent years, Haskell has emphasized professional training, particularly business and commercial subjects. While ideally an Indian should progress from day school through boarding school, dropouts occurred all along the continuum, long before the process was completed. The grade level of education achieved and the drop-out rate has been far greater among Indians, including Pueblos, than among students of the general population.

At present, the goal of the Bureau of Indian Affairs is to transfer the responsibility of educating the Indians to local public school systems. Public schools are now located among the Pueblos at Hopi, Zuni, Santo Domingo, and Laguna-Acoma. In other pueblos, Indian students are encouraged to attend the public schools nearest their homes. Since reservation Indians do not ordinarily pay school taxes, the government compensates local public schools for Indian students who attend with funds made available by the Johnson-O'Malley Act. It is apparent, however, that it will be a long time before the Bureau of Indian Affairs relinquishes its role as educator of American Indians for there remain many Indian communities in remote and isolated locations. It is important, too, that the Bureau-operated schools prepare the Indian children for a smooth transition into public schools. Most Bureau officials realize that it is their responsibility to help the student meet the change and adjustment to a new school environment as painlessly as possible. The following brief statistics quoted in a report on the Indian situation in New Mexico which includes Pueblo Indians is relevant here:

> Among Indians in general, out of each 100 high school students 49 usually finish. Twenty of these go on to college; but only seven (or 35 per cent of those entering) acquire degrees. Furthermore, of each 100 Indian college graduates only 10 usually go into "the professions," the other 90 ending up in lesser occupations. About 37 per cent of all Americans of college age attend college, with 60 per cent achieving graduation (Meaders 1963:17).

Educational organizations, institutions, and the Indians themselves are cognizant of the Indian students' low achievements, high drop-out rates, and other difficulties, and have set up programs of assistance. The Bureau of Indian Affairs provides scholarships for Indians; there are also a number of private organizations both national and local which provide scholarships and financial assistance for Indian students in higher education. Southwestern colleges and universities have either set up positions of "Indian advisers" or are prepared to furnish counseling services to Indians when needed. Finally, the tribes themselves have become aware of the importance of education and have organized financial assistance programs out of tribal funds to permit members to obtain college and university degrees. The Laguna Pueblo Council established an annual scholarship fund of $25,000. Other pueblos have set up liberal loan arrangements from tribal funds to assist those members of their communities going on to higher education. Pueblo Indians are active in educational organizations such as the New Mexico Kiva Club and the Indian Youth Council which conducts an annual conference managed and organized entirely by Indian students (compare Meaders 1963:17–18).

As a by-product of formal schooling, Pueblo Indians have become introspective about their own culture. A resurgence in arts and crafts has been engendered. Despite the fact that this movement is recent, there is already a growing list of artists (compare Guthe 1925; Bunzel 1929; Adair 1944; Tanner 1957, 1968; Dutton 1963; Dunn 1968). Among recent or contemporary potters, Nampeyo (Hopi-Tewa), Maria Martinez (San Ildefonso), and Severa Tafoya (Santa Clara) are widely known. Among painters, the following is a limited list: Pablita Velarde (Santa Clara), Fred Kabotie (Hopi), Ben and Joe Herrera (Cochiti), Jose Rey Toledo (Jamez), and Awa Tsireh (San Ildefonso). Working with other media, Charles and Otellie Loloma (Hopi) have developed novel forms of jewelry and sculptures. Hopi and Zuni silverwork is as popular in the Southwest as the more widely known Navaho work; its style differs from that of the Navaho and from one another. The development of Pueblo arts and crafts is an interesting, important, and significant aspect of recent Pueblo culture. It is not possible to do justice to this vast field in this study; recently, however, a number of studies based on extensive research in art and anthropology have appeared (see especially Tanner 1957, 1968, and Dunn 1968). Various museums, both in and out of the Southwest, have fostered the work of Pueblo potters, weavers, jwelers, and other artists. Pueblo Indians have responded enthusiastically to encouragement from friends and organizations and are working creatively with media and materials unknown to them in the past.

Health

In initial contacts with Europeans, the Pueblos, like other Indians, were highly susceptible to smallpox and other contagious diseases. The Pueblo population table indicates periodic population losses attributable to smallpox epidemics. Large scale smallpox vaccination of Indians began in 1832, when Congress authorized the Secretary of War to provide vaccination and appropriated funds for the program (Raup 1959:1). Effective vaccination programs were not developed until much later, however; and for the Pueblos, smallpox remained the most dreaded disease until the first decade of the present century.

After the control of smallpox, gastrointestinal diseases remained the chief cause of the high mortality rate among Pueblos. There was also a high incidence of typhoid, tuberculosis, and blindness from a rather rare eye disease known as tracoma.

The discovery of sulfanilamide and its use for tracoma in 1938 either cured or arrested the disease (Raup 1959:15). In recent years, the Indian pueblos through the help of the Bureau of Indian Affairs and the Public Health Service have engaged in various sanitation programs and have brought down the incidence of diseases responsible for high death rates among Indians. There has been work done in all the pueblos to improve the water supply and provide for proper waste disposal systems. Hospital facilities specifically for Indians have been available in Santa Fe and Albuquerque since about 1900. Since then clinics have been established in Pueblo communities and health personnel serving the Indians has been increased. After the transfer of Indian health services from the Bureau to the Public Health Service in 1955, there has been an acceleration of the number and the quality of health services provided for Indians. The result of these improved health services has been a rapidly rising population. From 1900 to 1960, Pueblo population tripled; but the most spectacular increase has been in the last three decades. In 1950, the population was about 20,000; in 1960, about 30,000, and in 1970 the population is expected to rise to 40,000 of more (see population tables).

Community Life

Pueblo society and culture have undergone changes, but in spite of them the indigenous core of Pueblo life continues. Under Spanish domination the basic farming economy was not affected, although a number of material and technological innovations were added. Similarly, the Pueblos adapted to raising livestock and new crops such as wheat, alfalfa, and fruit trees (peaches, apples, plums). Among the Rio Grande Pueblos the church and Spanish-Catholic customs were added as a separate system, kept distinct from aboriginal practices. This was a reaction primarily, we believe, to Spanish suppression of the more sacred aspects of native Pueblo Indian religion and ritual. Under constant pressure by missionaries and civil authorities to wipe out every vestige of the indigenous core of the religion, the Pueblos responded by taking their own religion underground and offering only the public portions of certain esoteric rites and the borrowed Spanish-Catholic system as their religion. The latter became a convenient and acceptable facade behind which to pursue the cherished religion of their forefathers. Eventually, the Spanish-Catholic system became important too; but the two systems remained separate, partly because they had learned them that way, but also because of the fear of reprisal. This interesting reaction to Spanish conquest and oppressive colonialism has been discussed in greater detail elsewhere under the term "compartmentalization" (Dozier 1961:150–151, 175–178). Compartmentalization simply refers to the presence among the Pueblos of two mutually distinct and separate socioceremonial systems, each containing patterns not found in the other. The two systems are the indigenous and the Spanish-Catholic traditions.

The western pueblos—Hopi, Zuni, and Acoma—were less influenced by colonial officials and church authorities. After the revolt, these pueblos discarded most of the Spanish-Catholic social and ceremonial veneer they had acquired from their Spanish oppressors and returned to the practice of their indigenous rites.

The Rio Grande Pueblos have not been completely successful in keeping non-Indian elements from invading the areas of native dances and rites. In recent years, particularly, numerous changes in dress and costuming have taken place. It is remarkable, nevertheless, how much of the indigenous pattern has been retained; even the casual white visitor is struck by the essentially "Indian" character of the public dances. Of importance for the understanding of pueblo compartmentalization, however, is not so much the degree to which the Pueblos have succeeded in keeping out foreign elements from the indigenous ritual, but in the desire and the effort expended to keep the native system "uncontaminated."

Reaction to American contact has not been a duplication of the Spanish-Pueblo contact reaction. American contact has been experienced primarily in its economic, material, and technological aspects. Complete religious reform was not attempted by American contact agents; although, interestingly, United States government agents and Protestant missionaries did attempt to suppress Indian rituals because of their obscene or immoral features, not because they were pagan practices (the Spanish reaction). Spanish contact, as we have noted, did not affect the farming economy and, compared to American contact, the material and technological innovations introduced were minor. The latter were simply added to the total fund of Pueblo culture under Spanish domination rather than compartmentalized as with Spanish-Catholic nonmaterial introductiohs. Similarly, under Anglo-American control, material items and techniques have been freely incorporated. American contact has, however, brought drastic economic changes that are obviously threatening to pueblo integration. Thus far, however, the pueblos do not show any serious signs of disintegration. Protestantism invaded with force only Jemez and Zia; these pueblos solved the problem of conflict by simply expelling the Protestant converts. Santa Clara, Laguna, and Isleta may more appropriately indicate the trend in the future. These villages have separated religious and secular functions and remain united primarily on a secular and political level. In these villages, Protestant converts are permitted to live in the community. There is a fairly substantial and growing number of Protestants in the pueblos; some appear to be permanent adherents of the new religion; others, however, shift back and forth between attendance at Protestant services and participation in the traditional compartmentalized Pueblo religion.

Considerable borrowing from the past between the major linguistic groups —Tanoan and Keresans—is obvious in the social and religious organization. Thus, Tanoans gave the moiety concept—perhaps animal and hunt associations—while they received in return medicine associations, the Katcina cult, perhaps the clown associations, and some notions of unilineal organizations. There was, we believe, a shift among Keresans from clan to village-based units. This shift, we suggest, was brought about by ecological conditions, but later reinforced by Spanish contact. The Rio Grande and its tributaries made irrigation possible; but to realize the full potential of an irrigation society, even a miniature one, necessitates greater centralization of power. Both the Tanoans and Keresans, we propose, developed such societies. They incorporated governmental and religious functions into one or two social and ceremonial organizations. In addition, they formed a strong council of priests (the heads of ceremonial associations) and ruled with virtually absolute power. The western pueblos, particularly Hopi, Hano, and Acoma, remained less centralized; their village was a more amorphous unit than the Rio Grande pueblo counterpart (compare Titiev 1944:59–68).

Borrowing, from one another and from nomadic neighbors, is obviously an old practice among the Pueblos. The borrowed traits have become so well integrated and reworked that the original provenances of the traits cannot be established with complete assurance. Cultural exchange between these groups has not stopped. Interpueblo borrowing and ceremonial cooperation are active and vigorous at present; within the larger pan-Indian whole, borrowing is very much a live process. There is little doubt that the Pueblos were likewise receptive to Spanish introductions in the initial contact period. The insistence that the Pueblos give up their religion and substitute the introduced Spanish-Catholic system wholly was an alien concept. As we have noted, the Pueblos accommodated Spanish pressures by separating the ceremonial practices that offended the Spaniards and concealing them behind a facade of the imposed Spanish-Catholic patterns.

Neither Spanish attempts to civilize and Christianize the Pueblos, nor similar efforts under American rule to "Americanize" them, have succeeded. We believe that this is because the locus of Pueblo socialization, the extended family and the community itself, has not been undermined. The traditional network of kin and community relations have remained essentially undisturbed. Present conditions threaten this area of Pueblo communities, but they have not actually brought about reorganization, except perhaps in one or two villages. Thus, the socializing units that have fashioned Pueblo individuals from the time of initial white contact to the present have changed but little. Since these units have not been seriously disturbed, they have molded the same type of personality structure through the years and continued to produce individuals loyal to old Pueblos beliefs, values, and moral concepts.

The Pueblos have retained to a remarkable degree the basic outline of the traditional ceremonial and sociopolitical organization presented earlier. Nevertheless, membership in the ceremonial associations has declined and there has been a definite weakening in the influence of traditional leaders. At the present time, sufficient members remain in the important village and moiety associations charged with governmental and ceremonial functions to keep the majority of the pueblos operating in the old way. But, as key associations become extinct or membership in them drops to lower levels, a change to new patterns of civil and ceremonial organizations is likely to take place. Pueblos like Laguna, Isleta, and Santa Clara point in the direction which all pueblos are likely to go. Considerable interaction with non-Indians and particularly intermarriage with outsiders is bound to result in fundamental changes. Doubts about the efficacy of the old system in a modern setting and the rise of dissident factions provide conditions for change.

The native languages are still dominant, but English is now an important second language. Past generations of Pueblo speakers were also conversant in Spanish; just as they guarded the core of Pueblo ceremonialism against Spanish-Catholic contamination, so also they deleted designations of Spanish origin in the native language. Pueblo Indians are purists with regard to their language, a factor related to the phenomenon of compartmentalization. The native language is considered within the sacred core of the culture and must not be polluted with foreign loans. Pueblo speakers are keenly aware of borrowed words and tend to delete or restrict their usage in the presence of outsiders by finding suitable descriptive substitutes from their own native language.

The persistence of the indigenous languages and the retention of the large extended family and the community as primary units of socialization, we believe, have tended to foster the continuity of a highly uniform personality structure throughout the Pueblos. Similarly, the persistence of a set of essentially indigenous values and moral concepts may be attributed to the continuity of the native languages and the basic units of socialization. In recent years, particularly in the less conservative communities, the influence of the supernaturals, their impersonators, and the ceremonial priests have diminished, but the languages and the host of relatives involved in socialization have not changed significantly.

Pueblo society and culture is vigorous and enduring. While members may live for varying periods of time away from their pueblo, they return constantly to enjoy the rewards of community life. Economic changes and relations with non-Indians have affected Pueblo society and culture profoundly, but Pueblo culture is highly adaptive. Much of the ceremonial life and community living patterns that are uniquely Pueblo go on underneath an external surface of apparent acculturation to modern American culture.

PART TWO

PREHISTORIC
AND
HISTORIC BACKGROUND

Prehistory

THE AREA COVERED by sites of prehistoric Pueblo culture is vast; it is found over large portions of the states of New Mexico, Arizona, Colorado, and Utah. Pueblo culture is only one of a number of terminal cultural developments of a series of earlier prehistoric cultures. Archeologists have found evidence of man in the Southwest as early as 10,000 B.C. living contemporaneously with now extinct forms of the sloth, horse, elephant, and great bison. These early peoples hunted some of these animals; and two distinct patterns are identified on the basis of projectile points and plant extraction tools. In the eastern part of the area, extending into the Great Plains country, were the Paleo-Indians, or big game hunters. A second cultural pattern, the Desert Culture, extended southward from the Great Basin and covered most of the Southwest. Apparently also hunters of big game in the earlier periods, carriers of the Desert Culture appear to have adapted to the hunting of small game and to the gathering of plants as the large game animals disappeared.

The eastern expression of the Desert Culture pattern, known as the Cochise, is important for the early elaboration of plant extracting techniques. Grinding implements like the *metate* and the *mano* are numerous in Cochise sites, attesting to the extensive use of wild vegetable foods by these Indians. Corncobs have been found in east-central Arizona and west-central New Mexico as early as 3000 B.C. The occurrence of cultivated corn indicates diffusion of the technique of maize cultivation from Mexico, presumably along the corridor of the Sierra Madre. The maize appears to be a variety adapted to high altitudes; the sites in which it is found are all in elevations of 6000 feet. By 1000 B.C. squash and beans are added to the diet, yet curiously these foods made no profound changes in the way of life of these people; there are no permanent habitations or other indications of a settled life until about 300 B.C.

With the advent of pottery, about 300 B.C., archeologists recognize a new tradition—the Mogollon. This tradition reveals the earliest settled life in the Southwest. Mogollon peoples, about 1 A.D., erected quadrangular and rounded pit houses grouped into clusters of tiny villages. Shortly after 1 A.D., the bow and arrow make their first appearance, and to this must be added a complex of *manos*, *metates*, mortars and pestles, and implements made of stone, bone, and shell. Five periods are recognized by pottery types extending to about 1100 A.D. when the area becomes substantially reduced and acculturated to another tradition, the Anasazi or Pueblo as it is sometimes called. The Anasazi tradition begins later in what is now the four-state corner area of Colorado, New Mexico, Arizona, and Utah. This tradition exists parallel to the Mogollon tradition for many years and eventually absorbs the latter. We will return to a fuller discussion of the Anasazi after presenting the development of another important prehistoric tradition, the Hohokam, whose beginnings are later than the Mogollon but earlier than the Anasazi.

While the Hohokam tradition is outside the area of the eventual development of ancestral Pueblo culture, cross influences are obvious and it is probable that peoples carrying this cultural tradition eventually joined those of the Anasazi. The Hohokam, too, apparently grew out of the Cochise, but its locale was the

31

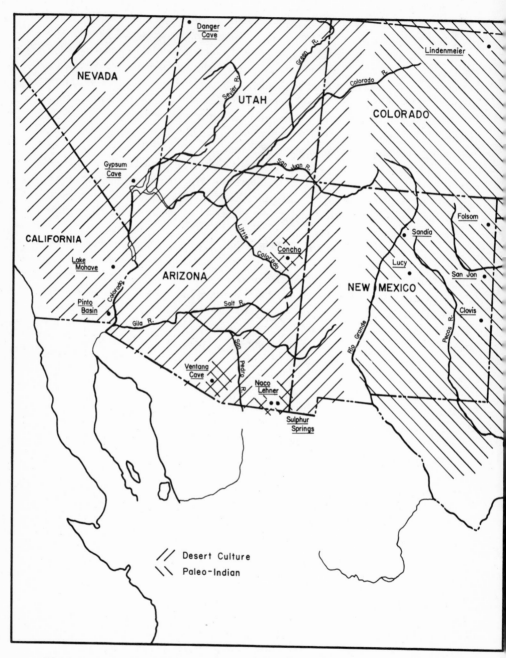

Figure 3. Prehistoric Southwest—Desert Culture and Paleo–Indian. C.A. 8000 B.C.

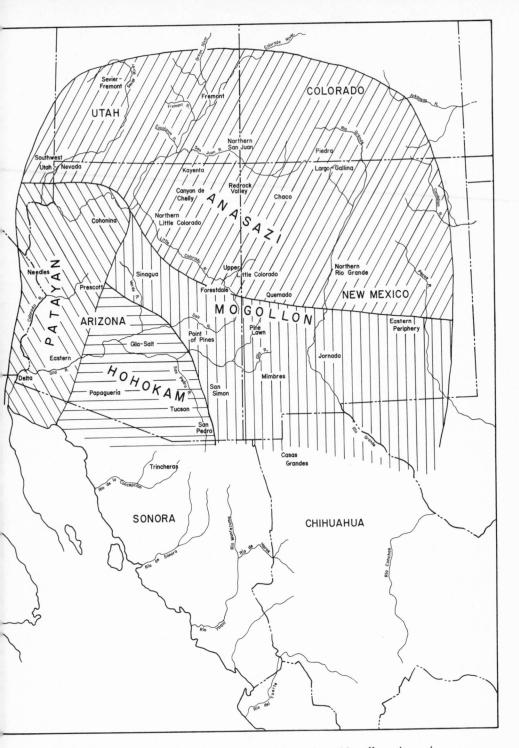

Figure 4. Prehistoric Southwest—Hohokam, Patayan, Mogollon, Anasazi.

33

desert region of central and southern Arizona. The Hohokam culture developed rapidly into a complex irrigation society along the lower reaches of the Gila River where long and elaborate irrigation canals were constructed. These water control achievements imply a well-developed sociopolitical organization, perhaps more complex than that achieved anywhere in the Southwest among the indigenous populations. Toward the end of the period, strong influences of the Anasazi tradition from the North are evident and the culture disappears abruptly about 1400 A.D. for reasons not yet solved by archeologists. Influences of the Hohokam are also evident in the lower Colorado River area in a subtradition known as the Patayan, or Hakataya. Whether the Patayan developed out of the Hohokam or directly out of the desert cultural pattern is not clear. The tradition, although sedentary, lacked permanent dwellings. The Indians built brush huts, cooked in stone-lined pits, and like the Hohokam Indians, cremated their dead. Flood farming rather than irrigation was employed. The Patayan never achieved the architectural or technological complexity of any of the other southwestern sedentary traditions.

Still another subtradition, the Sinagua, is recognized by archeologists in the area between the northernmost reaches of the Hohokam and the Anasazi on the northeast. The tradition was short-lived, beginning about 400 A.D. and ending by 1100 A.D. Influence from the Hohokam is evident in dwellings and ball courts, but like the Mogollon, it too acculturated to the Anasazi by 1100 A.D.

We may now return to the Anasazi or Pueblo cultural tradition. In prehistoric times the Anasazi covered the San Juan and Little Colorado river drainages as well as the northern Rio Grande region. Its most complex development was concentrated, however, in the four-state corner area of Arizona, New Mexico, Utah, and Colorado where the tradition reached a cultural florescence in the twelfth century A.D. During the final phases of the tradition, it absorbed the other traditions adjacent to it and, indeed, continued in recessed form in northern Arizona, western New Mexico and the northern Rio Grande Valley until historic times. It may have developed independently from the Desert Culture, but it undoubtedly borrowed agriculture from the Mogollon. The beginnings of the Anasazi appeared at least 300 to 700 years later than the Mogollon or Hohokam, but it surpassed both of the earlier traditions in architectural excellence. While lacking the complex water control achievements of the Hohokam, the Anasazi nevertheless practiced intensive agriculture by exploiting flood-water farming and a simple stream diversion type of irrigation. The potential development of another cultural peak by Pueblo Indians —diverting the waters of the Rio Grande and its tributaries—was arrested by Spanish conquest in the sixteenth century. This subject will receive additional attention in a later section.

Information on the prehistory of the Southwest reported in this section has been compiled from a number of recent summaries (Haury 1962; Jennings 1956, 1968; Willey 1966).

Contemporary survivals of the carriers of the archeological traditions we have surveyed cannot be determined with certainty. Anasazi and Mogollon traits are obvious in the social and cultural inventory of the present day Pueblos. The present Yuman speaking populations along the lower Colorado—the Havasupai,

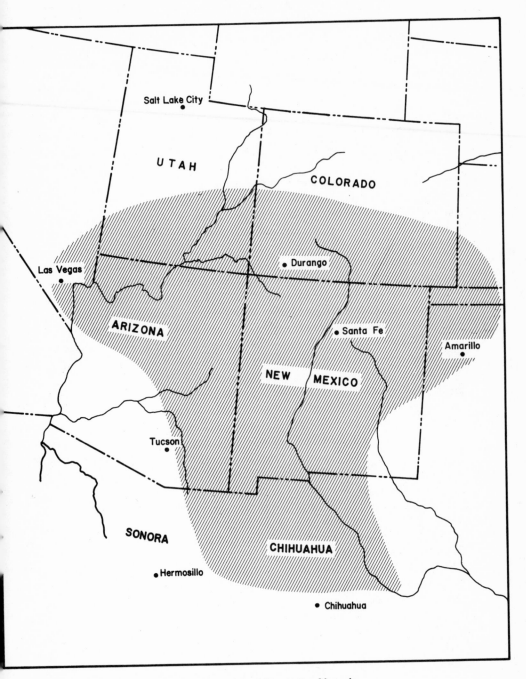

Figure 5. Extent of Prehistoric Pueblo culture.

Yavapai, Walapai, and the Yuman proper—are also believed to demonstrate a continuity of Patayan cultural characteristics, but not all authorities are agreed. Similarly, the contemporary Pima and Papago of southern Arizona are said to be cultural descendants of the ancient Hohokam. If Spanish influences on the surviving northern Mexican tribal peoples—like the Tarahumara, Opata, Yaqui, and Mayo— can be separated, these tribes may be linked to the Hohokam or Mogollon; but this may not be possible, for the imprint of Hispanic and Catholic patterns is extremely heavy on these groups. The fact that all of these northern Mexican tribal peoples speak Uto-Aztecan languages might be used as evidence that they stemmed from single or related traditions, yet linguistic unity is not always prerequisite to cultural relatedness. The Pueblos of Arizona and New Mexico are a case in point: all authorities appear to be agreed that these Pueblos are the cultural descendants of the Aanasazi tradition, with marked Mogollon characteristics, yet they fall into the four district language stocks of Uto-Aztecan, Tanoan, Keresan, and Zunian. It is important, therefore, to proceed with caution when we seek connections between contemporary language cultural groups and prehistoric cultural traditions.

In the northern periphery of the Pueblo area are the Paiutes and the Utes —nomadic peoples who may be considered continuities of the desert cultural pattern, or who may have reverted back to a hunting and foraging life after experiencing an early Anasazi sedentary life. During the historic period these people maintained a nomadic existence and, indeed, preyed on the settled farmers.

Another nomadic people who now comprise a majority in the population of the Southwest are obviously newcomers. The Apachean or Southern Athapascan peoples surrounded the Pueblo and the southern Uto-Aztecan peoples in late prehistoric and historic times. These Southern Athapascans are closely related linguistically to the Athapascans of interior Alaska and the Canadian Northwest. The earliest dependable archeological evidence places the Southern Athapascans in the Chacra Mesa and Governador regions of northern New Mexico early in the sixteenth century. The Southern Athapascans are divided at present into seven tribes: (1) Navaho, (2) Western Apache, (3) the Chiricahua Apache, (4) Jicarilla Apache, (5) Mescalero, (6) the Lipan, and (7) the Kiowa-Apache. The Navaho and the Jicarilla Apache are nearest the Pueblos and both have absorbed many Puebloan traits. Such traits were obviously borrowed in the sixteenth and seventeenth centuries from Pueblo Indian refugees who joined them to escape Spanish oppression, particularly after the Pueblo Indian Revolt of 1680 and the subsequent reconquest period of 1693–1696.

The term Pueblo was applied by the Spaniards to Indians living in compact villages who carried on a predominantly agricultural subsistence economy. During the sixteenth century, only the sedentary Indians of the middle Rio Grande and those of Zuni and Hopi fitted this term. When the Spanish explorers entered the Pueblo country in the middle of the sixteenth century, they found the Pueblos on the sites they now occupy but there were many more villages and they extended over a much wider area. There were numerous villages along the Rio Grande and along the eastern foothills of the mountains all the way from near El Paso in the south to Taos in the north. The Jemez area has as many as eleven villages; Acoma appeared to have been a single village, but both Zuni and Hopi had more villages than at present. The original Mogollon and Anasazi sites had long been abandoned when the Spaniards entered the Southwest; yet some of the village sites of the contemporary Pueblos have considerable antiquity. Settlements in the Hopi and Zuni areas go back to at least the eleventh century A.D. In the Rio Grande area, the prehistoric ancestors of the historic Tanoan and Keresan speakers settled in the region somewhat later. Continuities of both the Anasazi and Mogollon cultural traditions are evident in the modern pueblos as expressed in architecture, pottery, and by inference in their social and religious organization.

The present-day Pueblos are not linguistically uniform. At least three distinct stocks or phyla are represented among them. Hopi has been placed in the Shoshonean branch of the widespread Uto-Aztecan stock (Sapir 1913–1915). The Eastern Pueblos speaking Tiwa, Tewa, and Towa have been grouped along with Plains Indian Kiowa into Tanoan (Harrington 1909, 1910a; compare also Trager 1942; Miller 1959; Trager and Trager 1959; Hale 1962). In 1937, Whorf and Trager linked Uto-Aztecan with Tanoan in a superstock of phyla known as Aztec Tanoan. Keresan, the language spoken by the western New Mexico Pueblos of Acoma, Laguna, and by the Rio Grande Pueblos of Zia, Santa Ana, Cochiti, Santo Domingo, and San Felipe seems to be a distinct language with no clear relations outside the area, although Sapir (1929) placed it tentatively in his Hokan-Siouan super stock. In a recent comparative study of Zuni, Newman (1964a) suggested a remote relationship of Zuni to Californian Penutian. Thus, the Pueblos speak highly diversified languages; while the relationship of the languages of the Tanoan branch appear to be fairly close, they are not mutually intelligible. Indeed, within the Tiwa family, members of Taos, Picuris, and Isleta pueblos have difficulty communicating with one another in the native language. Rio Grande Tewa speakers of San Juan, Santa Clara, Nambe, San Ildefonso, and Tesuque do, however, converse freely in native Tewa; but the language of the Tewa village of Hano on the Hopi reservation is divergent and members of the two groups require a period of adjustment and familiarity with one another's linguistic differences before conversing with one another in the native language.

Archeologists and ethnologists are generally agreed in deriving the Eastern Keresan and the Tanoan-speaking Pueblos from two different prehistoric traditions, although there is yet no agreement on the particular archeological districts from which each stemmed (Reed 1949:182; Wendorf 1954; Wendorf and Reed 1955; Florence Hawley Ellis 1967). While the basic difference between these two groups of Eastern or Rio Grande Pueblos is linguistic, there are differences in political, social, and ceremonial organization as well. Such differences are probably the result of adjustments to differing ecological environments prior to settlement in the Rio Grande valley.

PREHISTORIC HABITAT AND ECONOMY

The Pueblos live in an area that is fairly uniform in altitude, climate, and in general topography. Elevations of village sites vary from approximately 5000 to 7000 ft. The climate is arid, more pronouncedly in the west than the east, but none of the villages have a rainfall in excess of 15 in. per year. The topography away from the Rio Grande is one of mesas and canyons, while the vegetation is typical of the Upper Sonoran life zone: cacti, yucca, grasses, and occasionally junipers and pinons. All the Pueblos have access to the flora and fauna of higher elevations, however. At distances of 20 miles or less are pine, spruce, fir, and aspen forests of the transition and Canadian zones. In these mountains, deer, bear, fox, and, formerly, antelope are fairly common.

Farming was a precarious occupation for the prehistoric and historic Pueblos. The mountain desert areas where food production initially began set definite limitations to farmers. High altitudes imposed a short growing season; arid conditions did not always provide enough rain for the maturation of crops, and the small, often intermittent, streams did not allow for the full development of irrigation. Hopi farming methods probably illustrate fairly accurately the way farming was carried on among the sedentary Mogollon and Anasazi dwellers. Except for a small stream which provides an irregular supply of irrigation water for the Hopi farmers of Moenkopi, none of the Hopi villages have access to permanently flowing streams. The plateau of the Black Mesa (on the spurs of which the Hopi villages are located) acts as a reservoir, however, and there are numerous springs at the base of the Hopi mesas that provide drinking water for the Hopi. In some springs the flow of water is abundant enough to permit the construction of small terraced gardens. These gardens add to the food supply, but the Hopi depend most heavily on crops grown on flood plains and alluvial fans. Maize, beans, and melons are planted near washes below the mesas where sands retain moisture and flash floods may hopefully irrigate the plants without uprooting them. In good years a fairly abundant harvest is taken in and stored to tide the Hopi over the lean years. But good years are the exception rather than the rule. Often there is so little rain that plants wither and die; at other times the rain falls in such torrents that the plants are washed away. The technology of the Hopi is so simple that little can be done in a practical way to solve the subsistence problem. To offset loss of crops by floods or insufficient moisture, the Hopi plant several plots in different areas so that if one crop is destroyed by flood waters or does not mature because of the lack of rain, another more favored by the exigencies of the weather may produce a crop.

In spite of the difficulties inherent in this type of farming, the late Mogollon and Anasazi farmers increased in population and developed more complex societies than the roving hunting and gathering people before them. In the late prehistoric period Pueblo-type cultures covered vast areas of the desert mountain terrain in the Sotuhwest. Large communities arose in certain favorable ecological environments, notably at Point of Pines in eastern Arizona, the four-corner area (Arizona, New Mexico, Utah, Colorado), and at Aztec and Chaco Canyon in New Mexico. Although these rather large compact towns did develop in areas where effective farming could be carried out, they were slow in coming. Haury comments succinctly on this interesting development in the Southwest:

> Settlement expansion from the hundred or so inhabitants of the village farming community to the large village or town of a thousand or more souls was ten

centuries in coming. With this increase we see also, especially among the *Anasazi*, formalized architecture, religious concepts made real to us by kiva architecture, expanding arts and crafts, with perhaps some specialists, some increase in trade, and public works in the *Hohokam* canals. At the root of these advances were, first, the food surplus, which permitted concentrated populations and, second, what Childe (1950) refers to as the "social surplus," members of the society who were not needed for food production. This level of attainment was maintained for 300–400 years, whence began a substantial reorientation of the societies, which took the form of shrinking boundaries accompanied by an increase in town populations. The Point of Pines ruin had a probable population of between 2,000 and 3,000 in the fourteenth century (Haury 1962:127).

Having achieved a cultural florescence in the fourteenth century, these towns were suddenly abandoned and the area of Pueblo population relocated and reduced to the areas occupied at the time of Spanish entry into the Southwest. The causes of this relocation and retraction were apparently due to drought and climatic changes in high desert areas which shortened the growing season for the maturation of maize. Abandonment of these earlier sites by the Pueblos has often been attributed to harassment by nomadic enemy peoples, but there appears to be little evidence for such a conjecture. The areas into which the Pueblos moved were open sites, less easily defended than the mesa and canyon locations of their ancestors. Even the Hopi were found by the early Spanish explorers at the foot of the mesas, for the most part, rather than on top where they might better defend themselves against enemy attacks. It was not until after trouble with the Spaniards that they moved to the top of the mesas. The factors of arroyo cutting, drought, and diminution of the growing season which prevented the growing of maize seem sufficient reasons to explain the migration of the Pueblos to the later historical locations (Hack 1942; O'Bryan 1952; Martin, Longacre, and Hill 1967).

Only the pueblos of Hopi, Zuni, Acoma, and Laguna (the Western Pueblos of today) occupy an environment comparable to those areas in which the prehistoric Mogollon and Anasazi culture was a period of readjustment and migration. This was a time of major settlements in the Rio Grande area and the beginning of building extensive irrigation systems by diverting the waters of the Pecos and the Rio Grande and its tributaries. While some of the villages were still on fairly high elevations, the majority of the Pueblo villages in New Mexico were cultivating the lower Rio Grande valley with elevations below 5000 ft. with ample water resources and a long growing season.

The major villages along the Rio Grande had been there for perhaps no more than 200 years when the Spaniards entered the Southwest. There is evidence of movement into the area earlier and the establishment of small settlements, but the consolidation into larger communities did not take place until after 1400 A.D. (Ellis and Brody 1964; Mera 1940). This concentration of populations appears to be correlated with the development of irrigated farming on the Rio Grande and suggests as well a developing social and political organization commensurate with the demands of the incipient waterworks society. The Rio Grande Pueblos were well on the road toward economic surpluses and the development of a complex society. The prehistoric communities of the Hohokam and Anasazi had reached a cultural peak earlier, but had then suffered a quick decline and the large towns had been abandoned. There was probably a lapse of 200 years between the time of the abandonment of the prehistoric Anasazi sites and the rise of large towns along the Rio Grande. In the interim the Pueblos had moved about, experimented with irrigation, and were making the needed social and political adjustments necessary to an irrigation society when the Spanish explorers arrived. Excerpts from the reports of two Spanish expeditions indicate the use of irrigation and reveal the general prosperity of the Pueblos in the late sixteenth century. The following is a report from the expedition of Antonio de Espejo in 1582:

> On reaching the said pueblos, we proceeded upstream for two days and found ten inhabited pueblos on both sides of the river and close to its banks, in addition to others which seemed to be off the beaten track. Passing through these settlements, we estimated that they contained more than twelve thousand people, including men, women, and children. [Espejos party was among the Piro Pueblos (now extinct) along the Rio Grande just north of the modern town of Las Cruces, New Mexico.]
>
> As we crossed this province the inhabitants of each town came out to meet us, took us to their pueblos, and gave us quantities of turkeys, corn, beans, and tortillas, with other kinds of bread, which they make more skillfully than the Mexican people. They grind raw corn on very large stones, five or six women working together in a single mill, and from the flour they make many kinds of bread. Their houses are two, three, or four stories high, each house being partitioned into a number of rooms; and in many of the houses there are estufas for the winter weather. In the pueblos each plaza has two estufas, which are houses built underground, well sheltered and tightly closed, with benches inside to sit on. At the entrance to each estufa there is a ladder for going down into it, so that strangers may find shelter there, and a large stack of wood. [These plaza *estufas* are the ceremonial chambers of *kivas* of the modern Pueblos.]
>
> In this province some of the natives are clad in cotton blankets, buffalo hides, or dressed chamois skins. They wear their blankets like the Mexicans, except that over their privy parts they have small pieces of colored cotton cloth; and some of them wear shirts. The women have cotten skirts, often embroidered with colored thread, and over the shoulders a blanket like that worn by the Mexican Indians, fastened at the waist by a strip of embroidered material, with tassels, resembling a towel. The skirts are worn like slips, next to the skin, the lower portion loose and swishing. Each woman displays such an outfit to the best of her ability; and everyone, man or woman, wears shoes or boots with soles of buffalo hide and uppers of dressed deerskin. The women arrange their hair neatly and prettily, winding it with care around moulds at each side of the head. They do not wear any head covering.
>
> All the pueblos have caciques, allotted according to the number of inhabitants. Thus there are the principal caciques, who in turn have other caciques under them, that is to say, their *tequitatos*, the latter functioning like sheriffs to execute the orders of their superiors in various pueblos, exactly as in the case of the Mexican people. When the Spaniards ask for something from the principal caciques of the pueblos, these officials summon the *tequitatos*, who then proclaim the order aloud throughout the pueblo concerned and in a very short time all bring what they may have been asked to provide. . . .
>
> In every one of these pueblos there is a house to which food is brought for the devil. The natives have small stone idols which they worship; and also, just as the Spaniards have crosses along the roads, these people set up, midway between pueblos, their artificial hillocks (*cuecillos*) built of stones like wayside shrines, where they place painted sticks and feathers, saying that the devil will stop there to rest and talk to them. They have fields planted with corn, beans, calabashes, and tobacco (*piciete*) in abundance. These crops are seasonal, dependent on rainfall, or they are

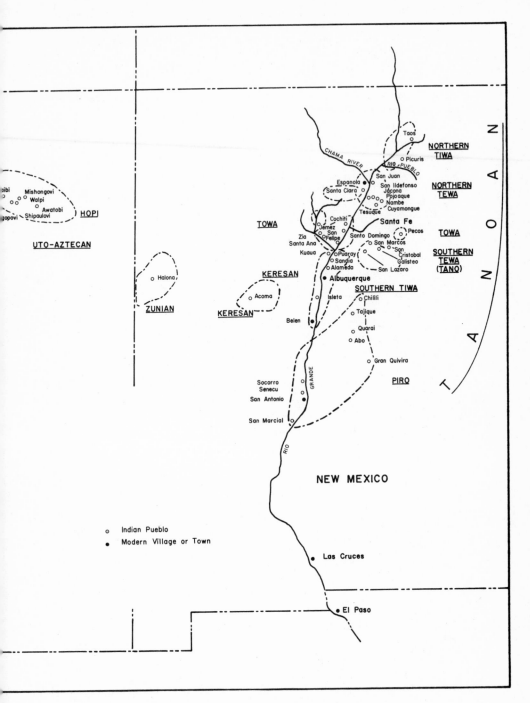

Figure 6. The Pueblos in the sixteenth century.

irrigated by means of good ditches. They are cultivated in Mexican fashion, and in each planted field the worker has a shelter, supported by four pillars, where food is carried to him at noon and he spends the siesta; for usually the workers stay in their fields from morning until night just as do the people of Castile (Hammond and Rey 1966:219–220).

Gaspar Castaño de Sosa's report of his travel and observations among the Tewa pueblos of northern New Mexico in 1591 also indicates concentrated populations, irrigated fields, and an abundance of crops. The following is excerpted from a daily journal Castaño kept on his party's expedition into the Pueblo country:

> On this same day [January 10, 1591] we went to sleep at another pueblo a league from there. [The pueblo where they spent the night was Jacona, about one league from the modern town of Pojoaque. Jacona was abandoned in 1696 and Pojoaque has been reduced to a population of only 23 Indians; it is no longer recognizable as a pueblo. See Schroeder and Matson 1965:117.] We were well received. They gave us in sufficiency all that of which we had need, and all was done that had been done in the others referred to before. All these six pueblos [including Pecos] are irrigated and have irrigation ditches, a thing [which would] not [be] believed if we had not seen it with our own eyes. A very great amount of maize, beans, and other vegetables is harvested. They dress in the manner of the pueblo [Pecos] previously described. They [the five Tewa pueblos visited to date] are small pueblos, although heavily populated. The houses are of two and three stories, all with such devices as hatchways and ladders which can be lifted up (Schroeder and Matson 1965:117).

In reading the early Spanish *entrada* accounts, one visualizes a picture of the Pueblos as a people with considerable vitality—an active, busy people, experiencing prosperity in abundant harvests, well-clothed and well-housed. The Pueblos were indeed the northern frontier outpost of civilization. Overshadowed by the rich culture of the Aztecs, perhaps, but compared to the crude, impoverished life way of nomadic peoples surrounding them, the Pueblos were a sophisticated folk. They were skilled weavers and potters. They possessed attractive jewelry of turquoise, shell, and coral. Their ceremonial life was rich. In the frequent rituals, men and women appeared beautifully dressed in embroidered cotton clothing of various colors with white moccasins and boots. Their walled towns were well-arranged and the houses sturdily built and warm in the winter. Back storerooms were filled with corn, beans, and squash—the New World food staples. When on rare occasions their nomadic neighbors were permitted to get a glimpse of Pueblo life, they must have marveled at the obvious wealth and comfort of these tillers of the soil.

A stage for the development of a more complex society by the Pueblos seemed imminent in the sixteenth century, but it never materialized. With Spanish colonization, oppression set in. Spanish civil and church authorities attacked the native religion and used the provisions and labor of the Indians to further their own interests. The Pueblos rebelled, held the Spanish at bay for a dozen years, but in the end, capitulated. In later years as Spanish power weakened, the Pueblos were able to hold their societies together; but ever afraid of retaliatory attacks on their customs, they became secretive and conservative. With the acquisition of the horse, the nomadic tribes wreaked havoc on both Pueblo and Spanish villages; but the

Pueblos survived. The promise of another Mexico in the northern frontier, however, remained unrealized. Eventually, writing, trade, mercantile centers, a money economy, the sciences, taxation—hallmarks of civilization—reached the Pueblos, but they were not the initiators of these new changes. Indeed, at times, they were not even partners, but passive bystanders. The unique culture of the Pueblos persists, however, and in an age where the promise of the tolerance and respect for different cultures looms as a possible value, the Pueblos may yet lead the way to the realization of that value.

We will relate in more detailed fashion the conquest of the Pueblos and assess the effects of Pueblo relations with Spaniards, Anglo-Americans, and other neighbors in the next section.

History 1539–1700

Most of the Indians of the Southwest have experienced the impact of three major representatives of Western European culture: Spanish, Mexican, and Anglo-American. These contacts brought about revolutionary changes unknown in contact relations involving Pueblo Indians and other Indians. The character of the organization and technological skills of Western European powers was beyond the comprehension of most of the Indian groups. Metal tools, wheeled vehicles, and firearms were revolutionary introductions, but equally important and far more disruptive was a new religion that tolerated no competing beliefs or rituals. Indians soon learned that Europeans had definite plans and programs of how they wanted to modify the Indian groups they invaded and eventually dominated. The goals and objectives of each of the three powers changed through time, but there were always definite plans and policies, often explicately stated in writing, as to how the Indian was to be brought into the dominant culture. Conflicts ensued, for what the intruders planned and put into operation was not always what the Indians wanted. In virtually all cases, cultural differences brought about misunderstandings which often resulted in hostile relations and sometimes broke out in open rebellion.

THE *ENTRADAS*

In the sixteenth century, after the conquest of Mexico, Spanish explorers were eager to find "another Mexico," a people who possessed an advanced culture similar to that of the Aztecs and their neighbors. The news of such a people was first triggered by the exaggerated report of Marcos de Niza in 1539. De Niza, a Franciscan priest, had made a trip into the northern country and from a distance caught a glimpse of the Zuni pueblos. He returned without setting foot in the pueblos, but his tale of cities and riches led the Viceroy of Mexico to authorize an expedition under the command of Francisco Vasquez de Coronado in 1540.

Coronado's party brought the first white men seen by the Rio Grande Pueblo Indians. The expedition was a spectacular one consisting of several hundred mailed and armed horsemen accompanied by Mexican Indian servants. Coronado and his men established headquarters in the pueblo of Tiguex near the present site of

Bernalillo, New Mexico. For two years the expedition was supported by provisions supplied by Tiguex and neighboring pueblos. From his central headquarters, Coronado sent expeditions to nearby pueblos as well as to the western pueblos of Acoma, Zuni, and Hopi. Initially, the relations between the Indian and Coronado's party were friendly, but as demands for provisions became more demanding the Indians staged a minor rebellion to force the Spaniards out of Tiguex. Coronado immediately put down the revolt and then "punished" the pueblo by executing several hundred of its inhabitants (Winship 1896:497). This news spread rapidly throughout the Pueblo country and laid the foundation for the mistrust and antagonisms that thereafter characterized relations between the Pueblos and Spaniards.

Upon his return to Mexico in 1542, Coronado dispelled much of the appeal for the new land with a sober report of the Pueblo Indians, who were neither as rich nor as advanced culturally as the indigenous populations in the valley of Mexico. But by 1580, the lure of the Pueblos was again uppermost in the minds of men of pioneering spirit in Spain and in Mexico. Priests and soldiers were moved by Christian ideals, service to the King, and the fortunes that might be made in the new land. Reports of towns two and three stories high whose inhabitants wore clothing made from woven cotton promised a highly advanced culture. The opportunity to save thousands of souls and at the same time finding riches for settlers in *encomiendas* (see section on the colonial period), mines, and ranches brought about appeals for a permanent settlement in the Pueblo country.

TABLE 1
IMPORTANT HISTORICAL DATES IN RELATIONS BETWEEN THE PUEBLOS
AND EURO-AMERICANS

1539	DeNiza's Expedition into western New Mexico.
1540–1542	Coronado's Expedition and explorations into New Mexico.
1581	Chamuscado-Rodriguez Expedition.
1582	Espejo's Expedition.
1598	The colonization of the Pueblo country by Oñate.
1630	Father Dominguez's report of conditions among the Pueblos.
1680	Pueblo Indian Revolt.
1693	Reconquest of the Pueblos.
1696	The second revolt of the Pueblos.

A small party under the command of Francisco Sanchez Chamuscado penetrated the northern frontier as far as the Tiwa Pueblos in 1581. In addition to Chamuscado, the party included Friar Augustin Rodriguez, two brothers of his order, and twelve soldiers. This expedition appears to have found Coronado's Tiguex and to have visited other pueblos in the central Pueblo area. When the party returned to Mexico, the friars were left among the Tiwa pueblos. Apparently the missionaries were put to death soon after Chamuscado's return for Espejo's expedition the following year found no trace of them.

Concern over the fate of the missionaries left among the Pueblos by Chamuscado's expedition prompted the next expedition under Antonio de Espejo in 1582. Espejo's party consisted of himself, fourteen soldiers, and one Franciscan priest. Actually, Spanish expeditions into New Mexico were larger than the personnel officially listed, for Indian servants always accompanied an expedition and such servants, if married, often brought their wives along. The Indians were not listed in the official rolls and only incidentally mentioned in the reports. Espejo and his soldiers all had one or more Indian servants. Most of the Indians who were taken on the expeditions were Mexican Indians; often they were taken from tribes through which the expedition passed on its way to New Mexico.

Although ostensibly to find out what happened to the friars left in New Mexico by the earlier expedition, Espejo was interested in exploring the Pueblo country for the possibility of establishing a permanent settlement. After learning that the missionaries had died among the Pueblos, Espejo remained to explore the area and to look for mines. He visited Zia, Jemez, Acoma, Zuni, and Hopi, and returned to the Rio Grande, passing through the Tiwa and Keresan pueblos again. He then visited the Tanos of the Galisteo Basin and returned to Mexico by the way of the Pecos River. Although unsuccessful in locating mining sites, Espejo reported favorably the conditions in New Mexico and petitioned for a contract to lead a colony of settlers into the Pueblo country.

As with members of previous exploring parties, Espejo and his men lived on the provisions furnished by the Indians. We have noted above the "punishment" given the pueblo of Tiguex for staging a protest or "rebellion" against the forced support of Coronado's party. Diego Perez de Luxan's account of the Espejo expedition gives a vivid description of another brutal punishment given the Indians of the Pueblo village that Espejo and his party used as headquarters on the Rio Grande. The pueblo is called Puala and is probably Puaray, a Tiwa village now in ruins across from modern Bernalillo. The following is Luxan's account of the incident:

> The people were all in the sierra except for some thirty Indians on the flat roofs of their houses. When we asked them for food, as they were our friends, they mocked us like the others. In view of this, the corners of the pueblo were taken by four men, and four others with two servants began to seize those natives who showed themselves. We put them in an estufa. And as the pueblo was large and the majority had hidden themselves there, we set fire to the big pueblo of Puala, where we thought some were burned to death because of the cries they uttered. We at once took out the prisoners, two at a time, and lined them up against some cottonwoods close to the pueblo of Puala, where they were garroted and shot many times until they were dead. Sixteen were executed, not counting those who burned to death (Hammond and Rey 1966:204).

It is clear that Spanish atrocities produced antagonistic reactions toward the newcomers long before a permanent colony was established in New Mexico. These attitudes become intensified when Spanish settlements become a reality in the seventeenth century and eventually culminated in the Pueblo Revolt of 1680.

Soon after Espejo's return to Mexico, he and others began to petition the crown for the colonization of the Pueblo area. While these requests were being considered, two unauthorized expeditions entered the Pueblo country. The first was made in 1590 by Castaño de Sosa, who established headquarters at Pecos and explored the Tewa, Keres, and Tano pueblos. A military expedition under the

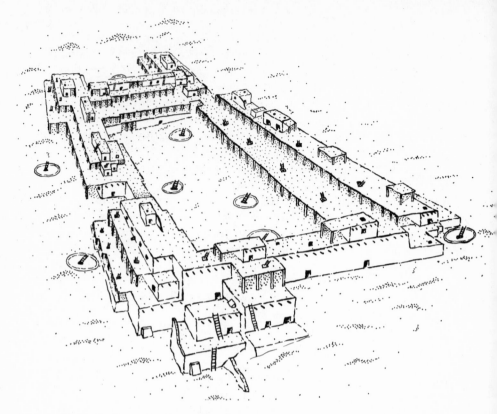

Figure 7. Pecos Pueblo—when the Spanish colony was established in 1598.

command of Captain Juan Morlete was sent to New Mexico and Castaño and his party were arrested and returned to Mexico. Two years later, two other Spaniards, Leyva de Bonilla and Antonio Gutierrez de Humana, tried to establish a colony at San Ildefonso pueblo, but both were killed while on an exploring trip into the Plains country.

COLONIZATION

The contract for the colonization of New Mexico was eventually awarded to Don Juan de Oñate in 1595. The recruiting of settlers, soldiers, servants, and other tasks of organizing the expeditionary force required three years before the colonizing party could begin the journey north. The party finally left southern Chihuahua on January 15, 1598 and reached the Pueblos late the same year. Headquarters was established at the Tewa pueblo of Yuqueyunque, which Oñate renamed San Gabriel. This pueblo was across the river from present-day San Juan; the site has been recently found and partially excavated by the University of New Mexico. In 1610, the seat of the provincial government was moved to Santa Fe, which remained the provincial headquarters during the Spanish period as well as during the short interlude of Mexican rule. Indeed, Santa Fe has continued to serve as the territorial and state headquarters under United States administration.

Oñate quickly embarked on a vigorous program of "civilizing" and Christianizing the Pueblos. Father Alonzo de Benavides, who directed the missionary program early in the seventeenth century, reported in his Memorial of 1630 that 60,000 Pueblo Indians had been converted and that ninety chapels had been built in as many villages. Oñate dealt brutally with any pueblo that resisted his program. Early in his visits to the pueblos to obtain their submission, he encountered resistance at Acoma, and in a skirmish with the Indians, his field officer was killed. Oñate retaliated by burning the pueblo and killing a large number of the Indians. For those who survived, he ordered one foot amputated from each man over twenty-five years of age and imposed a fine of twenty years of personal service. The men between twelve and twenty-five years escaped with twenty years of service. All the women over twelve years of age were likewise doomed to twenty years of servitude. Oñate considered his action as a warning to the other Pueblos that a rebellious act of any kind would be dealt with promptly and severely (Hammond 1926:461–462).

Oñate thus launched his colony by demanding strict obedience and submission to Spanish rule. We will note other instances of the cruelty, injustices, and abuses which characterized the actions of church and civil authorities toward the Pueblos during the seventeenth century.

The administration of the provincial categories may be conveniently described under three headings: the missionary program, the civil or secular governmental program, and finally, the military. Both the missionaries and secular authorities had definite plans and policies of how the Pueblos should be converted and how the labor and other resources of the Indian should be used for the benefit of a small elite among the settlers. The clergy and the civil administrators differed in the manner in which these programs should be implemented, however; in its proper place, we will discuss the conflict that ensued.

Missionary Program

The missionary program operated somewhat independently from the civil and military operations. The supreme authority in the new province was the governor and captáin-general, but the missionary head who supervised the activities of the missionaries occupied considerable independence and authority. No bishop had authority over the Franciscans in New Mexico during the seventeenth century. The superior of the missionaries of the province was called a prelate and had some functions of a bishop but his powers were much more limited. In New Mexico, a prelate could administer confirmation, confer minor orders, consecrate church buildings and ornaments, issue indulgences, and give dispensation in certain matrimonial cases. The commissaries and custodians of the Franciscans in New Mexico were the prelates of the New Mexican church. In New Mexico, the Franciscan who supervised the activities of the missionaries was known as the "commissary" until 1616. After that year, New Mexico was elevated to a "custody"—the Custody of the Conversion of St. Paul and of the Holy Gospel Province—and the Franciscan supervisor became known thereafter as the Custos or Custodio. Until 1610, while

Typical of the seventeenth-century mission establishments. Acoma Pueblo—western Keresan.

the provincial capital remained at San Gabriel, the office of the commissary or custodian was also at San Gabriel. When the capital was moved to Santa Fe in 1610, the headquarters of the Franciscan supervisor was established in Santo Domingo.

The commissary and later the custodian determined mission policy in New Mexico and was the intermediary between mission and civil activities in the province. From 1609 to 1674 there was a triennial mission caravan to Santa Fe, which brought supplies and replacements of personnel to New Mexico and returned goods and missionaries due for a transfer back to Mexico. Missionaries were constantly shifted from one place to another in the Pueblo area and also returned to Mexico. The shifting of missionary personnel was avowed policy of the Franciscan Order during the seventeenth century. It was a practice to prevent close ties between the friars and the Indians to whom they administered. Intimate relations between Indians and missionaries were considered harmful to the missionary program. For the same reason the missionaries in New Mexico were not encouraged to learn the native languages and only in rare cases did the friar learn the native idiom of the pueblo or pueblos under his jurisdiction.

The whole missionary program differed considerably from the missionary programs in other areas of Mexico. Spicer (1962:167) summarizes the primary differences between missionary work in Sonora and Mexico, on one hand, and that among the Rio Grande pueblos, on the other:

> Spanish-Indian relations in New Mexico differed from those in the south chiefly in the following respects. The imposition at a single time of the whole program over all the various groups of villages contrasted with the tribe by tribe advance in the south. Within a few years missions operating from a central administration in Santo Domingo had been set up over the whole of New Mexico. There were no preparations for missionary work with the different language groups, as the Jesuits had

prepared themselves through preliminary explorations and the gathering of materials for language study. Without such preparation the contacts of the missionaries must have been superficial and forced during the early years. There was no period of native request for missionaries with a waiting interval during which Indian leaders could prepare their people for receiving the missionaries—something which characterized the Jesuit situation, whether intentional or not, in the south.

The number of priests serving the pueblo area varied during the first century of Spanish rule. When Oñate entered New Mexico he brought eight Franciscan friars, two lay brothers, and three Mexican Indians dedicated to the Order, but who had not yet taken their final vows. In 1631, the royal treasury set the total number of friars to be supported in the Province of New Mexico at sixty-six. This quota may never have been filled; at the time of the Pueblo Revolt, there were only thirty-three missionaries in the province, of whom twenty-one were killed in the rebellion.

Soon after the colony was established, the entire country was divided into seven missionary districts, and missionaries were assigned to the various pueblos. The main task of the missionary program in its initial stages was a mammoth program of building churches and chapels, and in certain of the larger pueblos, in addition, a mission compound. These mission establishments were imposing walled compounds within or just outside the Pueblo village. The construction was supervised by the friars, perhaps with the assistance of a colonist and large numbers of Indian laborers. The walls of the mission compounds along the Rio Grande were of adobe brick; but outside the valley, notably among the Eastern Tiwa and Piro and the Western Pueblos of Acoma, Zuni and Hopi, the materials tended to be sandstone slabs set in adobe mud. The roof beams were enormous pine trees cut in the forested mountains several miles from the village and hauled to the mission sites by the Indians.

The missionary centers served a number of functions. They contained workshops where the Indians were taught weaving, leatherwork, blacksmithing, and a variety of other tasks. The mission employed a large number of Indians. Some served as cooks, maids, and servants; others served as herders for the sheep and cattle maintained by missionaries and kept on grazing lands outside the compound. Gardens and orchards were also the special pride of the resident missionary or missionaries and characteristic of the missionary compounds.

The force with which the missionaries pursued their building programs is indicated by the report of Father Benavides in 1630 that there were ninety chapels in as many villages. The duties of the friars consisted in saying Mass, conducting prayer services, performing baptism and marriage, and conducting burial services. Some of the Indians were taught how to serve the priest at Mass, perform other services connected with Catholic ritual, and in some instances, to lead the Pueblo congregation in reciting prayers. In each pueblo, a member of the civil government system, the *fiscal* (see below), was made responsible for all duties connected with the church and services. He had the responsibility of enforcing the villagers to attend Mass. In pueblos where there was no mission and no resident priest he kept the keys of the church, was responsible for the maintenance of the building and grounds, and made the church ready for the periodic visits of the priest.

Beyond the responsibility of keeping the mission and church establishments in constant repair, supervising workers in the workshops, and performing religious duties, the missionaries also attempted to carry out the task of making the Pueblos into "good" Christians. This task consisted primarily of the attempt to eradicate Pueblo indigenous religious beliefs and practices and the endeavor to substitute Catholic counterparts. In these efforts, missionaries enlisted the aid of the governor and the military organization. The missionaries were especially disturbed by the persistence of the Indians in holding ceremonies which were considered idolatrous. The masked Katcina dances in which the Pueblos represented mythological beings were particularly vexing to the missionaries, and such dances were eventually prohibited. The Indians continued to hold the dances and other sacred rituals in secret behind closed doors, however. But news of the performances of such prohibited rites often became known to the friars, whereupon soldiers were called to enter Pueblo ceremonial rooms and punish the performers and their leaders. The missionaries employed drastic disciplinary measures in their attempt to wipe out the native religion. They whipped native religious leaders and executed repeated offenders. Periodically, Pueblo homes were raided for Katcina masks, prayer sticks, prayer feathers, and other objects considered sacred by the Indians.

As a result of the suppression of native beliefs and practices, resentment swelled among the Pueblos. They did not give up their beliefs or even their sacred rites, but became more careful in concealment and secrecy. Under coercion they took over the externals of the new religion without understanding the deeper spiritual values of Christianity. Their own religious beliefs and organization fitted, as it were, to their own folk culture continued to have more meaning for them. Pueblo religion is founded on the belief that supernatural forces control daily activities and that such forces must be placated and propitiated to obtain the needs of existence. Special institutions existed for a successful hunt, for a bountiful harvest, for warding off illness, thwarting the enemy, and for achieving harmonious social relations within the community. The new religion provided no institutions for relief from these immediate and pressing anxieties of daily life. Instead, the new religion dwelt on incomprehensible rewards or punishments in the life after death. In Pueblo belief, conduct in the temporary world did not determine the kind of existence one might have in the hereafter. There was no concept of heaven or hell; one lived on after death, but no rules existed here and now for improving or worsening one's position in the next world. Life was difficult enough in this world; let the future take care of itself. So loyalty in the native beliefs and rites persisted. The Pueblo Indian accommodated himself to the external practices of the new religion for the simple expedient of survival, but his own indigenous religion was not abandoned.

This kind of accommodation might have persisted, but another branch of the colonial administration also threatened the Pueblos. For more mundane and selfish reasons, the secular arm of the civil government competed with the missionaries for the labor and services of the Indians. Eventually, the oppression became too much to bear even for a people who cherished their community independence. Taking advantage of the bickering between the missionaries and the secular authorities, the Pueblos achieved an unprecedented unity of purpose and organization to force the missionaries and the alien settlers out of the area. We will discuss the revolt in greater detail later because of its historic relevance and its importance in understanding the nature of Pueblo social and cultural integration.

The Hopi pueblos were also a part of the Spanish province of New Mexico, but great distance and the general inhospitality of the environment for mining or farming isolated these Indians from the seat of Spanish government in Santa Fe. The major Spanish expeditions had all visited the Hopi villages. In 1540, a party of the Coronado expedition spent several days among them; and in 1582 the Espejo expedition also visited these villages. Oñate, the colonizer of New Mexico, obtained the formal submission of the Hopi pueblos in 1598. Between 1629 and 1641, missions were established at Awatobi, Shongopovi, and Oraibi. Visiting chapels were built at Mishongnovi and Walpi. For a period of about fifty years, the Hopi Indians experienced the coercive Spanish missionary program and submitted to labor demands and to the imposition of the Catholic religion. These pueblos along with those on the Rio Grande killed their resident missionaries and destroyed the missions in the Revolt of 1680. The Pueblo rebellion and the abortive revolts of 1696 brought refugees from the Rio Grande. The Hopi welcomed these Indians, undoubtedly in order to better resist the Spaniards and also to fight off the increasing raids of nomadic Indians.

Both the Hopi and Zuni pueblos could violate Spanish civil and church

Pueblo homes—Old Oraibi, Hopi. A Western Pueblo.

edicts more openly because of distance and isolation. During the first century of Spanish rule, both groups took over a considerable number of cultural elements from the Spanish, particularly livestock and material items. They also appear to have accepted Catholicism, at least externally. After the revolt, these Pueblos reverted to their own native beliefs and practices.

Secular Organization and Civil Policies

The settlers who came in with Oñate were a diverse group in terms of ethnic or national backgrounds. Spaniards were a minority in the population; probably the majority were Mexican Indians and *mestizos* or mixed bloods of European and Indian parentage. The non-Pueblo population never exceeded 3000 people during the seventeenth century. In the beginning there was also a sprinkling of such non-Spanish Europeans as Portuguese, Flemish, and French. Toward the end of the century, however, 80 to 90 percent of the population was composed of natives of the province itself. The majority were mixed bloods, representing all of the strains listed above; but there were also a considerable number of Pueblo Indians who, by associations with the colonists or through work in the missionary workshops, had abandoned the Pueblo way of life and preferred to live like the newcomers.

Scholes (1935:97–98) has described the characteristics of the seventeenth-century colonial population from an examination of the documentary reports, as follows:

> The reader of the contemporary documents cannot fail to notice the incidental statements and evidence indicating that mixing of blood was frequent, and that many a man of pure European blood married an Indian, a mestiza, or even a Negro caste. This was inevitable in a community which not only lived with the Indians and was outnumbered by them, but which received comparatively few new colonists. Moreover, many of the colonists were themselves mestizos.
>
> . . . But despite the easy and free intermingling of classes and despite the fact also that no man could attain any great measure of wealth in New Mexico, there was clearly a well defined local aristocracy based on family, service to the Crown, and worldly possessions.

Pueblo Indians, during the first century of the Spanish colonial period, came into contact with newcomers in two types of contact communities: (1) the Pueblo villages, some of which had resident missionaries, perhaps a few soldiers, and a missionary workshop, and (2) three main areas of Spanish settlement. The most important settlement was Santa Fe, where the provincial governor and the garrison of soldiers resided; a second settlement was La Canada, near present-day Santa Cruz in the Tewa Basin; and the third settlement region extended from Santo Domingo pueblo to approximately the position of modern Socorro. The pueblos of Acoma, Zuni, and Hopi had no direct contact with the areas of colonial settlement, but mission compounds were built in all three areas. Among the Hopi, missions with resident priests were established at Awatovi, Shongopovi, and Oraibi, with chapels at Walpi and Mishongovi. All of the Indians in these pueblos were, of course, subject to the labor recruitment and paid tribute.

While the most intimate and intense relations with the newcomers occurred in the contact communities outlined above, all of the Pueblos became involved in the activities of the missionaries and civil authorities. Tribute and labor were constantly drawn from the Indians for maintenance of the missions and chapels, as well as for support of the civil government and military organization.

The provincial government system included the governor and captain-general (appointed by the viceroy), the secretary of government and war, the lieutenant governor, and the *alcaldes mayores*. The last three were appointed by the governor and held office at his pleasure. Closely associated with the civil government system was the military organization. The military group consisted of a group of professional soldiers who, along with the governor and his staff, formed the political and social elite of the province. None of the officials below the governor received salaries, but they all profited from the collection of tribute and from the labor of the Indians. In addition to these offices, the villa of Santa Fe was governed by a *cabildo*. This was a town council and consisted of four councilmen and two magistrates. The soldier-citizen group dominated the membership of the *cabildo*—hence, the civil government and military organizations consisted of a small closely knit group with the governor at its head.

The duties of the colonial officers were as follows: The governor was the highest authority in the province. It was his duty to promote an administration founded on justice, to defend the province against internal revolt and from attack by outside enemies, to protect the Indians under his jurisdiction (this applied specifically to the Pueblos) from abuse and exploitation, and, finally, to support the missionary program. The governor was the civil head, the commander-in-chief of the military organization, as well as the chief legislator and judicial officer. The secretary was in charge of all documents and papers issued in the governor's name and also his adviser and companion. The lieutenant-governor substituted at all functions which the governor could not attend or duties which he could not perform. During the latter part of the seventeenth century, the lieutenant-governor assumed control over the southern district—the Rio Abajo—from Santo Domingo south to near Socorro. The *alcaldes mayores* were in charge of subdivisions of the province (during the seventeenth century there were six or eight such units in the Pueblo country). These were the officials that the Indians most frequently came in contact with for they dealt directly with the people, both Indians and settlers.

The governors were rarely men of integrity. During the seventeenth century almost every one of the governors used the position selfishly for his own interests and benefits. They engaged in a variety of economic ventures in which the labor and products of the Indian were used. Pueblo Indians were put to work weaving cloth and blankets in workshops in either the pueblos or Santa Fe. When there was a piñon crop, Indians were made to collect large quantities of the piñon nuts, which were sold in Mexico City and brought handsome profits to the governors. Still other Indians built wagons and carts for special caravans to Mexico to ship out the accumulated goods. In the caravan trains, Pueblo Indians served as servants and muleteers. A trade invoice which was found in the Spanish archives and translated by Bloom (1935:242–248) indicates the tremendous amount of goods shipped out by Governor Rosas from Santa Fe to Mexico in 1638. Usually the Indians were forced to perform these services without compensation; even when wages were paid, they were far below the standard scale of pay. Mendizabal, who was governor from 1659 to 1669, ruthlessly exploited Indian labor. Through the complaints of the missionaries, Mendizabal was tried and found guilty, but there is evidence that other governors were equally as unscrupulous and abusive of Indian labor (see Scholes 1935:74 ff).

Although the salary was fairly good, compared to other salaries in New Spain for official posts, it did not attract men to the post of provincial governor. Opportunities for profitable engagement in stock-raising and trade, where the labor of Indians was used, were the primary attractions.

The governor received full support in his economic ventures from the professional soldier-citizens. These men, whose number was set at thirty-five, comprised the military organization of the colony. They received no regular salary, but were granted *encomiendas* which, in New Mexico, entitled a soldier-citizen to the services of a number of Indians. Some of the Indians assigned to a soldier-citizen were used as household servants, but the main service of the Indians came from the farms and livestock which they cultivated and tended on special tracts of land near the Indian pueblos. Although the *encomendero* was forbidden by law to live on the land, nevertheless, he received most of the proceeds that came from the livestock and produce. Since the governor allocated the *encomiendas* to the soldiers and determined the revenues to be derived from them, the soldiers became indebted to the governor and naturally supported and often joined him in his economic enterprises.

Both the missionaries and the governor's clique vied for the labor and products of the Indian. It is not surprising that conflict soon developed over this competition. The missionaries accused the civil authorities of making illegal profits and taking the Indians away from their agricultural activities. They claimed that the operation of the missions was hampered by recruiting workers who would ordinarily be serving the missions. The missionaries claimed also that so much time was spent by the Indians serving the governor and his cohorts, the Christianization program was becoming seriously affected. On the other hand, the civil authorities accused the clergy of setting up little kingdoms where the missionaries lived in comfort at the expense of the Indians.

Most frequently the governors called attention to the drastic measures used by the missionaries in suppressing the Indian religion. Cases of severe punishment to the Indians by priests and of sexual misconduct on the part of the missionaries were exposed by civil authorities. Some of the governors openly opposed the suppression of native religious rites and often disregarded the petitions of the missionaries to help them stamp out the native customs. In the mid-1650s Governor Lopez stated publicly that the Katcina ceremonies were harmless and gave official permission to a number of the pueblos to hold such rites in public. Although the missionaries were opposed to participation by the settlers in some of the Pueblo dances, Governor Lopez condoned such participation. Governor Lopez also objected to the frequent invasion of Pueblo homes and ceremonial rooms to seek out ceremonial paraphernalia. These conflicts between civil and missionary authorities contributed to the demoralization and disorganization of the New Mexico colony and, in part at least, paved the way for the Pueblo rebellion toward the end of the century (Scholes 1942).

As indicated earlier, the pueblos of Hopi and Zuni, being removed by distance and isolation from the center of colonial activity along the Rio Grande, were able to avoid the more serious effects of Spanish oppression. While a veneer of Spanish-Catholic culture also was painted over their indigenous religious system, after the Pueblo revolt these pueblos were able to wipe off the veneer and return to their native beliefs and practices.

On the eve of the revolt, the Pueblos still held primary allegiance to their traditional way of life. The Pueblo villages were not reduced as in other parts of Mexico. Had the Pueblo villages been broken up and the populations reestablished in locations nearer the Spanish settlements, social and cultural disorganization might have set in and the Pueblos modified into Ladino-type societies. The situation might then have been similar to that in parts of Mexico where Indian cultures exist as amalgams of Spanish and Indian elements. In New Mexico, the Indians were permitted to remain in their villages and hence able to retain their old customs and rites despite periodic raids on native religious objects and the punishment of their religious leaders. Forceful techniques to suppress the native religion were essentially one-sided; the friars received only sporadic help from civil authorities in stamping out the native rites. While the activities of the missionaries engendered considerable fear and hostility, attempts to wipe out the native religion and to substitute Catholic beliefs and practices were largely ineffective as they were not consistently applied with sufficient force. The provincial government, even if completely willing to use force to implement the missionary program, did not have the personnel to accomplish the task. A revolutionary change in the tactics of the missionaries—a change, for example, from permissive to noncoercive methods of missionization— might also have advanced the Christianizing and civilizing program among the Pueblos. Such methods were used by the Jesuit missionaries among the Yaquis with notable success (Spicer 1961). The Franciscans failed because they used forceful methods; their missionary efforts produced instead a people hostile to Spanish Catholicism and civilization.

THE PUEBLO REBELLION

By the middle of the seventeenth century, the Pueblos were fully aware of all the aspects of Spanish oppression and were determined to do something to put an end to the terrible suffering. A number of minor rebellions were staged in several of the pueblos which the military organization was able to repress. Although these protests against the severity of Spanish rule were unsuccessful, they enabled Indians to test the colonial forces and to note their strengths and weaknesses. It became clear that only a united effort in which all of the Pueblos were engaged in the overthrow of the alien population was likely to be successful. Such unity was foreign to the Pueblos; each Pueblo community was an independent political unit and no mechanisms had even been developed to unite them. Still, no common threat had ever faced them. In pre-Spanish times occasional attacks from nomadic tribes had been a nuisance, but the individual Pueblo villages had been able to cope with them. In the centuries to come the nomads would become a real threat, but in the seventeenth century the Pueblos were more than a match for these raiders. Indians on foot, armed with bows and arrows, were at a distinct disadvantage in attacking a fortified Pueblo village. The horse as well as firearms in the hands of these same nomads was another matter, however; toward the end of the first colonial period and increasingly in the next century, the nomadic tribes were to become formidable enemies.

The Revolt of 1680 was the result of careful and elaborate plans; the Pueblos took advantage of their previous failures in overthrowing Spanish rule and assessed both the power and the nature of Spanish resistance extremely well. Although the Pueblos greatly outnumbered the colonists, they were aware of the Spanish garrison's superiority both in organization and in the possession of superior weapons. The leader of the revolt is identified in contemporary documents as Popé, a "medicine man" from the Tewa pueblo of San Juan. As a medicine man, Popé could have occupied any one of a number of positions in Tewa socioceremonial organization. He may have been one of the moiety priests, hence having both ceremonial and governmental responsibilities in the pueblo. He may have been a member of a curing association, of which there are several in each pueblo; or a member of the hunt association; or even a member of the warrior association. All of these associations perform "cures" and its members comprise the ceremonial and sociopolitical elite of the Tewa pueblos. At any rate, Popé was obviously a man holding an important office in the traditional socioreligious organization and hence acquainted with other such men in the other pueblos.

Pueblo Indians value village sociopolitical autonomy and respect the autonomy of other villages. There is not much interaction between the pueblos and, hence, until recently, few interpueblo marriages; village endogamy was definitely a characteristic of the pueblos. However, ceremonial interaction among members of Pueblo associations is another matter. Attendance and participation in the esoteric rites of the village associations are open only to members, but members of such organizations from other villages are welcome to attend the meetings and rites of the associations. Identical or analogous ceremonial associations are to be found in every village despite linguistic differences. Because of rigid membership qualifications and long and involved initiation rites, the size of membership in these ceremonial associations is small. As a result, the number of members who come together in a meeting, even in interpueblo gatherings of these associations, is likely to be small. Throughout the Pueblo country the meetings and ceremonial rites are kept secret from children, women, and nonassociation members. Therefore, the date and the time of meetings are carefully guarded.

Because of the nature of Pueblo ceremonial associations and the secret character of their meetings, Popé was able to map out the strategy of the revolt so well and to enlist the aid and cooperation of virtually every pueblo, including those of Acoma, Zuni, and Hopi. But the best of plans often go awry; news of the revolt leaked out before the day of its execution and it had to be put into operation prematurely.

Popé established headquarters at Taos pueblo, where the revolt started, but it soon involved all the pueblos with the exception of Isleta, which harbored refugees living in the southern district. The revolt was to have been put into operation on August 11, 1680; but the capture, on August 9, of two Tesuque Indian messengers who were carrying the details of the uprising to the pueblos south of Santa Fe necessitated an immediate change of plan. The pueblo of Tesuque, learning that its messengers had been intercepted, sent additional messengers requesting the pueblos to put the rebellion into execution immediately. The general instructions that Popé and the other leaders conveyed were simple: On a given day at a given time, kill all the friars and the settlers. All the pueblos apparently received the revised message so that the killing of the missionaries and the colonists began at dawn on August 10 rather than on the eleventh, as previously planned. Fortunately for the colonists, however, an alert had been given so that some of the friars and settlers were able to flee before the Indians attacked them.

The Northern Pueblos, after killing the friars and colonists who had not escaped to Santa Fe, laid siege to the capitol where over a thousand colonists and missionaries had taken refuge. The Indians who initially attacked Santa Fe were the Tanos (Southern Tewa) and the Towa of Pecos. Later, these Indians were joined by the Northern Tewa and the Tiwa of Taos and Picuris (Hackett and Shelby 1942:xxxix–xli). All these Pueblos are members of the Tanoan linguistic group. Living nearer Santa Fe, they had perhaps more than any of the others suffered from the abuses and injustices of Spanish civil and church administration. Thus, they entered the rebellion with fury, determined to drive the colonists out of Santa Fe and out of the Pueblo country. So fierce were the Tanoan warriors at Santa Fe that after nine days of battle, Don Antonio de Otermin, governor and captain-general of the province, decided to leave the city and join the colonists in Isleta. The beleaguered colonists left the city on August 21, 1680. The following is an excerpt of a statement issued by Governor Otermin describing conditions within the Villa of Santa Fe during the siege and reporting the decision of the friars, military officers, and civil authorities to abandon the capitol:

> Many Indians who were captured have declared that all the nations of the kingdom that laid siege to the villa were confederated with the heathen Apache enemy so that, going to the siege to join them, they might destroy his lordship, the religious and all the Spaniards and persons who were besieged, who comprised the greater part of the kingdom. Many settlements have been laid waste and destroyed, and it is known that from Los Taos to the pueblo of Isleta, which is a distance of fifty-one leagues, all the people, religious, and Spaniards have perished, no other persons being alive except those who found themselves besieged within the *casas reales* of the villa, and there is information to the effect that the residents of *Rio Abajo* have fortified themselves and assembled in the said pueblo of Isleta. For which reasons, and finding ourselves out of provisions, with very few horses, weary and threatened by the enemy, and not being assured of water, or of defense, since the few horses and cattle are dying from being shut up day and night within the said *casas reales*—and on taking them out for water and to graze a little, it was necessary to leave the *casas reales* undefended because of the small number of soldiers, most of whom went out armed on horseback to guard and defend the said beasts and cattle—and because of many other inconveniences that followed, and of the holy church and all the houses of the Spaniards and the Mexican Indians and others being burned—for all these reasons, it was requested unanimously by the reverend father preachers, Fray Francisco Gomez de la Cadena, minister guardian, and Fray Andres Duran, *definidor*

habitual, and Fray Francisco Farfan, all clerical ministers, and by the *alcaldes ordinarios*, military officers, and soldiers, that his lordship, looking to the better service of the two Majesties and the safety of the people, arms, horse, and cattle which have remained where it is not possible to maintain them, decide to withdraw, marching from this villa in full military formation until reaching the pueblo of La Isleta, where it is said that the residents of *Rio Abajo* are gathered with the lieutenant general of that jurisdiction . . . (Hackett and Shelby 1942, Vol. 8:17–18).

The uprising in the central area (the Keres and Jemez districts) and in the southern Tiwa district (the Rio Abajo) followed a pattern similar to that which took place north of Santa Fe. Since the friars were nearest the pueblos, they were the first to be put to death. Next, the Indians attacked the colonists living on isolated ranches in the area. However, forewarned by messengers dispatched by Governor Otermin and by others fleeing from the besieged pueblos, the refugees began to work southward toward the pueblo of Isleta. The Isletans, through fear of the colonists, permitted their pueblo to be used as a gathering place. The lieutenant-general, Alonso Garcia, of the Rio Abajo district, scouted the southern area for survivors and brought them to Isleta. He was assisted by Luis de Granillo, alcalde Major and Captain of War of the Jemez and Keres districts, and several soldiers who had escaped from the Indians. Having collected as many of the settlers of the district as possible, Garcia sent repeated messages to Governor Otermin, but none of them reached him. On the other hand, the attempts of Governor Otermin to communicate with the colonists of the Rio Abajo district had also failed. The rumor that all of the colonists north of Santo Domingo were dead compelled Garcia to abandon Isleta and march south. The southern group of survivors, numbering about fifteen hundred set out for El Paso on August 14, 1680 (Hackett and Shelby 1942:lxvii–lxx).

When Otermin reached Isleta on September 3, 1680, he found the pueblo deserted. After the survivors of the Rio Abajo left, the Indians, apparently fearing both the Spaniards and the rebellious Pueblos, also abandoned their pueblo. Otermin sent messengers ahead to the retreating colonists instructing Garcia to wait for the northern contingent. On September 13, the two groups of refugees met at a place called Fray Cristobal, approximately sixty miles south of Socorro. The combined group of refugees then proceeded southward.

The destitute refugees were moved along by the happy knowledge that a wagon train was enroute north. Father Francisco de Ayeta, Custodio of New Mexico, was bringing clothing, food, firearms, ammunition, and troop reinforcements. Finally, at La Salineta, about fifteen miles above El Paso, on September 29, 1680, Father Ayeta and the group of refugees met. Here, almost immediately, meetings were held and plans made for a reconquest of the Pueblos; but complete pacification of the Pueblos was not to come for another thirteen years (Hackett and Shelby 1942:xc–cvi).

As for the Pueblos, they were free. After almost a century of forced labor and forced attendance at church services, of constantly "sweeping and putting the missions in order," the Pueblos had finally driven out their oppressors (Hackett and Shelby 1942:xc–cvii).

Although the revolt was rather bloody when we consider the slaughter of the *padres* and families in the *haciendas*, once the Indians realized the colonists were leaving they conducted themselves with compassion. They did not attack the retreating survivors. Both the northern and southern groups of colonists were poorly armed, many of them ill and weak. Such a destitute group moving along slowly would have been easy prey, especially in the open where the Indians could swoop down upon them in the fighting style in which they excelled. Certainly, the Pueblos must have realized how vulnerable the refugees were, but they let them go, watching their movements closely but not attempting to harm them. In comparison to the atrocities of the Spanish, the Pueblo behavior was humane. The missionaries constantly berated the Pueblos for their attachment to pagan beliefs and practices and attempted to substitute the more "enlightened" virtues of Christianity by force. Yet the Pueblos rarely matched the cruelty meted to them by Spanish officials. From any kind of behavioral standard, Pueblo conduct throughout the Spanish period demonstrates a higher ethic than that of the intruding population.

During the revolt, the Pueblos had killed twenty-one missionaries out of a total of thirty-three, and about 380 settlers out of a population of about twenty-five hundred colonists. The Tewa (including the Tano), the Northern Tiwa, and the Pecos Indians were the most active in the revolt and suffered the most casualties. In the attack on Santa Fe alone, 300 Tanoans were killed, while forty-seven others were captured and executed. Isleta and the Piro pueblos south of Isleta did not take part in the revolt; indeed, fearing retaliatory attacks from the others, they fled south and established new villages near El Paso. Only the Tiwa of Isleta returned after the revolt to reoccupy their village; the Piro and other Southern Tiwa pueblos were never reoccupied. All of the other Pueblos, including those of Acoma, Zuni, and Hopi aided the general revolt by killing their resident missionaries and other Spaniards or colonists living in or near these pueblos. Apparently the nomadic Apache did not actively participate; but the Spaniards, believing them to be in the revolt pact, gave up more readily. Everywhere among the Pueblo villages, Spanish houses, missionary establishments together with church records and furnishings were burned or otherwise destroyed. Statements given by Pueblo Indians captured in an abortive reconquest attempt in 1681–1682 by Governor Antonio de Otermin indicate that the leaders of the rebellion wanted to wipe out every vestige of the Catholic religion and Spanish culture. The testimony of two brothers, natives of San Felipe pueblo, questioned by Governor Otermin's lieutenant, Juan Dominguez de Mendoza, described the conditions among the Pueblos after the revolt:

> Asked what happened after the said rebellion [the two brothers] said they saw that the said Indian, Popé, came down to the pueblo of San Felipe accompanied by many captains from the pueblos and by other Indians and ordered the churches burned and the holy images broken up and burned. They took possession of everything in the sacristy pertaining to divine worship, and said that they were weary of putting in order, sweeping, heating, and adorning the church; and that they proclaimed both in the said pueblo and in the others that he who should utter the name of Jesus would be killed immediately; and that thereupon they could live contentedly, happy in their freedom, living according to their ancient custom. . . .
> They declared further that by order of the said Popé and Alonso Catiti, governor and head of the Queres nation, they were commanded to place in the pueblo and

its environs piles of stones on which they could offer corn and other cereals and tobacco, they saying that the stones were their God, and that they were to observe this, even to the children, giving them to understand that thereby they would have everything they might desire. They say that they have passed over many other things that they do not recall, but they saw that as soon as the senior governor and the rest of the Spaniards had left, the Indians erected many estufas in the pueblos and danced the dances of the cazina and of losse [masked Kachina and the clown or Koshare dances], which are dances instituted by the devil . . . (Hackett and Shelby 1942:251).

It is clear that some Mexican Indians, as well as others of mixed blood, joined the rebels and remained in New Mexico after the colonists left. Indeed, some of these mixed bloods appear to have had a leading role in the revolt. Alonso Catiti and an Indian with the nickname El Ollita are mentioned as leaders of the central pueblos in the revolt and both are said to have been mestizos. On January 1, 1682, Governor Don Antonio de Otermin, after receiving the report of his lieutenant about conditions in New Mexico, reported: "Many *mestizos, mulattoes,* and people who speak Spanish have followed them [the rebellious Pueblo], who are skillful on horseback and who can manage firearms as well as any Spaniard" (Hackett and Shelby 1942:355).

THE RECONQUEST

Governor Otermin made an unsuccessful attempt to regain the Pueblo area in the winter of 1681–1682. Although he failed in reconquering the Pueblos, he gathered considerable information that was useful later to De Vargas in the latter's successful reconquest of the area. The testimonies collected by Otermin from the Pueblos contributed to an understanding of the reasons the Pueblos revolted and helped to reconstruct the plans and organization of the revolt. We have noted that a considerable number of the leaders of the revolt were mixed bloods; it is obvious then that many of the settlers sympathized with the natives and that some of them were courageous enough to join the Pueblos in resisting Spanish oppression. The information given to Governor Otermin revealed that soon after the revolt, the unity of the Pueblos was broken and groups of the villages became actively hostile to each other.

There were two other unsuccessful forays into the Pueblo country, one by Governor Pedro Reneros de Posada in 1688, and another by Governor Domingo Jironza Petris de Cruzate in 1689. Don Diego de Vargas became governor of New Mexico in 1690 and in 1692 he made a preliminary entry into the Pueblo area. In this initial expedition, De Vargas received the formal submission of twenty-three Pueblo villages and freed a number of Spanish captives held by the Pueblos. De Vargas' first expedition into New Mexico and the earlier ones by Governors Otermin, Posada, and Cruzate had softened the Pueblos. The conquerers in all of these expeditions killed hundreds of Pueblo Indians and set fire to a number of their villages. The second expedition of De Vargas in 1692 reached Santa Fe in 1693. After the revolt of 1680, many of the Pueblos, anticipating punitive or reconquest expeditions, had abandoned their pueblos and retreated to more defensible areas in the mountains and mesas. Some of the Tano Indians moved north into the Tewa country while others entrenched themselves in Santa Fe, where De Vargas found them in 1693. These Indians threatened resistance. De Vargas, with over a thousand soldiers, colonists, and Indian servants, camped for two weeks outside the gates of the walled city. He made repeated demands for the Tanos to surrender; finally, he stormed the city and won the fortified stronghold with the loss of only one soldier.

In both his initial entry into the Pueblo country in 1692 and his final reconquest of the area in 1693-1694, De Vargas used Pueblo Indians to bring about the submission of the Pueblos. Perhaps the most valuable of these Indians in the reconquest period was a Zia Indian by the name of Bartolomé de Ojeda. Jones (1966:39-40) credits the part played by Ojeda in facilitating the reconquest:

> Accompanying the force [De Vargas' expedition of 1692] was a very important Pueblo Indian, Bartolomé de Ojeda. Fray Silvestre Escalante later noted that this Zia warrior had previously fought very well against Spanish soldiers who had attacked his pueblo. He then had come voluntarily to El Paso to join the *conquistador*. Ojeda was "muy ladino" [fluent in the Castilian language] . . . and knew how to read and write. Not only was he invaluable as an interpreter for the Spaniards, but he was at all times a reliable informant concerning the state of affairs among the Indians.
>
> Ojeda reported that the province of New Mexico was torn by anarchy and civil strife among the natives. The Keres of Zia, Santa Ana, San Felipe, Cochiti, and Santo Domingo, together with the Jemez, Pecos, and Taos Indians, feared the Tewa, Picuris, and Acoma Pueblos. In addition, the Zunis and Moquis (Hopis) were at war with the Keres, and the Apaches were causing considerable fear and devastation among the Pueblos in general. This disunity accurately reported by a Pueblo Indian, made the situation opportune for the reconquest, since Vargas could now take advantage of the existing factionalism to employ the technique of "divide and conquer" in the re-establishment of royal authority in New Mexico.

Other leaders and participants in the Pueblo Rebellion of 1680 who came to De Vargas to offer their assistance for the pacification of the Pueblos were Luis Tupatu and his brother, Lorenzo from Picuris, Domingo Romero from Tesugue, and Don Felipe of Pecos. Like Ojeda, Romero and Felipe spoke Spanish and acted as interpreters for De Vargas in the latter's attempt to get the Tanos and Pecos to submit peaceably to the Spaniards (Jones 1966:61). Later, these Pueblo leaders became valued *capitánes mayores de la guerra* in punitive expeditions against the nomadic tribes (Jones 1966:80).

Troubled by the dissension among the Pueblos and the increasing raids of the nomadic tribes, Pueblo leaders were anxious to establish peace with the Spaniards. De Vargas knew the strength of the enemy and, as he was experiencing difficulties of housing and feeding his small group of colonists, he welcomed these men. While camped outside the walls of Santa Fe during the siege of the city in the winter of 1693-1694, De Vargas had lost twenty-one of his group. Even after the successful capture of Santa Fe, the province was far from being subdued; the provisions of the colonists were running dangerously low, and the cold weather threatened even greater hardships. De Vargas, with the aid of the missionaries, spent months pleading with the natives to submit peacefully. In his visits to the pueblos, he was accompanied by the Pueblo leaders. Eventually, with the promise of forgiveness for the rebellion, reassurance that the rebels would not be punished, and agreeing to enlist their aid in forming a common resistance to the nomadic tribes, the Pueblos returned to their villages from mountain strongholds and reestablished residence in the pueblos. In a few months, settlers, missionaries, and the Indians had resumed a relationship similar to the prerevolt period.

De Vargas did not live up to his promises, however. In the capture of Santa Fe itself, De Vargas executed seventy of the enemy leaders. A large number of the Tano defenders and their families were, in addition, turned over to the soldiers and colonists as virtual slaves and servants. The remainder of the Tano population was dispersed among the Tewa pueblos, north of Santa Fe. De Vargas was equally severe in his campaign to subdue the other Pueblo communities. Thus, the situation continued to be tense and new outbreaks seemed constantly imminent. Finally, in 1694, the Tano and some of the Tewa moved to the top of Black Mesa near San Ildefonso. From this stronghold, the rebels harassed the Spanish settlements. De Vargas laid siege to the mesa for nine months and was finally able to effect a truce; the Indians then returned to their pueblos.

On June 4, 1696, a number of the pueblos again rose in a rebellion that was rumored to be another general uprising. The following pueblos were actually involved in the conflict: Taos, Picuris, the Tewas, the relocated Tanos pueblos north of Santa Fe, Santo Domingo, and Cochiti. The rebels killed five missionaries and twenty-one Spanish settlers and soldiers. In addition, the Indians burned and desecrated the mission churches and then fled into the mountains. De Vargas pursued the rebels and was able to get the Pueblos to sue for peace and persuaded the majority of the Indians to return to their pueblos; others, however, fled to the Navaho and Hopi country (see Espinosa 1940:39; Dozier 1961:133–134).

By the end of 1696 De Vargas with the aid of Pueblo leaders and the assistance of a growing number of Pueblo allies secured the submission of all the Pueblos in New Mexico. The western pueblos remained to be subdued, and indeed the Hopi pueblos were never really to be again brought under Spanish rule, although a number of attempts were made in the first two decades of the eighteenth century. In July 1697, Don Pedro Rodriguez Cubero took over the governorship, for Vargas' five year appointment was not renewed. Apparently, for some of the atrocities committed against the Indians and because of his stern rule of the colonists, De Vargas was thrown into prison in 1697. Governor Cubero and the *cabildo* displayed unusual power in thus punishing the reconquerer of the Pueblos. De Vargas, however, was later fully exonerated and, in 1703, he again resumed his post as the governor of New Mexico (Espinosa 1940:40–41).

The Pueblos settled down into outward peaceable relations with the Spaniards after the abortive revolt of 1696. While De Vargas' methods in pacifying the Pueblos were severe, even brutal, he did succeed in bringing the Indian leaders into partnership with the colonists in reestablishing Spanish authority in New Mexico. Cubero continued this practice and later De Vargas, in his second term as governor and subsequent governors after him, brought the Pueblos into full partnership with the colonists in a coordinated defense of New Mexico against the nomadic enemies. In addition, the Franciscans and the civil authorities modified their treatment of the Pueblos and the extreme coercive policies gradually gave way to more humane treatment of these Indians in the succeeding century. The relations between the two peoples will be discussed later in greater detail; at present, it is important to consider the effects of the first century of Spanish rule in New Mexico.

EFFECTS OF SPANISH RULE

A century of close contact brought many changes among the Pueblos. There were more profound changes in the east than in the west, but all of the Pueblos were strongly affected. The population of the Pueblo Indians in 1600 was possibly between 30,000 and 40,000. The number of Indian villages slowly decreased toward the end of the century so that at the time of the revolt, the population had dropped to half, or about 16,000 (Hackett and Shelby 1942:xxxi). New diseases, particularly the periodic smallpox epidemics, were probably the main cause of population diminution. The forced labor program of the Spanish civil authorities also took a large toll of lives, but much of the population loss resulted from migration to the Hopi, Apache, and other Indian communities, and movement into the colonists' villages. The latter was brought about not only by the recruitment of servants for Spanish households, but also by the addition of Hispanicized Pueblo Indians, who, through the efforts of the missionaries, became converted to the new religion and culture and preferred to live with the settlers. The revolt reduced the population still further as a result of deaths at the hands of Spaniards and losses by migration to sympathetic Hopi, Navaho, and Apache Indians. At any rate, by the end of the revolt, the population was probably no more than 14,000.

The number of Pueblo villages had been drastically reduced by 1700. All of the Piro settlements were deserted by the end of the century, as were the Tiwa villages east of the mountains and south of Isleta pueblo. This pueblo was resettled after the revolt when its inhabitants returned to New Mexico from El Paso after the reconquest. The only other Tiwa pueblo, Sandia, was created by the return of the Tiwa refugees from Hopi in 1741 (Thomas 1932:160). The Tanos just south of Santa Fe spoke the same languages as the Tewa north of the capital city and were closely identified with the latter in culture. These Indians, being nearest to the seat of Spanish government in Santa Fe, suffered the most from Spanish oppression and understandably took the most prominent part in the revolt. Despite the lead in resisting Spanish rule, however, the Tanos cooperated rather closely with the Tewa throughout the revolt period. The Tanos occupied four or five villages in the Galisteo Basin in 1600. At the time of the reconquest, all of the pueblos had been abandoned. Some of the Tanos had moved into Santa Fe and, as we have noted earlier, De Vargas executed a number of them, distributed others among the colonists as servants and dispersed still others among the Tewa pueblos. Prior to the reconquest, other Tanos had moved north to settle among their Tewa linguistic relatives. Two villages, San Lazaro and San Cristobal, were established on the Santa Cruz creek east of present-day Espanola. Shortly after the reconquest, De Vargas resettled the populations of these two villages to make room for a new villa of colonists, Santa Cruz de la Canada. The name San Cristobal was retained to apply to the community of both groups of Tanos. After the abortive revolt of 1696, the Tanos of San Cristobal fled west to Zuni and from there to the Hopi country where they established a village on First Mesa. One of the original Tano pueblos, Galisteo, was later resettled by Tanos living in the various Tewa pueblos, but disease and nomadic Indian raids rapidly decimated the population; between 1782 and 1794, the few surviving Galisteo Tanos moved to the pueblo of Santo Domingo (Dozier 1954:273–274).

A number of the Tewa pueblos prominent during the seventeenth century did not survive the reconquest and the revolt of 1696. Cuyumungue, between present-day Tesuque and Pojoaque, was abandoned, as was Jacona, another pueblo near San Ildefonso. The Tewa pueblo where Oñate established his first capitol, Yuqueyunque, was apparently abandoned before the revolt of 1680, its inhabitants joining Okeh or San Juan across the Rio Grande (Shroeder and Matson 1965: 114–134).

Towa speakers occupied a number of pueblos in the upper Jemez river drainage above Keresan speaking Zia pueblo at the time of Oñate's entry into New Mexico. After the revolt of 1680 and subsequent difficulties with Spanish authorities, large numbers of these Indians joined the Hopi and Navaho, while the remaining population settled in one village—the present Jemez pueblo. Pecos, whose inhabitants also spoke Towa, was the largest Rio Grande pueblo during the first century of Spanish rule, but its population diminished rapidly after the reconquest. Occupying a marginal position on the eastern edge of the Pueblo country, Pecos suffered continuously from Apache and Comanche raids. Finally, in 1838, the few Pecos survivors joined their linguistic kin at Jemez to form one pueblo (Hodge 1912:221).

The northern Tiwa villages of Taos and Picuris survived the revolt of 1680 and 1696 and endured through the subsequent two centuries, although greatly reduced in population. After the revolt of 1696, most of the Picuris Indians fled northeastward and joined a band of Apaches in the neighborhood of Pueblo, Colorado. The Apaches enslaved the refugees and in desperation the latter asked the Spaniards to rescue them and return them to their pueblo. Governor Francisco Cuervo y Valdez authorized a rescue party under the command of Sergeant Juan de Ulibarrí, with a force composed mostly of Pueblo Indians. The combined Spanish-Pueblo expedition successfully returned the refugees to Picuris during the summer of 1706 (see Jones 1966:73–77).

The Keresan pueblos along the Rio Grande and the lower Jemez river survived the difficult period between 1680–1700.

A number of Keresan Indians, however, moved west after the revolt, apparently in an attempt to get farther away from Spanish domination, and founded Laguna. The Zuni Indians combined their several villages into one large pueblo. Among the Hopi, the principal villages remained, although greatly reduced in population. Awatovi, the most eastern of the Hopi villages, survived the revolt only to be destroyed in 1701 by hostile Hopi and Tewa warriors because the village had again received Franciscan missionaries. The survivors of Awatovi were dispersed among the Hopi villages and Awatovi was never reoccupied.

Material Introductions and Changes

The first century of contact with Spanish religion and culture primarily brought about material changes. Aside from the mission compound, the Catholic chapel and workshops and the changes in architecture and village layout plan were not revolutionary. These additions, although intended by Spanish authorities to be central features of the villages, rarely became such. In all but a few pueblos the center of the community was moved away from the missionary buildings, and the village courtyard where the ceremonial chamber or chambers (*kivas*) were rebuilt continued to be the hub of social and ceremonial life. No improvements were made on house construction. While better molds for making adobe bricks may have been introduced, there is archeological evidence of the use of adobe bricks in prehistoric times (see Smith and Ewing 1952:9; Winship 1896:520). Documentary evidence for the use of adobe bricks in pre-Spanish times is also available in Gaspar Castaño de Sosa's Journal 1590–1591. In the same journal is the mention of wood ovens among the Pueblo villages. These ovens, prominent features of Pueblo architecture, have been thought to have been introduced by the Spaniards (Schroeder and Matson 1965:117–120). Architectural introductions, therefore, do not seem to have been as impressive. Indeed, the colonists adopted the adobe structures and the compact village plans from the Pueblos for their own communities.

The most tangible changes brought about by Spanish contact affected the economy. This was primarily through the addition of new crops and domesticated fowl and animals. There were little or no changes in farming techniques; the Pueblos already possessed a rather advanced agricultural economy based on irrigation. Besides, the Spaniards detested farming. The historian Beck's comments on the agricultural activities of the colonists is revealing:

> Several factors account for the agricultural backwardness of the Spanish settlers. First of all, the Hispanic attitude toward hired labor in the field restricted manpower to the Indian slaves or to the peons. No gentleman would condescend to such work; therefore, there was little interest in improving the agricultural techniques. Secondly, the Spanish methods of agriculture were obsolete, such practices as crop rotation, common even to medieval Europe, being unheard of. Farming implements were crude and ill adapted to extensive use. . . . Third, as the cultivated land was not closed with fences, for cultural reasons as well as the fact that fencing material was seldom available, growing crops were subject to frequent devastation by the flocks of roaming sheep owned by one of the *patrones*, who had little respect for such farming efforts. Fourth, during most of colonial times, outlying districts were subject to periodic Indian raids. . . . Fifth, the lack of markets discouraged hard work in the fields (Beck 1962:263–264).

Metal tools such as hoes and shovels lightened the task for the farmer, but such tools were scarce and not available to all Indians. Oxen and plows also permitted larger areas to be farmed, but unfortunately an economy based on forced labor for the benefit of Spanish officials did not leave a surplus of foods for the Indians. A variety of new crops was introduced, namely, wheat, melons (canteloupe and watermelon), apples, peaches, pears, tomatoes, and chile. The last two were aboriginal foods in Mexico, but new to the Pueblos. Again it is unlikely that the Indians benefited from these crops for the produce was used to feed the clergy and the families of the Spanish elite. The animals and fowl introduced also gained profits for the newcomers rather than the Pueblos: mules, horses, cattle, donkeys, goats, sheep, and chickens. Most of these animals simply added to the burden of labor for the Indians. During the whole of the first colonial period in New Mexico, the Pueblos were denied the use of horses (and firearms), for the Spanish authorities were afraid that the use of horses by the Indians would provoke uprisings. The introduced crafts meant simply additional work for the Indians: weaving in wool, blacksmithing (iron, tin, copper, bronze, and silver), and wood-working. Along with all of these introductions went an assorted complex of tools

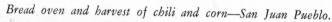

Bread oven and harvest of chili and corn—San Juan Pueblo.

and equipment like saddles, bridles, harnesses, metal knives, sickles, needles, axes, and so forth. The Pueblo Indian during the seventeenth century was kept so busy working to produce enough for his support and the support of a substantial part of the colonial population that he must have viewed these new additions to his culture as techniques to exploit his labor rather than as items to enrich his economy. Many Pueblo Indians, however, working as herdsmen, cowboys, smiths, and weavers for Spanish civil or church authorities, became skilled in their tasks. Important Spanish officials vied for their services and, as a result, a few Pueblo craftsmen and artisans escaped the abuse and exploitation which was the usual lot of the common Pueblo Indian worker. The skills learned in the workshops were passed on to succeeding generations and the disciplined and well-organized Pueblo societies of the eighteenth and nineteenth centuries owe much to the first century of Spanish colonization.

The silhouette of Pueblo villages changed too. The Catholic chapel, usually the largest and tallest structure in the pueblo, became a prominent feature in each village. Until recently—certainly throughout the eighteenth and most of the nineteenth centuries—the mission compound, with its complex of gardens, workshops, and so forth, was a constant reminder of the output of Indian labor. During the closing decades of the last century and in some pueblos until recently, the ruined buildings of these missions still lingered; but they are now gone except perhaps for mounds of dirt where these imposing structures once stood. Among the Rio Grande Pueblos the chapel or church has remained, for these Indians consider themselves to be Catholics and are advocates of their native religion as well. The church, like the *kivas*, is an important religious structure where the worship of two sets of deities are conducted separately.

Nonmaterial Introductions and Changes

The amount of borrowing and acceptance that has taken place in the less tangible areas of social organization, religion, and values is difficult to assess. It is evident that rather early in the seventeenth century a civil government system was introduced to facilitate church and civil affairs. This was a procedure followed by Spain elsewhere in the New World. Indeed, even before the establishment of a colony in New Mexico, Castaño de Sosa, in his expedition among the northern Pueblo Indian villages in 1590–1591, had appointed a governor, *alcaldes* (councilmen), and *alguacil* (constable) in each of the villages he visited (Schroeder and Matson 1965). This act was part of a formal ceremony of obedience and submission which Castaño carried out in the pueblos. It is doubtful that the Indians of this time understood fully the meaning of the formalities and very likely they paid no attention to the officers appointed. Castaño's visits to the individual pueblos were brief, no more than a few hours in each village. It was not until the seventeenth century that the full complement of secular officers was established and that the pueblos began to relate to Spanish authorities through these officers. The set of officers given here is a generalized list: a governor, a lieutenant governor, *alguacil, sacristan, mayordomos,* and *fiscales.* There is some variation in the names, functions, and even numbers of the officers among the individual pueblos. The Spanish and missionary authorities expected rather specific kinds of services from these officers. The governor was to represent the village in all important dealings with Spanish authorities. The lieutenant governor was to serve as assistant to the governor and represent him when absent; and, in the event of the governor's death, succeed him. The *alguacil* was to maintain law and order within the pueblo; the *sacristan* was church assistant and aid to the priest; the *fiscales* were responsible for mission discipline; while the *mayordomos* were ditch superintendents.

Another position, *capitán de la guerra*, was apparently established after the revolt, for no mention is made of the position earlier. The use of Pueblo Indian leaders in the reconquest and later to check nomadic enemy raids made the position imperative. Most of the pueblos had at least two *capitánes*, others as many as four; apparently the number of such military leaders depended on the size of the village. These officers were in charge of the soldiers recruited from each pueblo in military expeditions sent against enemy Indians or else commanded Indian warriors in the defense of their pueblos in the case of an attack. Frequently, during the eighteenth century, as enemy raids increased and large retaliatory expeditions were organized by the provincial governor, one of these "war captains" was put in charge of all the Indian auxiliaries (Jones 1966:54–55; 78–80).

All the pueblos have, in addition to these officers, a group of sociopolitical and ceremonial leaders who are the de facto governing group. This native governmental organization will be described in some detail in the section on Pueblo social and ceremonial organization; at present, it is important to note only that the officers of the civil government system are recognized in all the pueblos today as an imposed set. This is not to imply that the latter are unimportant, for these officers are crucial in dealing with profane matters and the outside world. In addition, the officers of the civil government system are useful in masking the identity and activities of the native officers who are additionally concerned with ceremonial matters that have, in the past, generated considerable difficulties with Spanish authorities, particularly the missionaries. Hence, a set of officers, formally approved and sanctioned by Spanish and now by Anglo-American officials, permits the Pueblos to conduct secular matters separately, while their ceremonial activities are under the direction of leaders unknown to outsiders. Not all the pueblos have separated "church" and "state" affairs, however. Indeed, in most pueblos, the religious officers select and appoint the secular officers, a practice not ordinarily known to outside administrators. Generally, then, the secular affairs of a pueblo are controlled by a hierarchy of native "priests" who make primary and ultimate decisions for the pueblo. The secular officers simply carry out the decisions and instructions of the priests. As we will see, some of the pueblos have challenged this type of government, but at present most of the pueblos still operate under it. During Spanish times, the dual system of government was essential in order to preserve the rich and complex ceremonial life of the Pueblos. The set of secular officers served as a convenient facade behind which the more important and vital organization of native priests carried out the social and religious functions of the pueblo.

Spanish officials must have also introduced a set of civil officers among the Hopi Indians, for the system is known as far west as Zuni. The Hopi do not now, nor in the recent past, have such an organization. Certainly, the Tano pueblos conducted their affairs with Spanish authorities through a set of secular officers during the seventeenth century. Hano, the Tano speaking village on First Mesa, whose antecedents were Tano (Southern Tewa) refugees, has no vestige of this organization. If the officers no longer exist among the Hopi and at Hano, we may propose that the organization was not deeply rooted among the pueblos in the seventeenth century. If such officers were important in the social and political organizations of these pueblos, then we would have expected the organization to have survived to the present, at least in some rudimentary form. The organization has survived and perhaps even increased in importance among the Rio Grande pueblos, we believe, because of the following reason: It served to keep the identity and activities of the native religious system secret from Spanish civil and church authorities. But among the Hopi and at Hano, in later years, there was no need to mask the religious organization and its activities from the Spanish, for affairs in the Rio Grande, particularly the raids of the nomadic tribes, kept civil and church authorities too busy to concern themselves with the pueblos of the western frontier.

A set of pageants and dances which are of obvious Spanish or Mexican derivation have a definite place in Rio Grande Pueblo ceremonialism, although their foreign derivation and separateness from native Pueblo ceremonies is recognized. Included in this complex are the Horse, or Sandaro Dance, the Pecos Bull, and the Matachina dances. Associated with these dances are masked clowns, called Chapio (also Khapio, Tsabiyo), who speak Spanish and Indian in falsetto. The masks have no resemblance to those used by the Katcina impersonators and are obviously of Spanish or Mexican provenience. The masks do, however, resemble the Chapaiyeka masks of the Mayo-Yaqui ceremonies and other masked clowns associated with festivals at Eastern time in many towns and villages in Mexico. The Matachina pagaent itself, in variant form, is danced by Tarahumara, Hucholes, and Mayo-Yaqui (see Parsons 1939:852, 1005–1007). The Matachina is also popular in a number of Hispano villages, namely: Bernalillio; San Antonio, east of the Sandia Mountains; and Alcalde, north of the pueblo of San Juan. For an interesting and significant study of the Matachina and similar ceremonies, see Kurath 1949. Both the Hispanos and the Pueblo Indians believe that the Matachina pageant was "introduced" by the Aztec priest-god, Montezuma. Among the Rio Grande pueblos, where Montezuma is variously known as Bocaiyany (Santa Ana), Poshaiyanki (Zuni), and Poseyemu (Tewa), he is a culture hero. Montezuma may assume different physical forms, as well as speak diverse languages, perform miracles, and foretell the future. He told the Pueblos of the coming of Europeans, but admonished them to keep their own indigenous beliefs and ceremonies. Parsons suggests that "the Pueblos heard a good deal about Montezuma from their early Mexican Indian visitors and later found Montezuma a 'god' that might be mentioned conveniently to white people." Parsons' suggestion is intriguing for it fits the Pueblos' passionate desire to deflect attention away from their own rich mythology and ceremonialism. Dances connected with Montezuma are, unlike Katcina ceremonies (see section on Pueblo society and culture), open to public observation. They appear to be well integrated into Rio Grande Pueblo ceremonialism and, hence, were likely introduced during the early years of contact. It is interesting that these dances were either not introduced to the Hopi or not accepted by them. The Zuni have the Montezuma legend, but not the dances.

The Spanish language became an important additional language to the Rio Grande pueblos very early. Not all Pueblo Indians, obviously, learned Spanish, but it is clear that during the revolt and after the reconquest communication between the Pueblos and the Spaniards presented no difficulties. In later periods Spanish became a *lingua franca* among Pueblo Indians speaking unrelated languages. Whether the Western Pueblo Indians at Zuni and Hopi were also proficient in the use of Spanish during the seventeenth century is unknown. In subsequent centuries, when contact between these pueblos and the settlements along the Rio Grande was severed, these Indians also lost knowledge of the Spanish language. Among the Rio Grande Pueblos knowledge of Spanish made possible the use of their indigenous languages as tools for retaining and perpetuating cherished and closely guarded customs and beliefs. A study of the Pueblo languages today reveals how effectively borrowing from the Spanish language has been resisted (see Dozier 1956).

The missions of the Rio Grande pueblos were rebuilt soon after the revolt, but Spanish attempts to revive missionary activity among the western pueblos were not as successful. Only one of the three missions originally constructed at Zuni (Halona) before the revolt was repaired and used sporadically in the eighteenth century (Kubler 1940:97). Acoma, closer to the center of Spanish activity, rebuilt its mission, but it too had difficulty in maintaining a resident missionary (Kubler 1940:96–97; 94–95).

The Spaniards failed to reestablish the missions among the Hopi, although they partially succeeded at the village of Awatovi. The opposition of the Hopi to Spanish missionary activity is dramatically related in a documentary account of the destruction of this Hopi village:

> At this time [1700], his people being infuriated because the Indians of the pueblo of Aguatubi [Awatovi] had been reduced to our holy faith and the obedience of our king, he [Espeleta, the chief of the Oraibi] came with more than one hundred of his people to the said pueblo, entered it, killed all the braves, and carried off the women, leaving the pueblo to this day desolate and unpeopled. Learning of this outrage, Governor Don Pedro Rodriguez Cubero made ready some soldiers to punish it, and in the following year of 1701 went to the said province of Moqui, taking with him the aforesaid religious, Fray Juan Garicochea and Fray Antonio Miranda. With his armed force he killed some Indians and captured others, but not being very well prepared to face the multitudes of the enemy, he withdrew and returned without being able to reduce them, especially as the Moquis had with them the Tanos Indians [Tanos, the Southern Tewa of the Galisteo Basin in New Mexico who fled to the Hopi country after the revolt of 1696—see Dozier 1954, 1966], who, after committing outrages had taken refuge among them and had risen at their command . . . (Navaréz 1937:386).

Pueblo Indians appear to have absorbed very few Catholic beliefs and values during the first century of contact with Spanish culture and the Catholic religion. They performed the external acts required of them such as attendance at Mass, vespers, and so forth. Some were baptized, married, and even buried by the friars. Such acts were done under compulsion, however, and it is unlikely that any of the church concepts were really understood and believed. That the Hopi Indians, similarly exposed to Catholicism for a century, were able to slough off all vestige of Christian training in the centuries following the revolt indicates that the Rio Grande Pueblos did not really become Catholics either. The coercive methods of the friars in teaching them the new religion and the efforts to stamp out the old folk customs merely drove the Pueblos deeper into their own indigenous religion. Scholes has characterized the reaction of the Pueblos to the Christianizing efforts of the missionaries admirably:

> But drastic disciplinary measures . . . could not force full allegiance to the new order. The efforts of the clergy to abolish the old ceremonial forms and to set up new standards of conduct merely caused greater resentment on the part of the Indians. . . . The Pueblos were not unwilling to accept externals of the new faith, but they found it difficult to understand the deeper spiritual values of Christianity. Pueblo religion served definite material and social ends, viz., the propitiation of those supernatural forces which they believed controlled their daily existence. They expected the same results from the Christian faith. But they soon realized that the new ways were no more successful in obtaining a good harvest than the old, and

they realized too that the efforts to abolish their traditional ceremonials and destroy the influence of the old native leaders whose functions were both social and religious, raised serious problems concerning the entire fund of Pueblo civilization. Bewilderment soon turned into resentment and resentment into resurgence of loyalty to the traditional norms of folk-culture.

Under Spanish rule for a century, the Pueblos added to their society and culture an impressive array of material items, domesticated animals and plants, and learned a variety of craft techniques. But the Pueblos did not become Christians; they remained essentially neophytes, deeply attached to their indigenous beliefs and customs.

History 1700–1800

DECLINE OF SPANISH POWER AND INFLUENCE: PUEBLO-SPANISH MILITARY COOPERATION

It is not always possible to measure the extent and the severity of material losses, the suffering of the maimed and injured, or the mental anguish of the survivors of a rebellion for freedom. Nor can anyone say that such losses and suffering are worth the price of a better society. While better relations between Pueblos and the intruders were established during the eighteenth century, the Spaniards were back and, as we will see, Spanish oppression was not a thing of the past. Many of the objectionable aspects of Spanish rule and the mission programs continued. Perhaps the most important cause of the revolt, the *encomienda* system, was, however, terminated. The Spaniards or their heirs who lost their servants at the time of the revolt never regained the traditional right to collect tribute from the Pueblo Indians. There was only one exception, De Vargas, who was granted a large *encomienda*; it was never put into operation and finally, in 1726, De Vargas' heirs had it changed into a pension (Espinosa 1940:38).

PUEBLO RELATIONS WITH THE CHURCH AND CIVIL AUTHORITIES

Pueblo resentment of the clergy and the civil authorities remained. The animosity which the Pueblos bore the friars arose from the strict mission discipline and the periodic punishments they meted out through the *fiscales*. But the large-scale mission building programs of the prerevolt period were gone; repairs and maintenance of the missions did not entail the long hours and physical suffering of building the enormous religious structures. Apparently the Pueblos also encountered less resistance in the performance of their sacred ceremonial dances, particularly the Katcina dances that had so irritated the friars. The latter opposed these dances because they considered them a deterrent to their Christianization program. Civil authorities have generally been more relaxed about the matter. Just prior to the revolt of 1680, however, some of the governors sided with the friars and prohibited the ceremonies (Adams and Chavez 1956:258, footnote 27). The accelerated efforts to stop the ceremonies of the Pueblos and the harassment and punishment of native religious leaders quickly led to the revolt.

During the seventeenth century no serious attempts were made to compel the Indians to stop their native ceremonies and we have no record of the destruction of sacred paraphernalia. Indeed, it is rather surprising to find the *custodio* and a number of the friars supporting not only the right of the Pueblos to bear firearms, but also the Pueblo warriors' right to continue the custom of painting their faces while fighting enemy Indians. Both of these topics were raised in a special *junta* (meeting) called by Governor Flores Mogollón in 1714. The governor and a majority of the settlers opposed the *custodio*, Fray Juan de Tagle, and friars from Pecos, Santo Domingo, Cochiti, Santa Clara, Taos, Jemez, and Laguna. The latter declared that the Pueblos needed the arms to protect themselves. As for painting, the friars pointed out that the Indian custom was no worse than the practice of Spaniards who often painted themselves and put feathers in their hats to wear to church (Jones 1966:87–89).

The sincere desire of Spanish authorities to bring the Pueblos into partnership with the provincial government is illustrated by the appointment of a "protector general" of Indians. In an important meeting called by Governor Francisco Cuervo y Valdez on January 6, 1706, the protector general, Captain Alfonso Rael de Aguilar, was introduced to a gathering of influential Pueblo Indians. Pueblo governors and other leaders from all the pueblos except Hopi were present including Don Domingo Romero Yuguaque, governor of the pueblo of Tesuque and *capitán mayor de la guerra* of all the Christian Indian nations of New Mexico. Romero addressed the meeting in good Castilian as did many of the others, while a few spoke through interpreters. The purpose of the meeting was to cement the good relations that everyone expressed already existed between Spanish authorities and the Pueblos (Hackett 1937, Vol. III, pp. 366–369).

With the pressure on the suppression of their religious rites relaxed, the Pueblos were enjoying a rich ceremonial life as is evident in the records of the late eighteenth century. The pagan rites disturbed the friars, but it is obvious that they did not have the authority to stop them. The following statement by Fray Dominguez in 1776 is a rather apathetic report of the failure of the friars to convert the Pueblos:

> Even at the end of so many years since their reconquest, the specious title or name of neophytes is still applied to them. This is the reason their condition now is almost the same as it was in the beginning, for generally speaking they have preserved some very indecent, and perhaps superstitious, customs. . . .
>
> Their repugnance and resistance to most Christian acts is evident, for they perform the duties pertaining to the Church under compulsion, and there are usually many omissions. They are not in the habit of praying or crossing themselves when they rise or go to bed, and consequently they have no devotion for certain saints as is customary among us. And if they sometimes invoke God and His saints or pray or pay for Masses, it is in a confused manner or to comply in their confusion with what the fathers teach and explain.
>
> They use *estufas* [kivas], of which some pueblos have more, others less. . . . [Estufas] are the chapter, or council rooms, and the Indians meet in them, sometimes

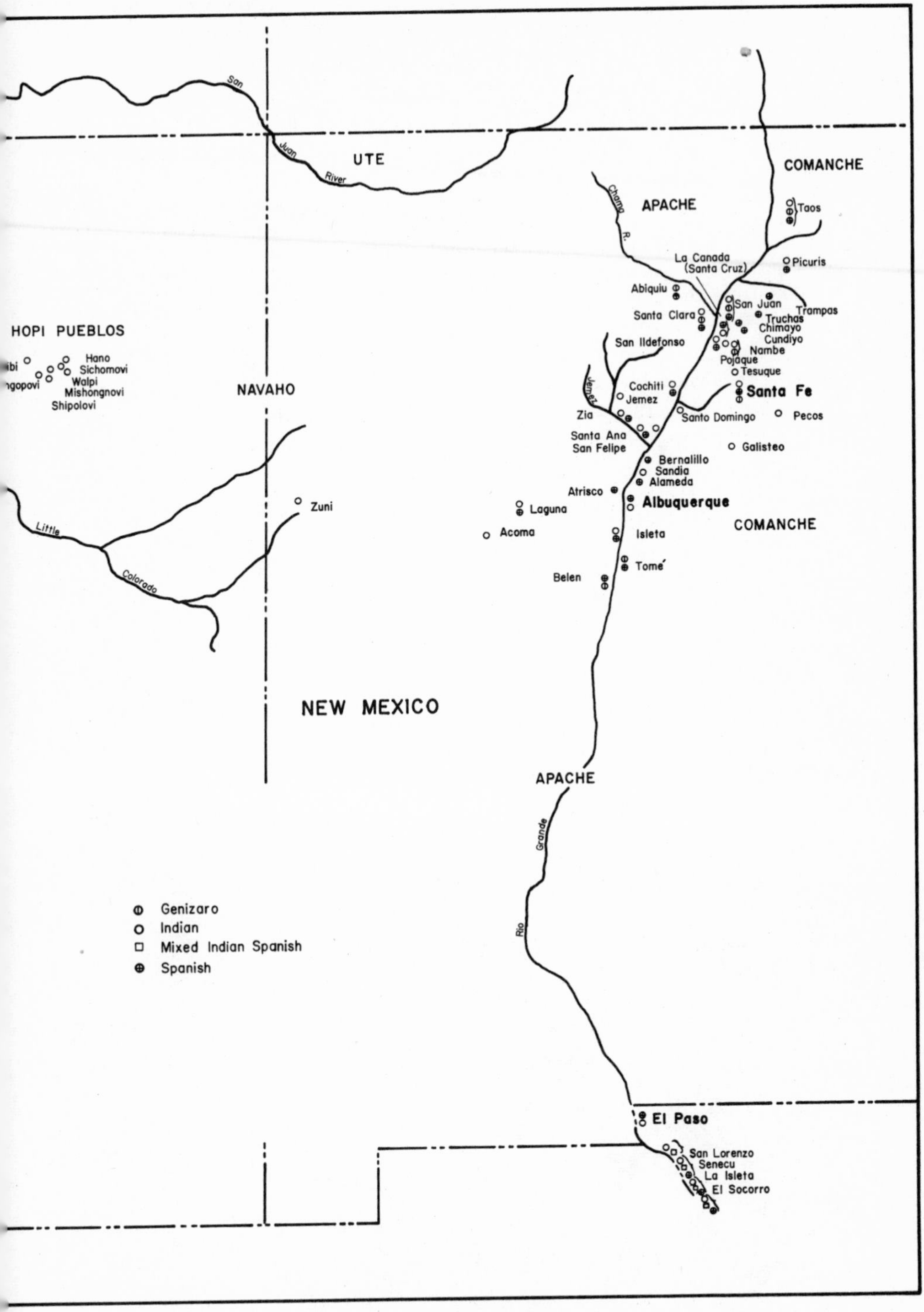
San
Juan
River
UTE
COMANCHE
Chama
R.
APACHE
Taos
La Canada
(Santa Cruz)
Picuris
Abiquiu
San Juan
Trampas
Santa Clara
Truchas
Chimayo
Cundiyo
HOPI PUEBLOS
San Ildefonso
Nambe
Pojaque
Hano
Sichomovi
Walpi
Mishongnovi
Shipolovi
Tesuque
NAVAHO
Jemez
Cochiti
Jemez
Santa Fe
Zia
Santo Domingo
Pecos
Santa Ana
San Felipe
Galisteo
Bernalillo
Sandia
Alameda
Atrisco
Zuni
Albuquerque
Laguna
COMANCHE
Little
Acoma
Isleta
Colorado
Tome
Belen
NEW MEXICO
APACHE
Grande
Rio
Genizaro
Indian
Mixed Indian Spanish
Spanish
El Paso
San Lorenzo
Senecu
La Isleta
El Socorro

Figure 8. The Pueblo country in 1750.

to discuss matters of their government for the coming year, their planting, arrangements for work to be done, or to elect new community officials, or to rehearse their dances, or sometimes for other things.

Their customary dances usually resemble contredances or minuets as danced in Spain, or they are scalp dances.

There are other general customs observed by the Indians of these regions, but I have mentioned only the most noteworthy. I note, indeed, that although I stated above that the contredances, or minuets, do not appear to be essentially wicked and are usual on solemn occasions during the year, here in the scalp ceremonial the dances are tainted by the idea of vengeance. The fathers have been very zealous in their opposition to this scalp dance, but they have received rebuffs, and so the fathers are unable to abolish this custom and many others, because excuses are immediately made on the ground that (the Indians) are neophytes, minors, etc. (Adams and Chavez 1956:254–258).

The dances that Father Dominguez reports as resembling contredances and minuets are clearly the so-called Corn or Tablita dances of the Pueblos. Scalp dances, also described by Father Dominguez, were performed in the memory of the oldest informants among the Tewa; indeed the women's scalp society reenacted activities similar to those described by Dominguez well into the present century and the society is still active in some of the Tewa pueblos (Parsons 1929:212–214).

Since no mention of *kiva* and medicine association rites (particularly masked

Tewa Tablita or "Corn" Dance—Santa Clara Pueblo.

Katcina dances) are made in the descriptive reports of the Pueblos in the eighteenth century, we may assume that the practice of concealing the more sacred dances and ceremonies from observation by non-Pueblo peoples was already in operation. This practice becomes an important aspect of Rio Grande Pueblo society in later periods. Of significance, too, is that the descriptions of the dances reveal no Catholic elements; on the other hand, Catholic ritual also was free of native ceremonialism. Already at this time the Pueblos were insisting on the separation of Catholic from native rituals and guarding against a mixing of the two. This is a phenomenon of Pueblo culture that we have elsewhere called "compartmentalization" (Spicer 1961: 94–186). Compartmentalization is an accommodating device developed by the Rio Grande Pueblos to permit them to enjoy and practice indigenous rites objectionable to Spanish authorities. Those dances and rites that aroused no opposition or displeasure from the non-Indian population were given openly and frequently, indeed as if these activities were all that remained of their indigenous culture. But behind closed doors, or in heavily guarded areas, there was the performance of another set of complex rites shorn of all borrowed elements from the intruding culture. These were the ceremonies that in their pagan glory offended Spanish civil and church authorities.

It is clear from reading eighteenth century historical accounts that the Pueblos resented church discipline more than any other aspect of the missionary program. To a people who did not internalize the deeper meanings and values of Christianity and who had only a vague and indefinite conception of the teachings of the church, the activities of the friars were simply another form of Spanish oppression. As for the missionaries, frustrated in their efforts to convert the Indians, they emphasized proper behavior in the church and compulsory attendance at church services. The following account of Mass and religious instruction at Jemez pueblo by Father Joaquin de Jesus Ruiz about 1773 is believed to be typical of church services among the Pueblos during the eighteenth century (Hackett 1937, Vol. III, p. 42):

> The bell is rung at sunrise. The married men enter, each one with his wife, and they kneel together in a row on each side of the nave of the church. Each couple has its own place designated in accordance with the census list. When there are many, the married couples make two rows on each side, the two men in the middle and the women on the sides. This may seem a superficial matter, but it is not, for experience has taught me that when these women are together they spend all the time dedicated to prayer and Mass in gossip, showing one another their glass beads, ribbons, medals, etc., telling who gave them or how they obtained them, and other mischief. Therefore the religious who has charge of the administration must have a care in this regard. After all, it is a house of prayer, not of chitchat. . . .
>
> The petty governor and his lieutenant have their places at the door so that the people may not leave during the hour of prayer and Mass.
>
> When all are in their places, the fiscal mayor notifies the father, who comes down with his census lists and takes attendance to see whether everyone is there, whether they are in their proper places, and whether their hair is bound. If anyone is missing, the petty governor goes to fetch him. If he is not in the pueblo, it is indicated by the thong and he is punished on the following Sunday or holy day of obligation. If the truant is a woman, her husband is sent to fetch her. . . .
>
> After Mass is over, if the minister thinks that some have left, he summons them

in accordance with the list and punishes anyone who does such a thing. He severely reprimands the petty governor who permits it. . . .

The lists of married men and widowers are so arranged that if anyone is guilty of absence, this was indicated by the thongs. . . .

Punishment was still employed by some friars in the eighteenth century, but such occasions were rare. The influence and power of the church in New Mexico had obviously diminished from the previous century. During the height of the missionary program in the mid-seventeenth century the triennial mission was authorized to bring the number of priests assigned to the area to the full quota of sixty-six (Scholes 1930). A century later, in 1760, Bishop Tamaron reported only thirty friars serving the entire province. Six of the priests were in the pueblos of the El Paso area and only twenty-four in the interior (Adams 1954:77). Sixteen years later, the number of friars serving the interior—the Pueblo area—had been reduced to twenty (Adams and Chavez 1956:217). Some of the main pueblos like Pecos, Galisteo and Tesuque had no missionaries in 1766. In addition, the fathers were now responsible for a rapidly increasing non-Pueblo Christian population which was almost double the size of the Pueblos (Bancroft 1889:279).

In the previous century, the Christianization program was a monopoly of the Franciscan order. The *custos* or *custodio* virtually had the power of a bishop, since no bishop had authority over the Franciscans in New Mexico during the seventeenth century. This priest made the assignment of friars to the missions, received and distributed the provisions needed by the missionaries, and was the intermediary between mission and civil concerns in New Mexico. But early in the eighteenth century, the friars came under the supervision of the bishop of Durango. In 1730, the bishop of Benito Crespo made a visit to New Mexico. It was the first official visit of a bishop to the province. Two other official visits by bishops followed: Elzaeocochea, in 1737; and in 1760, Tamaron, whose well-recorded tour has been preserved and is an excellent source of information on the missions and the people of New Mexico in the seventeenth century (Adams 1954).

Bishop Tamaron was appalled by conditions in New Mexico and severely criticized both the missionaries and civil authorities. He reported that the Pueblo Indians, after almost 200 years of contact with missionaries, had only a superficial conformity to Christianity and did not really understand or have an interest in the religion. Tamaron believed that the language barrier was the main reason for failure to convert the Indians. The friars had not learned the native idioms, nor had they been successful in teaching the natives to speak Spanish (Adams 1954:31). The second problem which alarmed Tamaron was the ineffective defense system against the depradations of the nomadic Indians (Adams 1954:33).

To make matters worse for the Franciscans, civil authorities were also critical of the conduct of the priests and the results of the Christianization program during this period. Hackett (1937, Vol. III, pp. 38–39) summarizes the main points of criticism made against the clergy by Don Juan Antonio de Ornedal y Masa, who was sent by the viceroy to New Mexico as presidial *visitador*:

The charges which Ornedal made against the religious of New Mexico included the following: The religious almost totally neglected the Indians, even failing to say mass for them for months on a stretch. The missionaries, in violation of the law, had failed to learn the Indian languages and to teach the Indians the Spanish language; indeed, no minister since the conquest of the province had applied himself to writing a vocabulary of the many and diverse Indian tongues. As a result even the sacrament of penitence had to be administered to the Indians by an interpreter. The missionaries forcibly took grain and sheep from the Indians who were also compelled to weave for them wool and cotton without pay. The religious, because of their poor and irregular pay, were tempted or obliged to engage publicly in trade "among themselves and the Indians, in such goods as the country affords." They also arbitrarily took from the Indians the "buffalo skins that they obtain for sheltering themselves, and the buckskins that they sell and give away among each other." When the Indians complained of this to the civil authorities they were threatened with whippings and other punishments.

The missionaries were incensed by the Ordenal report and other criticisms made of them and the missionary program by civil authorities. They in turn unleashed a series of reports accusing the governors and *alcaldes* of profiting from the labor of the Indians and in the process of enriching themselves while subverting the work of the missionaries. Excerpts from a lengthy and vituperative report of the Father Provencial, Fray Pedro Serrano to the viceroy in 1761 is a strong indictment of the civil authorities of New Mexico (Hackett 1937, Vol. III, pp. 484–486):

In each town where weaving is done they [the governors] leave a portion of . . . wool, allotting to the Indians the task of washing, combing, carding, and spinning it, and making the blankets, all to be done within a certain number of days. When the work is finished, the distributors of the wool return for the blankets, and the unfortunate Indians, as a reward for their labor, are forced to toil further in taking the blankets, either on their backs, afoot, or on their horses if they have them, to the governors palace. . . . The same thing happens in the transportation of tithes throughout the kingdom, for the poor Indians themselves collect and carry them in groups, under the *alcalde mayor* or the lieutenant of the pueblo, gathering from ranch to ranch, and from house to house, grain, seeds, calves, sheep, and hogs (where there are any) chile, wool, onions, etc.

This immense labor does not stop here, for when corn is to be shelled for the soldiers' rations, the alcalde or lieutenant asks for a half a pueblo of Indians—men women, and children—who go to the place where the corn is shelled, with great labor, by striking or rubbing one ear against another with the hands, producing in this way fifteen or twenty *fanegas* of corn. To this another task is added for both men and women, for out of the great amount of wheat or shelled corn they have to grind by hand fifteen or twenty fanegas into flour for the señor governor, and the poor Indians have to carry it to the villa, each one traveling with his horse a distance of thirty leagues or more, over rough roads and through very dangerous country. . . . For none of these immense labors do [the Indians] receive any . . . reward, wage, or recompense. . . .

This example set by the governors is followed as well by *alcaldes mayores* and their lieutenants. . . . These alcaldes never conduct themselves in any way that yields any benefit to the Indians or aid to the missionaries for the encouragement of religion, for they never go to church to see whether they [the Indians] fail to attend mass. On the contrary, what happens most often is that we religious suffer many injuries, outrages and afflictions from the alcaldes if we try to defend the unfortunate Indians in any way. . . . The alcaldes laugh, for they alone are favored and protected by the governors, for whom the best alcaldes are those who oppress the Indians most.

From an impartial point of view, it is difficult, from this distance in time, to tell which source of oppression—clergy or civil—was the most abusive and generated the most suffering. It is clear from the records that conditions were not as bad for the Pueblos during the eighteenth century as in the preceding one. We have already noted that the power and the influence of the missionaries had been sapped. They were not as brutal in enforcing Catholic doctrine and practices as before the rebellion. As for the civil authorities, the depredations of the nomadic tribes were diverting the attention of the governors and alcaldes away from the Pueblos. Indeed, the Pueblos were now being brought into a partnership with the Hispanicized population in controlling enemy Indians. It soon became apparent that mounted and armed Pueblo warriors were necessary to insure the continuity of the sedentary communities along the Rio Grande, whether those of the Indians or the colonists. The value of the Pueblos as military allies of the Spaniards is emphasized by Jones (1966:177):

> The greatest benefit Spain derived from her close affiliation with the Pueblos was the establishment of unity in a province formerly torn by internal dissension and native hatred for the conquerors. This early disunity, so prominent in the seventeenth century, ultimately resulted in the expulsion of the Spaniards from New Mexico for nearly a dozen years. Beginning with the reconquest, Pueblos gradually were attracted to the cause of the Iberians, thus forming a nucleus for future development and expansion. Without the unification of the Pueblos and their subsequent association with the Spaniards, Spain could not have controlled New Mexico with the limited resources she maintained in that area. Except for rare occasions in the early part of the period when conspiracies were reported, Spain in the eighteenth century never again had to worry about her Pueblo allies rebelling against her imposed authority.

The sense of partnership and participation in the wars as important and prestigeful allies of the Spaniards offset the abuses that the Pueblos suffered. Their scapegoat position and bottomrung status in the social ladder of New Mexico, too, was being displaced by a rapidly growing population of captives (Genizaros) from enemy tribes. Not the least of the good fortune that came to the Pueblos in their military partnership was a sharing in the booty recovered in warfare; they even acquired captives as servants and were also rewarded by Spanish authorities with titles and privileges (Jones 1966:175).

THE PUEBLOS AS WARRIORS

Anthropologists, historians, and others have long held a view of the Pueblos as a docile, nonaggressive people. Ruth Benedict, in "Patterns of Culture" (1934), has given this Pueblo stereotype its widest currency; labeling the Pueblo personality type as "Apollonian," she characterizes the Pueblo Indian as controlled and unassertive, eschewing excesses of all kinds (compare Chaves 1967:86–87). Such Indians could have hardly staged a rebellion of the character and dimensions of the Pueblo revolt of 1680. Actually, this stereotype of the Pueblo Indian is controverted by the historical record of the more detailed ethnographic studies now available. Popé, the Tewa Indian who started the revolt, was an unusual individual yet he was not atypical; there were and are assertive and aggressive Pueblo Indians.

During the revolt we know of three other Pueblo Indians who emerged as aggressive rebels but who later cooperated with De ·Vargas and facilitated the reconquest of New Mexico. These were Alonso Catiti from Santo Domingo, Bartolomé de Ojeda of Zia, and Luis Tupatu from Picuris. All three of these men, like Popé, wielded considerable influence among the Indians and were courageous, forceful leaders. There is ample evidence of the alleged non-Pueblo type characteristics of the rebels in the statements collected from captured Pueblo Indians by Lieutenant Juan Dominguez de Mendoza during the winter of 1681–1682 (Hackett and Shelby 1942:232–403). That some of these rebels may have been mixed bloods surely must have added to the vigor of the Pueblos, but such mixed bloods were products of Pueblo culture as well. By 1680, much mixing of blood between Pueblos and settlers had taken place (Scholes 1935:97–98). Some of these mixed bloods, growing up among the Hispanicized settlers, threw their lot in with the colonists; those who were born and raised in the pueblos grew up with primary allegiance to Pueblo life. This is a process that has been going on as long as these two peoples have lived as neighbors. Culturally, the two populations are quite distinct; racially, they are predominantly Indian despite allegations of racial purity espoused, sometimes rather heatedly, by each group. It is unfortunate that the Pueblos and Hispanos do not take pride in their mixed heritage; instead, the latter boast of Spanish culture, while the Pueblos emphasize their indigenous background. Both have deep roots in native America and should proclaim their inherent right as native Americans—a claim most Euro-Americans cannot make.

We have a long history of Pueblo involvement in conflicts which attest to the aggressive traits of these Indians. If active participation in warfare is indicative of aggressive personality characteristics, then there is ample evidence of such activity among the Pueblos (compare Ellis 1951a:177–201). The bloody massacre of the inhabitants of the Hopi village of Awatovi in 1701 after Awatovi had again received Franciscan missionaries by a party of Hopi warriors and the Tewa of Hano is indicative of Pueblo aggressiveness (Navarez 1937:386). Warfare has not been simply a defensive activity with the Pueblos either. Spanish documents of the eighteenth century and early nineteenth century record Pueblo Indian auxiliaries accompanying Spanish soldiers and settlers in campaigns against the nomadic marauders. The Pueblos turned out to be dependable and courageous warriors. Indeed, Spanish military leaders consistently reported the Pueblos to be better fighters than the settlers. During the remainder of Spanish rule, every major Spanish retaliatory or punitive expedition against the Apache, Navaho, and Comanche contained Pueblo Indian auxiliaries. Usually in these campaigns the number of Pueblo Indians exceeded the regular soldiers as well as men recruited from the settlers. A number of Indians became extremely able leaders and were given the title of *capitán major de la guerra*. During the first two decades of the eighteenth century, three Pueblo Indians were consistently mentioned as capable leaders in the campaigns against the nomadic enemies: Domingo Romero of Tesuque, Don Felipe of Pecos, and Jose Naranjo of Santa Clara. Jones (1966) has presented an excellent account of the contributions of the Pueblo Indians toward the control of the nomadic tribes following the Pueblo revolt. Excerpts from his book dispel the image of the Pueblo Indians as docile tribesmen unfit for war:

By 1729 there was no longer any fear of Pueblo Indian uprisings. Unity among these natives had been established in support of Spanish policies in New Mexico. Control of these friendly Indians had been effectively demonstrated, particularly on the more regularized and organized campaigns. Pueblo assistance on these expeditions had provided the necessary strength with which to meet the many widely scattered enemies. Indeed, as the period progressed, the number of auxiliaries seemed to increase until, at the end of the era, a larger proportion of the combined force was recruited. In addition, problems of organization were gradually worked out during this period. Likewise the Pueblos furnished numerous other forms of assistance as scouts, interpreters, and informants. Their ready supply of foodstuffs and equipment, their effective fighting techniques, and their willingness to offer their villages as rendezvous points for campaigns were other contributions of the Pueblos. Certainly, they provided an attractive example to other Indians such as the Jicarilla and Sierra Blanca Apaches. This formative period provided the basis in New Mexico for an intersocietal exchange which increased and endured until the end of the Spanish authority in the province. . . .

Pueblo auxiliaries served as the most consistently reliable element in the pacification of hostile tribes and the defense of New Mexico during the eighteenth century. The presidial force at Santa Fe, numbering only eighty troops during the major portion of this era, was too small to control the province adequately by itself. Militia forces were unreliable, poorly equipped, and often untrained and undisciplined. From [governors] Vargas to La Concha, authorities complained of the reluctance of the settlers to serve in defense in the province. At the same time they praised the loyalty, self-denial, and military preparedness of the Pueblos in fulfilling their obligations to defend the kingdom. Of unusual importance is the fact that both civil and religious authorities seemed to agree that the natives contributed greatly to the defense of the province (Jones 1966:108–109, 178).

In 1752, the Pueblos possessed three times as many horses as the Spanish soldiers and settlers. Also, at this time, they had many more men-at-arms, more lances, and a larger number of leather jackets for individual protection. The Spaniards had more swords and, possibly, firearms, although some of the Pueblos also possessed them. It is interesting that the pueblos of Laguna, Acoma, and Zuni each possessed more horses than any Spanish settlement, and that Laguna had almost as many as all of the colonists together (Jones 1966:123).

Other evidence of the aggressive behavior of the Pueblos may also be mentioned in order to destroy the image of the Pueblos as passive and docile. In 1837 a group of Pueblo Indians and some Hispanos attempted to take over the government of New Mexico. The action was apparently brought about by the appointment of Albino Perez, the first non-New Mexico born governor under Mexican rule. This fact, plus a rumor that circulated among the poorer Hispanos and Indians that heavy taxes were to be levied upon poultry, dogs, irrigation ditches, and clothing, among other things, brought about the rebellion. The group of Pueblo Indians and Hispanos stormed Santa Fe and killed a number of citizens, including Governor Perez. They then elected one of their own participants, an Indian from Taos by the name of José Gonzáles, as the governor of New Mexico. Gonzáles' rule was brief; a force under Manuel Armijo recaptured Santa Fe and Zonzáles and several of his associates were captured and shot (Bancroft 1889: 317–319).

Pueblo Indians also joined Hispanos in the Revolt of 1847 against American occupation. According to most historians, these rebels were "lower-class" Mexicans and Indians (Bancroft 1889:432–437; Hallenbeck 1950:271–274); yet whatever their "class," the group demonstrated loyalty to Mexican rule and demonstrated the suspicion and distrust of Americans held by a substantial portion of the Hispano and Indian population during the period.

Warfare was an important activity in the past and war associations are found in every pueblo. Indeed, among the Tanoans there is a counterpart women's organization—the Women's Scalp Association. Until about a century ago when warfare was still a live activity, members of this association among the Tewa pueblos met a returning war party, took the enemy scalps from the victorious warriors and wildly chewed the scalps while emitting vindictive epithets at the enemy. Once at the pueblo, the returning warriors and the members of the Women's Scalp Society engaged in a frenzied dance of victory (Hill, manuscript). This is indeed very un-Appolonian type of behavior! During the eighteenth century, the pagan and orgiastic nature of these dances disturbed the Spanish civil and church authorities and they tried, unsuccessfully, to repress them (Adams and Chavez 1956:244–248, 257–258; Jones 1966:83–84).

Still another example of seemingly atypical Pueblo behavior is displayed by Pueblo Indians in factional disputes that are characteristic of all Pueblo communities. These factions are usually initiated by an individual who strongly opposes some aspect of life in the community. Village members take sides and, depending on the issues involved, there may be two or more dissident factions. Disagreement over religious matters are particularly frequent sources of conflict among the Pueblos. A number of studies of Pueblo factionalism now exist; in all the cases reported, highly individualistic and aggressive behavior is noted as characteristic of the factional leaders (see Dozier 1966; Fenton 1957; Fox 1967; French 1948; Siegel 1949; Siegel and Beals 1962; Titiev 1944; Whitman 1940, 1947).

While factionalism appears to be an old and continuing characteristic, Pueblo villages persist as distinctive communities. In the prehistoric past, nonconformists were probably evicted or else moved out voluntarily to found new communities. During the Spanish-Mexican period, such malcontents joined the more permissive nomadic Navaho or one of the neighboring Hispano villages. In recent years, particularly since World War II, those who could not tolerate the authoritative rule of the pueblos have moved into urban areas, becoming a part of a growing urban Indian population in the Southwest. It is rare, however, that a whole pueblo has dissolved. One obvious explanation for the persistence of these communities is the "skimming off" process by which malcontents drop out of the villages, thus leaving Pueblo communities organized along traditional lines. Another reason that pueblos never completely break up may be that factions are only one type of segmentary division; each village is made up of kinship units—as many as six associations—and among the Eastern Pueblos, organized into dual divisions or moieties, as well. These units cross-cut the village population in membership with the result that two people are rarely in two units together. Friction in one of these units may bring opposition between two individuals, but such individuals may need to support one another in a second or third social unit. Finally, it is important to realize that Pueblo Indians value the rewards inherent in group living and like to participate in the frequent ceremonials and communal projects. Most Pueblos compromise and submit to authority rule rather than give up these rewards. Pueblo individuals do air their objections and so factional disputes arise, yet such conflicts may be important to societies that are surrounded by a social environment which is in a constant flux of change. The Pueblos must constantly achieve an adjustment between neighboring societies and their own; factional disputes therefore may help in this accommodation process.

THE NON-PUEBLO POPULATION

The non-Pueblo colonial population during the eighteenth century was far from being uniformly Spanish. The settlements contained a core of Spanish or Mexican settlers and a mixed population, often referred to as "gente de razon." (Adams 1954:34, footnote 61). To this population must be added the many Indian servants and workers for the settlers who, in time, also became a part of the colonial population. Finally, Pueblo individuals and families dissatisfied with Pueblo life also joined Hispanicized villages. The following dispute between the pueblo of Santa Clara and a Pueblo Indian family, the record of which was found in the Spanish archives of New Mexico, illustrates one case of an obviously Hispanicized family that had severed connections with the pueblo. This case went back to the original complainant, one Roque Canjuebes, in 1744. The issue, when finally settled in 1817, was resolved in favor of the pueblo against the grandchildren of Roque Canjuebes. The pueblo objected to Canjuebes living within the boundaries of the pueblo grant if he chose to lead a Spanish way of life. Some members of the family made as many as three trips to Durango to lay their claim personally before the Commandant General. The matter was eventually decided in favor of the pueblo. The Commandant General, Bernardo Bonavia, directed the provincial governor "to give the Canjuebes to understand that if they want to hold the lands [on the pueblo grant] they must go back and become part of the pueblo community; but if they want to retain their Spanish citizenship, they must buy the lands they need elsewhere, as do other citizens of the Province" (Twitchell 1914, Vol. I, pp. 77–78, 371–372).

The Canjuebes' case is special only in that the litigants expended considerable effort to achieve a settlement. Information collected in recent years indicates that many Pueblo Indians have, in the past, lost pueblo homes and land rights and either have been evicted from the pueblo or else have moved out voluntarily to seek their fortunes elsewhere (Dozier 1966:175–176; Hawley 1948: 273–280). Obviously there have been many cases of Pueblo Indians becoming genuinely converted to Catholicism and adopting the values of the neighboring Hispanic culture. Traditional Pueblo society and culture, however, prevents the free exercise of Catholic beliefs and practices at the expense of dropping indigenous beliefs and customs. All Indians who are members of the pueblo must conform to the native religious demands as well, and in many areas the two religious systems are in conflict. The only action open to the Pueblo Indian who cannot reconcile the two religious systems is to leave the pueblo and move into an

Hispanicized community. The commandant's decision in the Canjuebes' case gave official sanction to the right of an Indian pueblo to evict members who did not want to conform to its tribal customs. It is likely that this decision discouraged other Hispanicized Pueblo Indians from testing their pueblo's right to confiscate their property and evict them. Either they conformed to their pueblo's demands to abide by Pueblo customs or else they left the pueblo voluntarily to carry on an Hispanicized existence among the settlers. The population of the pueblos declined steadily during the eighteenth and nineteenth centuries at the same time that the population of Spanish-American villages was increasing. The inference is that this diminution and upsurge in population in the two types of communities is the result of the movement, at least in part, of Pueblo Indians into the Hispanicized communities (Hodge 1912:327). Undoubtedly this process started soon after the friars began active missionary work, as it certainly was well established in the eighteenth century (Jones 1966:178–179).

During the early part of the eighteenth century, a separation between the people of predominantly Spanish blood and the mixed and Indian groups was maintained. The former had the best lands and the most livestock. It was this group that made an effort to keep up the Spanish way of life, as much as this was possible in the isolated frontier of New Mexico. The mixed bloods and the Indians in the settlements were in a menial position, both socially and economically. They looked up to the Spanish elite and took their cues of life, faith, and proper behavior from them.

The composition of the mixed population living with the Spanish minority and eventually absorbing the latter is described by Swadesh (1966:52–53) under the term "castas":

"Castas" were people of mixed ancestry, whose cultural identity and civil status permitted including with the Spaniards. The principal categories of castas were: "Mestizos" (mixed Spanish-Indian ancestry); "Coyotes" (in the eighteenth and early nineteenth centuries, at least, children of European, non-Spanish fathers and New Mexican, Spanish or Mextizo mothers); "Mulatto" (mixed Spanish-Negro ancestry), and "Zambo" (mixed Indian-Negro ancestry). An "Indio" was a person born in a specific tribe or Pueblo and the Genizaro settlements [former Indian captives, see below] were designated as Pueblos. . . .

Genizaros at first did not have *vecino* status [the status that entitled one to full colonial Spanish citizenship], any more than Pueblo Indians. It appears that the lower grades of castas, in menial positions, did not enjoy this status either. But, as the baptismal and marriage books of Abiquiu show, vecino status could be and was acquired. . . . The acquisition of tithable property was perhaps the key to social upgrading [see the Santa Clara-Canjuebes' case above]. Since property was such an important consideration in selecting a marriage partner, it also seems likely that an impoverished person of higher status would wed a lower-status person of means. The children would inherit the status of the higher-placed parent. Property considerations thus had the two-way effect of reducing the chances of marriage between people of vastly different status, while giving sufficient motive for marrying out of one's immediate group so that rigid castes did not crystallize.

From the earliest time of settlement, some high status people left children of mixed ancestry. . . . Current achievement, affluence and status earned in any generation apparently influenced choice of marriage partner more than ancestry in remote generations.

GENIZAROS

A substantial population in New Mexico consisted of *Genizaros*, Indians who were purchased or captured from nomadic tribes. The term is a Spanish transliteration of the Turkish word *yenicheri* (English *janizary*), literally "new troops" referring to a former body of Turkish infantry largely recruited from compulsory conscripts and converts taken from Christian subjects (Hodge 1912:489). The Genizaros of New Mexico are well characterized by Adams and Chavez (1956:42, n. 71):

> In New Mexico [the term *genizaro*] was used to designate non-Pueblo Indians living in more or less Spanish fashion. Some of them were captives ransomed from the nomadic tribes, and their mixed New Mexico-born descendants inherited the designation. Church and civil records reveal such varied derivations as Apache, Comanche, Navajo, Ute, Kiowa, Wichita and Pawnee. Many had Spanish blood, clandestinely and otherwise. They all bore Christian names from baptism and Spanish surnames from their former masters; belonging no longer to any particular Indian tribe they spoke . . . Spanish. . . .

The Comanches and Utes brought Indian captives from diverse tribes and, occasionally, French and Spanish captives to barter and sell to Spanish authorities at fairs held at Toas and Abiquiu. Father Dominguez, who made an inventory of the New Mexico missions in 1776, has a vivid description of the Taos and Abiquiu fairs, where in addition to captives, a variety of other items were sold and traded. Rather extensive excerpts are quoted from Dominguez' account for it is a unique report of on-the-spot observation of Plains Indian trading activities and of the items bought and sold or traded.

> When they are on their good behavior, or at peace, they enter Taos to trade. At this fair they sell buffalo hides, "white elkskins," horses, mules, buffalo meat, pagan indians (of both sexes, children and adults) whom they capture from other nations. [In Father Claramonte's time Christians from other places were also ransomed. He astutely cultivated the Comanche captain, his great friend, in order to get them out of captivity, for otherwise they carry them off again.] They also sell good guns, pistols, powder, balls, tobacco, hatchets, and some vessels of yellow tin (some large, others small) shaped like the crown of the friars' hats, but the difference is that the top of the hat is the bottom of the vessel. These have a handle made of an iron hoop to carry them. . . . They acquire these articles, from the guns to the vessels, from the Jumanas Indians (Wichitas), who have direct communication and trade with the French, from whom they buy them. The Comanches usually sell to our people at this rate: a buffalo hide for a *belduque*, or broad knife made entirely of iron which they call a trading knife here; "white elkskin" (it is the same [buffalo] hide, but softened like deerskin), the same; for a very poor bridle, two buffalo skins or a vessel like those mentioned; the meat for maize or corn flour; an Indian slave, according to the individual, because if it is an Indian girl from twelve to twenty years old, two good horses and some trifles in addition, such as a short cloak, a horse cloth, a red lapel are given; or a she-mule and a scarlet cover, or other things are given for her.
>
> If the slave is male, he is worth less and the amount is arranged in the manner described. If they sell a she-mule, either a cover or a short cloak or a good horse is given; if they sell a horse, a poor bridle, but garnished with red rags, is given for it; if they sell a pistol, its price is a bridle; if both together, a horse is given for them.

This is the usual, and a prudent judgment of how everything must go can be based on it. They are great traders, for as soon as they buy anything, they usually sell exactly what they bought; and usually they keep losing, the occasion when they gain being very rare, because our people ordinarily play infamous tricks on them. In short, the trading day resembles a second-hand market in Mexico, the way people mill about (Adams and Chavez 1956:252).

Father Dominguez describes the fair at Abiquiu where the Ute Indians come to trade:

Every year, between the end of October and the beginning of November, many heathens of the Ute nation come to the vicinity of this pueblo. They come very well laden [with] good deerskin, and they celebrate their fair with them. This is held for the sole purpose of buying horses. If one is much to the taste and satisfaction of an Indian (the trial is a good race), he gives fifteen to twenty good deerskins for the horse; and if not, there is no purchase. They also sell deer or buffalo meat for maize or corn flour. Sometimes there are little captive heathen Indians (male or female) as with the Comanches, whom they resemble in the manner of selling them. They usually sell deerskins for belduques [iron knives] only, and they are given two of the latter for a good one of the former. With the exception of firearms and vessels, the Utes sell everything else as described with regard to the Comanches, but they are not so fond of trading as has been said of the latter (Adams and Chavez 1956:252-253).

The retaliatory expeditions and the fairs described above added a significant population of captive Indians to the population of New Mexico by the middle of the eighteenth century. Initially these captives were assigned as servants to the homes of the settlers, but as their numbers increased, Pueblo auxiliary soldiers were also permitted to take captives to their pueblos. As the number of captives increased, those who served as servants in the homes of the settlers for many years and had become Hispanicized were settled in separate communities. The role these captives played in the defense of the colonial settlements and the service they performed along with the Pueblo Indians as auxiliary soldiers earned them the name Genizaros. Some were settled in a special *barrio* in Santa Fe, others separately near the villages of the settlers, while at least three *pueblos de genizaros* were established in the eighteenth century. These pueblos were at Abiquiu, Ojo Caliente, Tomé, and Belen (Hodge 1912:489); Jones 1966:139), and were by design of Spanish authorities placed in locations where they would receive the initial brunt of enemy attacks. The Apaches raided from the south; Tomé and Belen were the first two villages encountered from that direction. Abiquiu and Ojo Caliente were corridors for the raiding activities of the Utes and Comanches. The colonial settlements, thus, were buffered by either Genizaro or Pueblo villages. Acoma, Laguna, and Jemez pueblos received the first attacks of Navaho raiders, while the Galisteo Basin Pueblos and Pecos were exposed to the initial thrusts of Plains Indians. Inordinate demands were made on both the Pueblos and Genizaro villages to furnish warriors for punitive expeditions into enemy territory (Jones 1966:36, 98). New Mexico population identified as Genizaro showed a steady decrease in the late eighteenth century and finally disappeared as a separate category in the nineteenth century. Swadesh (1966:42) attributes the decline in part to the excessive military casualty rate, but primarily to their absorption into the Hispanicized population.

The class blood lines of the non-Pueblo population were to become increasingly blurred in the succeeding century, and they finally become crystallized into the Spanish-American or Hispano population. This population developed important cultural characteristics that will be described in the next section. The non-Pueblo settled populations grew rapidly in numbers, primarily by the continuous additions of Genizaros and disaffected Pueblo Indians. A comparison of the population from 1750 to 1799 is illuminating: in 1750 there were 3779 settlers and 12,142 Pueblos; in 1760, 7666 settlers and 9104 Pueblos; in 1793, 16,156 settlers and 9275 Pueblos; and in 1799, 18,826 settlers and 9732 Pueblos (Jones 1966:153). It is obvious that this terrific population by 1799—more than four times the population of 1750—is due to the addition of Indians to the Hispanicized population. Immigration from Mexico was at a standstill during this period; the frontier settlements in New Mexico were sealed off from population centers in the south by distant, hostile tribes, and the weakening of Spanish power and influence. While some increase may be attributed to a rise in natural birth rates, such an explanation is hardly tenable when we realize the periodic enemy raids and epidemic diseases to which both the Pueblos and Hispanicized populations were exposed. The only reasonable explanation is the addition of Pueblos and nomadic Indians, the latter as servants initially, but gradually being absorbed into the population as "Spanish citizens." It was not until the following century that the mixed population developed distinctive ethnic and cultural characteristics.

THE WESTERN PUEBLOS

While the Rio Grande pueblos established a reciprocal type of relationship with their neighbors after the revolt which continued through the eighteenth century, the Western Pueblos were neglected and virtually abandoned by missionaries and civil authorities during this period. As we have noted in the previous section, missionary activity among the Rio Grande was reestablished in the first decade of the eighteenth century, but Spanish efforts to revive the missionary program among the western frontier pueblos were not as successful. One of the missions at Zuni was rebuilt; but because of the increasing raids of the Apaches and Navahos, it was difficult to maintain the mission. Acoma also reestablished its mission after the revolt, but keeping a resident missionary was a constant problem throughout the eighteenth century.

During the first half of the eighteenth century, attempts to bring back the Rio Grande Pueblo Indians who had taken refuge among the Hopi highlighted Spanish activities. In 1707, Governor Cubero Valdez sent some soldiers under the supervision of Fray Juan de Mingues to bring back the "apostates" (as the Spaniards termed the Pueblo refugees). The expedition encountered resistance and returned to Santa Fe without any of the refugees. Next, in August 1716, Governor Felix Martinez went to the Hopi country with an army of Spaniards and Rio Grande Pueblo Indians for the same purpose. Martinez reported:

I explained to them [the Tanos and other apostates] the sole purpose for which I had come with the army, that is, that they should offer submission to the Divine and human Majesty and bring back all of the Indians who had rebelled, some in the year '80 [1680] and others in '96 [1696]; that they should return to their own pueblos whence they fled . . . (Bloom 1931:204–205).

The Indians refused to come down from First Mesa where they had established their village. Martinez attacked, and in the battle that ensued several Indians were killed and many others wounded. Then Martinez proposed to the Walpi (Hopi) chiefs to allow him to ascend the mesa to take the refugees prisoner. The Spaniards were told they could ascend the mesa, but apparently Martinez decided against the venture. Instead he ordered his soldiers to destroy the crops in the fields. For five days the army ambushed and seized people, cattle, flocks, "doing all damage possible to the Apostates" of First and Second Mesas. When all but a few "very insignificant" fields had been destroyed, the governor felt that "the enemies of our Holy Faith" had been properly punished and the army marched back to Santa Fe (Bloom 1931:192, 218).

The Southern Tewa (Tanos) remained on First Mesa despite repeated attempts of the Spaniards to induce them to return to the Rio Grande valley. The community of Hano, where the descendants of the original Tano immigrants now live, is a flourishing pueblo of over 500 inhabitants (Dozier 1966:22).

Competition between Franciscans and Jesuits over the jurisdiction of the Hopi pueblos brought about renewed Franciscan activity among the Hopi. In 1741, two missionaries, Fray Carlos Delgado and Fray Ignacio Pino, succeeded in returning 441 apostate Tiwa Indians and restored them to their old pueblos—Pajarito, Alameda, and Sandia—on the Rio Grande (Thomas 1932:160). Only one of these—Sandia remained at the time of Father Dominguez' visitation of the Pueblos in 1776. There were ninety-two families and 275 person in that year (Adams and Chavez 1956:144). At present, Sandia has a population of about 250; the other former Tiwa villages have not survived as Indian pueblos. Although the King of Spain had actually assigned the Hopi region to the Jesuits in 1719, the King reversed his royal order in 1745 as the result of the activities of the Franciscans (Thomas 1932:21).

In 1775, interest in an overland route from New Mexico to California stimulated concern for the Hopi. This interest, plus the hope of returning the Hopi Indians to the fold of the Catholic Church, brought Fray Silvestre Velez de Escalante, then the resident priest at Zuni. Father Escalante found the rugged country of northern Arizona and southern Utah impossible to penetrate, but he spent eight days among the Hopi and sent a vivid description of the Hopi and their neighbors to Governor Pedro Fermin de Mendinueta:

This province is bounded on the east by the Navajos, on the west and northwest by the Cosninas [Havasupai], on the north by the Utes, on the south by the Gila Apaches and on the southwest with others whom they call here Mescaleros. . . . The Moqui are very civilized, apply themselves to weaving and cultivating the land by means of which they raise abundant crops of maize, beans, and chile. They also gather cotton although not much. They suffer from scarcity of wood and good water . . . (Thomas 1932:150–151).

After Escalante's visit, the Hopi region experienced a devastating drought. Governor Juan Bautista de Anza, taking advantage of the deplorable condition of the Hopi, made a final attempt to convert them. He sent messengers offering assistance if the Hopi would come and build their pueblos in the Rio Grande valley. Although many Hopi are reported to have settled among the Navaho at this time, they did not accept the offer of the Spanish governor. Governor Anza himself visited the Hopi villages in 1780. His report indicated that starvation, disease, and migration of the Indians to the Navaho country had drastically reduced the population (Thomas 1932:221–245).

After Governor Anza's trip to the Hopi country, Spanish reports about the Hopi ceased. Distance, isolation, and the growing hostility of the nomadic tribes eventually separated the Hopi as well as the Zuni pueblos from the center of Spanish activity in the Rio Grande valley. The Spanish government was pre-occupied with troubles at home, serving the Rio Grande pueblos, and a growing Hispanicized Mestizo population as well. To make matters worse, the vigorous Comanche Indians, along with the Apaches, Navahos, and Utes, had begun to raid the settlers and the Pueblo Indians. The provincial government in Santa Fe was in no position to send missionaries to the western pueblos nor to provide military aid to the Hopi and Zuni, who were suffering from the periodic raids of Utes, Navahos, and Apaches.

This period of neglect and virtual abandonment of the Western Pueblos by church and civil authorities caused the people to remove almost completely the veneer of Spanish culture they had acquired during the century before. These conditions remained until the advent of Anglo-Americans in the nineteenth century.

History 1800–1900

THE MEXICAN INTERLUDE AND ANGLO-AMERICAN INTRUSION

Although New Mexico became a part of the Republic of Mexico in 1821 and United States rule was extended over the area in 1846, the impact of these changes did not seriously affect the Pueblos until after 1850. The neglect of the Pueblos by both civil and church authorities continued and reached a peak during the Mexican period. Spain's power in the New World weakened progressively and she was unable to reestablish the stronghold on the pueblos that she had maintained during the seventeenth century and the first half of the eighteenth. This was particularly true with regard to the western pueblos. The missions, as we have noted, were never rebuilt among the Hopi and only one of the missions at Zuni (Halona) of the three originally constructed during the seventeenth century was repaired and used sporadically until the first quarter of the nineteenth century when it was abandoned (Twitchell 1914, Vol. II, p. 640; Kubler 1940:97). The isolation of the Western Pueblos from the center of the provincial government became even more pronounced when Mexico gained its independence; indeed, contact with these pueblos virtually ceased until late in the nineteenth century when the United States government established relations with them.

PUEBLO RELATIONS WITH THE CHURCH
AND CIVIL AUTHORITIES

Pedro Bautista Pino, a prominent New Mexican and a representative to the Spanish Cortés, spoke of the deplorable religious situation in New Mexico in 1812. Pino reported that the twenty-six Indian pueblos and 102 villages of the settlers were served by only twenty-two priests. The number of priests available for meeting the religious needs of the Pueblos alone was inadequate, yet they were responsible for the religious welfare of a non-Pueblo population twice the size of the indigenous population as well. Pino indicated that the great distances between the pueblos where the missionaries resided and the communities of the settlers seriously impaired religious instruction and services to the latter. He reported that because of the tremendous distance between the seat of the bishopric (Durango) and the New Mexico settlements, no bishop had visited the province for fifty years. The need to establish a special bishopric for New Mexico was emphasized and Pino also made a plea for the construction of a college and primary schools (Carroll and Haggard 1942:50–51).

As a result of the recall of some of the Spanish priests, the number of priests in New Mexico was further reduced to seventeen shortly after Mexican independence. Most of the priests were old and even if they were in the prime of youth, they could hardly have been able to administer the services of the church to a rapidly increasing population spread out over a large area.

In 1832, neglect of the missions was even more acute. Antonio Barreiro, a Mexican lawyer residing in Santa Fe, reported as follows about the religious situation in New Mexico:

> The religious care of these pueblos rests in the hands of the missionaries of the province of the Holy Gospel of Mexico; unfortunately, however, there exists the most doleful neglect because only five of the pueblos (out of twenty listed) have missionary fathers. If the government does not take active steps to remedy this evil, the vacant missions will never be filled, and the salvation of the souls of these unfortunate Indians shall continue, as it has for a long time, to be woefully neglected (Carroll and Haggard 1942:29).

Barreiro observed that many people, both Pueblos and settlers, died without receiving the sacraments of confession and extreme unction. Corpses often were not buried for days and the baptism of infants delayed. It was not possible for all people to attend Sunday mass because of the distances involved between the settlements and the few chapels where mass was offered. Barreiro also remarked about the ruined condition of most of the chapels and mission structures (Carroll and Haggard 1942:53).

The religious decay described by Pino and Barreiro continued until the American period when John B. Lamy became archbishop of the newly created archdiocese of Santa Fe in 1851. Lamy not only increased the clergy, reformed the church in New Mexico, but also launched a progressive program of education. The Catholic church, during and after Lamy's long service in New Mexico, tried to persuade the Pueblos to give up their pagan beliefs and practices, but they did not employ the coercive methods of the Spanish Franciscans. Lamy's reforms did not reach the Pueblos of Zuni and Hopi. These Pueblos reverted back to their pagan beliefs and customs. Not until the latter part of the nineteenth century— this time through the work of Protestant missionaries—were the western pueblos again to experience interference in their indigenous religious practices. Indeed, except for making the services of the priests more available to the pueblos—a dubious benefit to most Indians—Lamy's activities affected the non-Pueblo population primarily. Archbishop Lamy reestablished a number of the missions that had fallen into ruin and constructed many others, some with schools and convents. In addition, Lamy brought respect to the church and its clergy from Catholics and non-Catholics alike.

The Pueblos also received little attention from civil authorities during this period. Under both Spanish and Mexican rule, local officials were busy with commerce and troubled with the threat of a Texan or American invasion and the constant ravages of the nomadic tribes. These factors, except for the raids of enemy Indians, did not affect the Pueblos. They continued through both the Spanish and Mexican periods to furnish men for the defense of the New Mexico settlements. As far as their internal affairs were concerned, the Pueblos were happy to be ignored by Spanish and Mexican officialdom. The surge of ceremonial activity, which had started in the last century, continued through the Mexican period. Just as the church was unable to restore contacts with the pueblos of Zuni and Hopi, so also the seat of civil government in Santa Fe made no attempt to reestablish relations with these pueblos during this period. The Navaho and Apache had formed a virtually impenetrable barrier between the Rio Grande settlements and the Western Pueblos. This state of affairs was to change with the increasing number of Anglo-Americans entering New Mexico; but for almost half a century, the pueblos were relatively free of outside interference.

HISPANOS

Sometime after the mid-eighteenth century, the mixed population which we have thus far designated alternatively as colonists, settlers, or the Hispanicized population, surpassed the Pueblos in population. The term "Hispano" although not an entirely satisfactory designation for these people, helps to differentiate them from more recent migrants from Mexico who are ethnically similar but whose history is not rooted as deeply in the region. "Hispano" is also a less awkward term than such hyphenated labels as "New Mexican" or "Spanish-American." The latter term is objectionable for other reasons as well; it implies pure Spanish heritage both racially and culturally. All the Spanish ancestors of colonial New Mexico entered via Mexico, the majority of the early settlers being *creoles* (Mexico-born whites), *mestizos* (Indian-white mixtures), or Mexican Indians. Further mixing took place in New Mexico with the indigenous population by the addition of Pueblo Indians, Genizaros, and former Indian servants. Hispanos, thus, have deep roots in the New World—earlier than other Europeans on the Spanish side and back many millennia through their indigenous forebears.

Shortly after Mexican independence, the population of New Mexico was estimated as 50,000 (Carroll and Haggard 1942:31). This estimate did not take in the nomadic Indians, but it did include the Pueblo Indians, whose population rarely exceeded 10,000 during the nineteenth century. Thus, there were approximately 40,000 Hispanos just prior to Anglo-American entry. By 1880, this population had doubled while the Pueblo population remained substantially the same (Bancroft 1889:723; Hodge 1912:325).

The Hispanos by the mid-nineteenth century, through intermarriage among themselves, represented a fairly uniform physical type in which Indian ancestry was marked. There was an "upper class" group who claimed "pure" Spanish ancestry; but, in actuality, this class represented the *ricos* or wealthy strata of the society rather than a group with any legitimate claim to descent from pure Spanish ancestors. The *ricos* owned large herds of sheep and cattle which grazed over vast areas of northern New Mexico. The livestock driven annually to markets in Chihuahua and Sonora brought substantial profits to the *ricos*.

The number of well-to-do stockowners were relatively few in the population. In 1867, this group was estimated to number about 500 to 700 families, and the rest of the Hispano population between 50,000 and 70,000. Most of the poorer Hispanos were held in bondage through the peonage of debt. Since the debts were passed down to descendants, the control of the majority of the Hispanos by a few *ricos* was a pattern that went on for many generations. In addition, in the same year (1867) the number of actual Indian slaves in New Mexico was estimated as between 1500 and 3000. Debt, peonage, and slavery in New Mexico were so serious that a Congressional Act was passed in 1867 to outlaw the practice (Ganaway 1944:9–12).

The characteristics of community life in New Mexico developed out of the practice of giving land grants, either to individuals or to communities, and the way in which this land was used. A land grant made to an individual, the *patrón*, and his family (with inheritance rights along the male line in his family) entitled the *patrón* to assume charge of the land and selection of the Hispano families to settle on the land. Even where land was granted to a specific community, an influential and well-to-do Hispano was made responsible for assigning houses and farm sites to the people settling on the grant. In practice, such an individual and his family also assumed *patrón* status, and in one case at least (the now famous Tierra Amarilla Land Grant case), the successful petitioner's children considered themselves heirs to the whole of the land grant—over half a million acres of land. Kluckhohn and Strodtbeck (1961:183–184) describe the patterns of land grants and land use among New Mexico Hispanos as follows:

> The older Spanish-American pattern was for whole villages to use the range lands which a *patron*, or occasionally a community, had received from the Spanish Crown [or Mexican government] in the form of a land grant. Usually, though certainly not always, the village families would own small plots of land for purposes of irrigation agriculture, but beyond this they were dependent upon the good will of the patron for the use of land for livestock, for firewood, and for any building

materials they might need. Where no water was available for irrigation agriculture, the average family frequently owned no land at all except a house site. But because the land grants had never been surveyed during the whole of the Spanish and Mexican colonial periods their boundaries were vague and indefinite. Moreover, only a very few New Mexican *patrones* became agricultural *hacendados* of the type so commonly found in Old Mexico. A majority of the *patrones* ruled over villages by means of a system of debt peonage rather than having peones who were bound to the land. The usual result of this system was that the village families who wished to run herds of livestock of their own were permitted to use the patron's land so long as they did not aspire to building herds of a size to threaten the patron economically. Many of the villagers also worked for the patron, of course, and most of them were dependent upon him for more than just land. Only the patron, for example, would have the shearing equipment or the dipping vats necessary for running a sheep business. He also usually had control of the essential but scarce watering places on the range. The system was, in short, one of great land holdings which were operated in accord with quite well defined patterns of limited permissiveness in the use of land and equipment.

In addition to using the services of the Hispanos on the land, setting up land use patterns, and assigning work patterns, the patron also assumed certain duties and responsibilities for the tenants. Again, Kluckhohn and Strodtbeck have succinctly reported:

> *Los patrones* of New Mexico always also assumed many responsibilities for the people under their control. Don Juan [the patron of the Hispano community studied by Kluckhohn], for example, seldom allowed any of those who actually worked for him to go without basic food supplies. He also managed, more or less completely, the affairs of many families and gave advice to others; he would occasionally take the ill or dying to doctors or hospitals in Railtown if requested (actually medical attention was seldom sought); and either he or members of his family performed many minor services as well. . . . The habits of dependence which a majority of Spanish-Americans—and Mexicans—are taught early and thoroughly by their family system, by patron control, and by a very paternalistic type of Catholicism are not easily abandoned (Kluckhohn and Strodtbeck 1961:204).

In the last sentence of the quotation, Kluckhohn and Strodtbeck have reference to the general dependency characteristics of Spanish-Americans who have been accustomed to depending on the services furnished by a patron. As the patron system began to disintegrate under the pressure of new economic pursuits in the 1930s, many Spanish-Americans experienced extreme difficulties in adjusting to Anglo-American life patterns. The "built-in" nature of the dependency system in early Hispano community life is apparent in the following excerpt from a description of Hispano culture:

> The patrilineal pattern of village social organization is . . . modeled after the strongly patrilineal system of the church, in which authority comes down from God the Father to the Pope, then to the priests, and then to the fathers of families. As guardian and sponsor to each village, a patron saint received the special veneration of the people; his image is kept in the church and his day is celebrated by a fiesta. In a relatively parallel position in the secular organization is the patron, usually the head of a large family and of more wealth, prestige, political power, and experience than the other villagers. In return for their loyalty and support, his duty is to supply

them with jobs, aid in emergencies, and proffer advice. He provides their contact with the outside world . . . (Hawley and Senter 1946:137).

Hispanos felt keenly the shortage of priests and the general void into which the region had lapsed in the early eighteenth century. During this period, an organization, in later times called the "cofradia de Nuestro Padre Jesus Nazareno" (more popularly known as the "Penitentes"), came into being. The organization was introduced either from the south, or developed from an organization which lay dormant through the seventeenth and eighteenth centuries and then suddenly experienced an enthusiastic revival. The origin of the cult is obscure. Its similarity to *cofradias* which developed in Spain during the medieval period is obvious, however. Foster describes these religious organizations as follows:

> The cofradia, in its earliest form, was a voluntary sodality formed by individuals motivated by the desire to worship or pay homage to a particular saint of their choice. From the beginning these associations had mutual aid as well as religious aspects, in that Christian burial and the requisite number of masses of the dead were provided for deceased members. Rumeu [see Rumeu de Armas 1944] calls this type the *cofradia religioso-benefica*, or "religious-mutual aid sodality." Membership was open to any man acceptable to the other members (Foster 1953:11).

Foster (1953:12–17) points out other functions of the *cofradias* of Spain: requirement to attend the funeral of each brother; determination of the needs of a brother who fell ill—if in debt, the *cofradia* paid all necessary expenses; brothers stayed with a sick brother to relieve his family; should death occur, the attendance of brothers at the wake was required; dowries for orphan daughters of members who died young were set up; members carried the image of their patron during Holy Week and sometimes in other fiestas, as well. Most of these functions are characteristic of the Penitente cult in New Mexico. While apparently the *cofradias* of medieval Spain were most often dedicated to saints, the Penitente's patron was Jesus of Nazareth, and perhaps as a consequence, emphasized the suffering of Christ. Woodward (1935:160) notes that the expiation of sins by corporal punishment, a central characteristic of the Penitente organization, was common among religious organizations in Spain during medieval times. Self-scourging was witnessed by Father Dominguez and Escalante in 1776 at Abiquiu but there is no mention of the existence of a distinct organization (Chavez 1954:109–110). It seems plausible then that while some of the customs inherent in *cofradias* were present early among the Hispanicized population in New Mexico, such customs did not become part of an organization until sometime during the first or second decade of the nineteenth century.

Much has been written about the more spectacular aspects of the Penitente cult: The activities during Holy Week of the Lenten Season when the passion of Christ was reenacted; the marching of men, with backs bare, whipping themselves until blood flowed; and finally an enactment of the crucifixion when one of their members is tied to the cross remaining bound for perhaps an hour. It is reported that often the man enacting the role of Christ died. Criticism of the cult for the severity of corporal punishment used by its members was made as early as 1833 by Bishop Jose Antonio Laureano de Zubiria during the bishop's official visit to New Mexico (Chavez 1954:110–111). Despite the criticism, however, the cult continued to grow, with chapters in most of the Hispanicized villages. After the establishment of American rule, American military and civil authorities voiced their opposition to the cult. Along with the Penitente cult, the few native priests of New Mexico were also viewed with disfavor by American authorities, since it was generally believed that much of the resistance to Americans came from members of the cult and from their leaders who were suspected to be native priests. When John B. Lamy assumed his duties as archbishop of the newly created archdiocese in 1851, he instituted a series of extensive reforms. He immediately encountered the opposition of the native priests and while he attempted to introduce his reforms gradually, he was obliged to excommunicate five native clergymen. Lamy replaced and increased the number of priests largely by bringing in foreign-born priests. In addition, Archbishop Lamy denied the Penitente cult the sanction of the church and antagonized a large proportion of the Hispanicized population of the territory.

The late 1840s and early 1850s were marked by the movement of the population into formerly unoccupied areas of New Mexico away from the Rio Grande. Swadesh (1966:77) believes that the establishment of communities in the San Luis Valley (southern Colorado) during this period was partly "to escape the opposition to folk religious practices on the part of elements hostile to Penitentism." This belief is supported by the fact that the majority of the San Luis Valley settlers were members of the Penitente brotherhood.

The resurgence of activity around the cult beginning in the second or third decades of the nineteenth century indicates that it was a conscious attempt by laymen to preserve religious devotion among the Hispanos (Chavez 1954:114–120; and Swadesh 1966:80–81). It was, thus, in certain respects a nativistic reaction (Linton 1940:232–233) or what Wallace (1956:267–268) calls a "revitalization movement." The rise of the Penitente cult was only in part a reaction brought about by the advent of Anglo-Americans; it was primarily an attempt to fill the spiritual void created by a shortage of priests and the diminution of church services. The care of the sick, burial of the dead, comforting the relatives of deceased members—all the life crises periods for which priests and the church provided special services were now drastically curtailed. The Penitente brotherhood stepped in to provide substitute services, especially those revolving around illness, death, and bereavement—the areas which are perhaps the most anxious and provoking among all people.

The Pueblos appear not to have experienced spiritual loss as the result of the events described above. With missionary criticism and intervention virtually removed during this period, the Pueblos began to relax their own surveillance measures. Ceremonies which were criticized by the clergy in former periods were once again given in the plazas and open to observation by non-Indians. Barreiro's comments on Pueblo dances indicate an active and full ceremonial life in the pueblos during the 1830s (Carroll and Haggard 1942:30). These remarks are even more true of the Western Pueblos who reverted back to their indigenous beliefs and ceremonies during this period.

While in the early years of the nineteenth century the Penitente brotherhood served essentially religious needs; once the Catholic church was reestablished in full power and influence and had regained the confidence of the natives, the religious functions of the cult subsided. Instead, however, the potential power of the cult to further the ambitions of a political candidate emerged. From the establishment of American rule to the end of the nineteenth century, the Penitente cult exerted tremendous influence on New Mexico politics (Beck 1962:218). Since members are sworn to assist and protect one another, it is clear that a Penitente candidate for a political office had the support of the order. Ambitious politicians during the latter part of the nineteenth and even into the twentieth century used the cult to their advantage. Jean B. Salpointe, who succeeded Lamy as archbishop, followed his predecessor in suppressing the activities of the cult by instructing parish priests to refuse to celebrate Mass in chapels attended by Penitentes and requesting them to deny the sacraments to members of the cult. Salpointe commented as follows on the use of the cult for political purposes:

> [The Penitente cult] has degenerated so that it is nothing today but an anomalous body of simple credulous men, under the guidance of unscrupulous politicians. Their leaders encouraged them, despite the admonitions of the church, in the practice of their unbecoming so-called devotions in order to secure their votes for the times of political elections (Salpointe 1898:161–162).

The Penitente cult apparently was never a Hispano-wide organization; nor was it even under the control of a single authority. Each community had its own chapter, with officers drawn locally. The brotherhood was finally given church sanction in 1936 by Archbishop Gerken. At this time, the Penitente cult designated Don Miguel Archibeque of Santa Fe as the Hermano Supremo. In 1960, there were 135 chapter houses in New Mexico and southern Colorado with an estimated membership of 2000 to 3000 (Holmes 1967:37–38).

While Hispano and Penitente influence on New Mexico politics appear to have been strong in the last half of the nineteenth century, such influences had weakened by 1916. In tabulating and analyzing the 1912 election returns in Hispano counties containing both Penitente-controlled precincts and those free of Penitente influence, a political scientist commented:

> Other things being equal a candidate bearing a name like Baca or Lucero could poll a heavier vote than a candidate named Smith or Bursum. And if a candidate of any name was judged "simpatico" by members of the Penitente fraternity that, too, could be traced in the election returns. . . . Voting in the Penitente precincts shared the characteristics of the voting in other Hispanic but non-Penitente precincts. In Penitente precincts those characteristics were etched a little more sharply; they were a little more discernible. But . . . in neither case do the characteristics measured describe an extreme reaction to the presence of particularly favored candidates. Other groups in the United States have frequently shown their responses to ethnic considerations much more sharply. In the New Mexico case the bonds of party have acted as a powerful restraint. The cases are legion in which a "Bursum" did defeat a "Baca" in the Hispanic counties, but in many the "Bursum" or the "Smith" may have trailed his ticket by a few points (Holmes 1967:42).

The influences exerted by both the Penitente brotherhood and the Hispano as a distinct ethnic group have continued to subside. Sometime in the 1940s the population of New Mexico bearing non-Hispanic names passed the group with Spanish surnames. By 1950, only 37 percent of the state's population and only ten of the thirty-two counties had an Hispano population of 50 percent or more (Holmes 1967:10).

With the lapse of its religious and political functions, the Penitente brotherhood has lost much of its prestige and influence. As New Mexico's Hispanos move to urban areas the cult continues to lost membership. The cult took root in rural communities and as with the Pueblos, the land no longer supports the population. Wage work and the products of an industrial society have replaced former agricultural subsistence patterns and locally produced goods. The land base no longer provides a livelihood and despite the satisfactions inherent in traditional Hispano village life, urban areas offer the promise of a life free from constant dependence on public relief services. In the process the uniqueness of New Mexico's Hispano communities are beginning to disappear.

During the nineteenth century, Pueblos and Hispanos shared a considerable number of social and cultural traits. They also cooperated when circumstances intervened to affect their mutual destiny. Toward the end of the century, however, the forces that drew the two groups together began to disintegrate and Pueblos and Hispanos drifted apart. These developments will be discussed in the section which follows.

PUEBLO-HISPANO RELATIONS

Perhaps even more than the Pueblos, the poorer Hispanos encountered adjustment problems as they were engulfed by Anglos and Anglo culture. Many of the *ricos* married early Anglo pioneers and adopted the lifeway of the newcomers, but for the majority of Hispanos, language and cultural barriers plus the intolerance of many Anglos brought about a sharp separation between the two groups. Movement of Hispanicized Pueblo Indians into Hispano villages continued throughout the nineteenth century, particularly into frontier areas where new Hispano settlements were being made. Intermarriage between members of the established Pueblo villages and the Hispano communities rarely occurred. Considerable European admixture, however, is evident in the Pueblo population, the result obviously of clandestine relations between native women and those Spanish officials (perhaps the priests as well) who lived close to the Pueblos. In the villages, Hispanos do not speak of their Indian heritage and object to marriages between themselves and individuals known to be Indian. Kluckhohn has described these attitudes appropriately:

> Although few Spanish-Americans either can or do claim to be pure Spanish in their blood heritage, there is a highly defensive attitude about being part Indian. They frown upon intermarriage with Indians and, when it occurs, express their disapproval by stigmatizing the children of the union with the terms *lobo* and *coyote* (Kluckhohn 1961:205).

In spite of the objection to marrying Indians, Kluckhohn notes that in the little Hispano village she studied three individuals of recent Indian heritage married into old and well established village families. One of these married a girl closely related to the family of the *patrón* in the village. Kluckhohn remarks that while there is considerable opposition to marriage with Indians, permission is usually granted and that distinction by blood seldom remains an issue for long (Kluckhohn 1961:205).

Although the cultures of the Pueblos and Hispanos differ radically, they shared and continue to share certain features marginal to the core culture of the Pueblos. This statement must be understood as applying primarily to the Hispanos and Rio Grande Pueblos; the Zuni and Hopi lost most of the Spanish patterns they had acquired during the height of Spanish rule in the seventeenth century. These Pueblos retained only livestock and material items of European provenience. The externals of Rio Grande Pueblo culture—that which these Indians revealed to Spanish civil and church authorities—involved services in the church, religious processions, baptism, marriage, and certain customs associated with funerals. These patterns are undeniably Spanish and in the observance of these customs they are often joined by Hispano neighbors. A wealth of other customs associated with the core culture of the Pueblos was and is carefully concealed from Hispanos. The latter as well as Anglos commonly know nothing about this wealth of indigenous Pueblo culture; they believe that the colorful public ceremonies which they are permitted to witness comprise the total fund of Pueblo culture. The Pueblos, of course, are happy to foster and perpetuate this deception. From painful experiences they have learned that a knowledge of these esoteric rites may bring about a suppression of their most sacred beliefs and practices.

The conditions in New Mexico during the nineteenth century bore little resemblance to those in effect during the first century and a half of Spanish contact. Suppression of native customs had ceased; and while the priests harangued the Indians constantly about church attendance and rebuked them for their participation in pagan rites, the Pueblos had learned to appear attentive and even remorseful on such occasions. Once the priest was gone they happily returned to the rich ceremonial life of their indigenous culture. On the other hand, the occasional contacts with the growing Hispano population was on a friendly and cooperative level. Each group preferred its own life; and although it did not understand or approve of its neighbors' customs, still it respected them. On feast days, Hispanos were received hospitably in Pueblo homes; and whereas reciprocal visits of Pueblos to Hispano village festivals appear not to have been as common, some intimate Pueblo-Hispano family exchange visits were typical (Marriott 1948:39-51). Where a pueblo used a common irrigation canal with a neighboring Hispano village, men of the two communities worked together in cleaning, repairing, and in allocating water rights. In the frequent retaliatory raids into enemy territory both groups furnished their share of warriors; together, they fought the enemy and, if victorious, reclaimed townspeople captured by the enemy and brought back enemy captives.

Pueblo Indians, Genizaros, and a segment of the Hispano population also staged a revolt in 1837, indicating that all three groups shared common grievances during the unsettled period just prior to American occupation. In 1835, Albino Perez became the governor of New Mexico, the first governor under Mexican rule who was not a native-born New Mexican. Apparently this fact, plus a rumor that heavy taxes were to be levied upon poultry, dogs, irrigation ditches, among other items, brought about the rebellion. Hostilities began at La Cañada (Santa Cruz) in early August 1937. Governor Perez gathered an army of about 150 volunteers, but the insurgents routed the governor's forces and the governor himself fled to Santa Fe and southward to El Alamo where he was overtaken, returned to Santa Fe, and killed. On August 10, the rebels took possession of Santa Fe and elected one of their own participants, an Indian from Taos—reputedly a Genizaro by the name of José Gonzáles—as governor of New Mexico. They also appointed other members of their group to minor government posts. The rebels ruled New Mexico only for a brief period. A force of "loyal citizens" under former Governor Manuel Armijo recaptured Santa Fe. Gonzáles fled to La Cañada where Armijo, with the help of troops dispatched from Chihuahua, caught up with the rebels shortly after the New Year, 1838. After a rule of less than six months, the only Indian governor of New Mexico under either Spanish or Mexican rule and several of his associates were captured and shot (Bancroft 1889:317–319; Chavez 1955:190–193; Gregg 1954:93–96).

There is much confusion about the organizational aspects of the revolt and the identity of the leaders in addition to Gonzáles and the three others executed with him. Former Governor Armijo, who put down the rebellion, along with the prominent priest from Taos, Antonio José Martinez, are believed to have had a part in planning the uprising (Gregg 1954:95). Padre Martinez seems to have been a popular leader and supporter of the sentiments and concerns of the poorer Hispanos and his involvement, or at least sympathy, with the revolt are understandable (Francis 1956:268). Armijo was an opportunist and he had both revenge and political advancement to gain from supporting the uprising. He was angry with Governor Perez and the latter's political associates for having been removed as a custom-house official. According to Gregg (Francis 1956:268), Armijo expected to be made governor by the insurgents when Perez had been deposed. After the temporary success of the revolt, it was apparent that the Hispano and Indian participants preferred Gonzáles as governor. When it was apparent that no special honors were to be expected from the Gonzáles regime, Armijo selected "loyal" citizens from the Rio Abajo district and led his counterrevolution.

That Padre Martinez and Armijo cooperated with the insurgent governor in the initial stages of Gonzáles' "regime" is confirmed by their participation in a meeting of the *asamblea general* on August 27–28, 1837, over which Gonzáles presided. Indeed, Gonzáles appointed Armijo and Juan Jose Esquibel (Esquibel was later executed by Armijo as one of the leaders of the revolt) to draft a statement containing the grievances of the people to be presented to the central government in Mexico (Twitchell 1963; footnote 403, p. 201). Obviously Armijo must have expressed sympathy for the complaints of the poorer Hispanos and Indians at this time; thus his later action in leading a counter-revolution can only be viewed as a betrayal of the trust Gonzáles, Esquibel, and members of the *asamblea* placed in him.

Armijo's arrogant and curt dismissal of Gonzáles when the latter appeared before him after his capture is an unflattering measure of the man. Gonzáles, having been admitted to Armijo's quarters, addressed the leader of the counterrevolution as follows:

> How are you comrade? I come to ask for guarantees for my people, that is, that no impost or taxation be placed upon them; and so I will keep the peace.
> Armijo replied:
> No part of what you ask will be considered by this government. . . . My object is to establish peace and order and this I shall do by the shortest road.
> Armijo then turned to Padre Martinez who was with him:
> Confess this half-breed so that they may give him five bullets (D. Pedro Sanchez's *Memorias*, quoted in Twitchell 1963: footnote 404, p. 201).

There is little information about Gonzáles and the other leaders of the revolt. Indeed, the affair is generally dismissed as a rather confused and meaningless uprising of "low-class" Hispanos and Indians (Gregg 1954:93–96; Twitchell 1912: Vol. II, pp. 65–67). The on-the-scene reporter, Gregg, and later Historians cannot believe that Gonzáles might have been a capable leader, representing the serious concerns of a substantial proportion of the Hispano and Indian population. While Armijo and Padre Martinez appear to have joined the leaders, probably for the reasons given above, there is no evidence that they furnished leadership. The fact that Hispanos and Indians alike selected Gonzáles as governor indicates that he was a popular leader among them. The causes of the uprising appear to be serious ones, particularly the matter of direct taxation. The proposed taxation aroused widespread fear among the poorer people that moved their leaders to draw up a "plan" of action to offset the impending regulations of the Mexican government. One of the points of the plan clearly stated: "to defend our country even to shedding the last drop of blood in order to secure the victory intended" (Twitchell 1963: footnote 397, p. 199). Governor Perez had little support and his own forces deserted to the enemy at the height of the revolt. Gonzáles apparently was in full control of the insurgents who besieged Santa Fe and the looting and pillaging anticipated by the American traders in the city never materialized. To the surprise of the Americans and the reporter of the historical events in Santa Fe, the "semi-civilized savages [committed] no outrage of any importance . . . upon either inhabitants or trader" (Gregg 1954:93–95). Apparently Gonzáles assumed his duties as governor with as much sophistication and competence for ruling as other governors before him. As noted above, shortly after taking office he appointed a committee to present the grievances of the people to the Mexican government. This act, together with his final interview with Armijo just before he was executed, demonstrates Gonzáles' goodwill. His behavior, at least in these two instances, suggests the thoughtful actions of a man concerned with the well-being of his fellow citizens. He apparently knew how to write for he signed the statement of grievances—incidentally, along with Donaciano Vigil, an intelligent, respected New Mexican, later to become governor of the territory of New Mexico under American rule.

Rumors of the greater significance of the revolt of 1837 and even of the involvement of Americans in the plot appear to be unfounded. Mexican authorities may have thought Americans were involved and also that the insurgents wanted to sever connections with Mexico, which was also rumored; but there is no evidence for such assumptions. There is also no basis to the rumor that the rebels proposed sending a deputation to Texas to seek protection. Analysis of the reports confirms the avowed claims of the leaders; they rebelled because they wanted to remove the fears engendered by the new regulations emanating from the Mexican government (Gregg 1954:93–96; Read 1912:237–238).

The rather enthusiastic response of Pueblo Indians and Genizaros to the uprising may have been engendered, however, by the action of Governor Perez shortly before the revolt. The governor disbanded the Indian troops because he had no funds with which to pay them. The Indians valued their status as warriors and also eagerly anticipated the booty to be recovered in the retaliatory raids (Read 1912:371–372). They obviously resented being disbanded and no doubt blamed Perez, an outsider, for bringing it about. The Genizaros occupying the peripheral areas and exposed to the attacks of the enemy were especially unhappy with the governor's orders. These Indians were naturally hopeful that the overthrow of Governor Perez's regime would place in command a governor and a group of government officials who would be more aware of their needs and who could help them. The coup d'etat almost succeeded; indeed, it might have without the intervention of Armijo, the political opportunist.

Pueblo Indians and Hispanos also cooperated in the revolt of 1847 against American occupation. Again, most historians have depicted these rebels as "lower-class" Mexicans and Indians (Bancroft 1889:432–437; Hallenbeck 1950:271–274). This characterization, however, in no way detracts from their sincerity and desire to reclaim their land recently occupied by foreign intruders. In the events at Taos, where Governor Charles Bent was killed, and in other skirmishes in the northern part of the state the actual fighting was done by Indians and poor Hispanos. It is clear that prominent Hispanos were involved in the pact, but they kept in the background and escaped punishment. Later, many of the leading conspirators served in important American governmental posts (Twitchell 1963:275–287). The majority of the casualities—both killed and wounded—were Pueblo Indians. One of the leaders, a Taos Indian by the name of Tomas, was shot by a soldier; others, whether leaders or implicated in one way or another with the revolts, were tried either by court martial or by a civil court. The charge was murder or treason against the United States. At Taos, an eye witness to the trial and sentencing of the rebel leaders described the reaction of the Pueblo Indian as follows:

> Not a muscle of the chief's face twitched, or betrayed agitation, though he was aware [that Mrs. Bent's evidence] sealed his death warrant. He sat with lips gently closed, eyes earnestly centered on [Mrs. Bent], without a show of malice or hatred—an almost sublime spectacle of Indian fortitude, and of the severe mastery to which the emotions can be subjected. Truly, it was a noble example of Indian stoicism!

The relations between Pueblos and Hispanos began to change after American occupation. As competition for land and the specialized treatment of the Pueblos became established, friction between the two peoples developed. The Spanish crown gave the Pueblo Indian land grants and provided protective measures, particularly the alienation of land. During the seventeenth century, Pueblo lands remained in the possession of the Indians, simply because the Spaniards were not tillers of the soil. Instead, under the *encomienda* system and the missionary program, the Indians provided for the support and economic gain of the intruders from the proceeds of their own land and labor. After the reconquest, the *encomienda* system was abolished and the Hispanicized population itself began to settle down to farm. Throughout the eighteenth century, however, the population remained small and the Pueblos did not enter into serious competition for arable land. During the Mexican period, however, with an increasing Hispano population, encroachment upon the lands of the Pueblos became a problem and loomed into critical proportions after the first half of the nineteenth century. While most of the squatters on Pueblo lands were Hispanos, Anglos also began to settle on these lands after the mid-nineteenth century. The land problem and the special programs introduced by the United States government specifically for the Pueblos will be discussed in a later section. It is appropriate now to pick up our historical narrative and sketch the entry and increasingly dominating role of the Anglo in New Mexico during the nineteenth century.

ANGLOS

The term "Anglo" is generally used to designate a non-Spanish, non-Indian United States citizen of white European descent. It will be used with that designation in this book.

A Creole trader, Baptiste Lalande, was the first United States citizen to enter New Mexico in 1804 (Bancroft 1889:291). Lieutenant Zebulon Pike, who spent the winter of 1806–1807 on the northern frontier of New Mexico with a small party of soldiers, was, however, the first American to describe the country and the characteristics of the people of New Mexico to the American public. Pike and his soldiers constructed a block house on the Rio Grande near the mouth of the Rio Conejos in what is now southern Colorado. Although Pike had entered Spanish territory illegally and, indeed, was arrested and ultimately released, his report informed Americans about the nature of the country and drew a number of traders into the region. Most of these traders were "mountain men." New Mexican authorities attempted to stop these intruders, but the mountain men were an independent lot and remained in the area. Some of them lived with Indians; others with the Hispanicized population. They lived the life of the frontier—wild, free, and irresponsible. They were trappers and fur traders—the main furbearing animal they trapped was the beaver. While the beaver was abundant—during the first quarter of the nineteenth century—life for the mountain men was prosperous. They sold or traded their furs either at Bent's Fort or the Hispano town of Taos. About 1830, the fur trade began to wane, partly because of the rapid decline of beavers, but primarily because of changes in the market for beaver pelts. For the most part, the mountain men remained in New Mexico, in the villages where they had taken wives and made their homes. These men and the families they had established were a strong support for American rule later. Some of these traders and trappers attained prominence in later times: Kit Carson; Jebediah Smith; the Bent and Sublette brothers (Cleland 1952).

The mountain men paved the way for other Anglo-Americans to follow. Mexican independence and the ambitious frontier businessmen eventually brought about the opening of the Santa Fe Trail. William Becknell of Franklin, Missouri is generally credited with laying out the route and officially establishing trade with Santa Fe in 1822. The Santa Fe trade had a tremendous impact on New Mexico. It made it possible for Hispanos and Pueblos to share in the variety of goods brought from east of the Mississippi and provided as well an outlet for their own products. Santa Fe became a redistribution center; a considerable amount of the products received from the East went south to California and Chihuahua, while products from Mexico eventually found their way into New Mexico and some were traded again for items coming from the East. The fear that Anglo-Americans might take over the region caused Mexican authorities to periodically raise custom fees; but once an appetite for American goods had been created, trade was never cut off completely (Gregg 1954).

For over half a century, the Santa Fe Trail brought a tremendous amount of products to New Mexico. These goods were largely manufactured products that were exchanged for hides, skins, and wool. The coming of the railroads in the latter part of the nineteenth century eventually stopped the trade over the famous trail. Many of the early Americans who entered New Mexico to engage in business became Mexican citizens and some married Hispano women. Perhaps the most renowned of the latter were Kit Carson, Charles Bent, and St. Vrain. While these and other former Americans cherished their homes and families, when the opportunity presented itself for Americans to take over the region, they promptly helped to bring it about.

ANGLO-PUEBLO RELATIONS

Mountain men and the early traders had little contact with Pueblo Indians. The few contacts appear to have been generally friendly, although one unfortunate encounter between the Hopi Pueblos and two companies of Rocky Mountain Fur Company trappers is reported by Joseph Meek in 1840. Some of the party plundered Hopi gardens and upon being discovered, fired upon the Hopi, killing fifteen or twenty Indians (Victor 1871:153). This unpleasant initial experience of the Hopi with Americans was somewhat tempered a few years later when Mormons pushed their settlements into Arizona and tried to convert the Hopi (Bailey 1948:200). Of all the missionary groups, the Mormons have made the most favorable impression; like the others, however, they have made few converts among the Hopi. Zuni, Acoma, and Laguna remained similarly isolated until after the middle of the nineteenth century. The Eastern Pueblos perhaps saw these early Americans with greater frequency, but typically, such contacts were casual and fleeting. The Taos Indians may have been an exception. Since the Hispano town of Taos was an important trade center during the first half of the nineteenth century, these Indians obviously had more contact with Anglos.

With American occupation, the isolated life of the Pueblos began to change, slowly at first but with accelerated tempo toward the end of the century. We have noted the rather unfortunate results of Pueblo participation in the

Revolt of 1847. Later, the Pueblos realized that conditions in their lifeway were no worse and in many respects better under American rule than under previous governments. Initially, at least, they lost no land to the newcomers; their labor was not exploited, and no demands were made for their products. Indeed, they gained a powerful ally to battle the Navaho and Apache raiders. They had long ago lost faith in the Mexican military organization to control their nomadic enemies, much as the young Pueblo warriors enjoyed participating actively in the campaigns. But even this last had been curtailed during the Mexican period and the few Pueblos who went on the expeditions were denied a share in the booty taken from the enemy.

Shortly after the American occupation, James C. Calhoun was appointed the first Indian agent for the Territory of New Mexico. The Western Pueblos sent delegations to ascertain the "purposes and views of the government of the United States towards them" and to complain "bitterly of the depredations of the Navahos." Calhoun assured the Hopi delegation that the government wanted to establish friendly relations with them and sent them home with gifts (U. S. Dept. of Interior, 1894, p. 171, U. S. census of 1890).

Navaho raids during the mid-nineteenth century were particularly devastating to the Western Pueblos, but they also plundered Rio Grande and Hispano farms and took large numbers of livestock from the *ricos* and Anglo ranchers. In 1863, as the result of the continued raiding activities of the Navaho, the United States government authorized the removal of the Navahos from their homeland to the eastern part of New Mexico. Colonel Christopher Carson was commissioned to put the task into operation.

Over the next twenty years, United States troops carried on an intensive campaign against the Comanches and the various bands of Apaches. By 1880, Indian raiding activities and resistance to the better armed and better organized American soldiers were at an end. All of the nomadic tribes had been placed on reservations and the Indian menace was over. The policy of most of the commanders during this period was virtually one of extermination; in the end, more humane operations won out, but there was much useless killing, often of women and children along with the men. The following instructions to Colonel Kit Carson by General James H. Carleton when Carson had been placed in charge of removing the Navaho expresses the opinion generally shared by military commanders:

> The Indian men . . . are to be killed whenever and wherever you can find them: the women and children will not be harmed, but you will take them prisoners. . . . If the Indians send in a flag and desire to treat for peace, say to the bearer; [they have broken] their treaty of peace, and murdered innocent people and run off their stock: that now we are going to punish them for their crimes, and that you are there to kill them wherever they can be found. We have no faith in their broken promises and we intend to kill enough of their men to teach them a lesson.
>
> I trust that this severity in the long run will be the most humane course that could be pursued toward these Indians (Quoted in Beck 1962:189).

While the nomadic Indian problem was put to an end, drought and smallpox epidemics continued to plague the pueblos, particularly those in the far western part of the territory; they periodically presented these problems to the Indian agent in Santa Fe. Reservations were established in all of the pueblos including the western pueblos by 1890 and local Indian agents were appointed who tackled and solved many of the problems. In the wake of these developments, new problems appeared, particularly with the advent of Protestant missionaries, schools, and the whole spectrum of government control and supervision. These events which increase in intensity in the twentieth century will be discussed in the next historical period. Here, as a finale to almost a century of Anglo-American contact, a brief description of Pueblo life in the late nineteenth century will be presented.

OUTLINE OF PUEBLO CULTURE ABOUT 1900

We indicated a Pueblo population figure at the end of the previous century of 9732 (Bancroft 1889:279). Pueblo numbers fell to an all-time low in the 1850s to about 7000 but had gained again by the end of the nineteenth century to 9026 (Hodge 1912:325). These figures do not include the Hopi which varied between 2000 and 3000 during the nineteenth century. The low population figure at mid-century was very likely the result of the movement of Hispanicized Pueblo Indians into Hispano settlements which appear to have increased in the period just before American occupation.

The location of the pueblos was on the sites they had occupied during the eighteenth century, although much reduced in population. Pecos steadily dwindled in numbers as the result of enemy raids and smallpox epidemics. The pueblo was finally abandoned in 1838 when its seventeen survivors moved to Jemez, a pueblo whose inhabitants spoke the same language. During this period the Genizaro populations of Tomé, Abiquiu, and Belen became a part of the general Hispano population. At the end of the century the Pueblos were slowly increasing in numbers, but they were separate geographically and socioculturally from a rapidly growing Hispano population. The native-born citizens of New Mexico with Spanish surnames numbered about 150,000 in 1900.

Architectural features of Pueblo homes had changed little in 200 years. The description given in the previous section might well serve for the following one provided by John C. Bourke who visited the Pueblos in 1878 and again in 1881. On his first visit through the Pueblo villages, Bourke wrote in his journal:

> We observed on our way that the chimneys of the houses were made of earthenware pots, placed one upon another and coated with mud, that upon the roofs in nearly all cases were bake-ovens, and that to enter any house it was necessary first to ascend a ladder to the roof of the first story and then descend to the living rooms . . . the walls were not, as with us, flush with the front walls of the edifice. They receded in such a manner as to leave a platform in front; this was the roof of the first story and was formed of round pine logs, covered with small branches and afterwards plastered smoothly with mud (Bloom 1935:313).

By the 1880s the Pueblos and their villages had been photographed; some of these early photographs are reproduced in this book. These, together with the descriptions of Pueblo houses and villages, may be compared with the sketches of Pueblo Bonito and Pecos. The sketches have been reproduced by an artist from site plans worked out by archeologists and they are believed to depict rather faithfully the architectural features of these prehistoric and historic villages. The changes are remarkably slight over a period of some 400 to 600 years, indicating a record of extreme conservatism in Pueblo architecture. These are, of course, in gross features. What appear to be minor changes, however, are evident in the photographs. Small windows of glass and doors indicate that for several years now inhabitants of these villages have not experienced an enemy raid. As the Pueblos become convinced that the attacks of the nomadic enemy have ceased, the ladders and upper story dwellings steadily disappear in the villages.

Agriculture remained an important occupation for the Pueblos throughout the nineteenth century. Contact with Anglos brought no revolutionary introductions in either new crops or agricultural techniques. The tools they introduced were vastly superior to those previously available, however—plows, shovels, hoes, rakes, pitchforks, and spring wagons were present in fairly large numbers by the end of the century. These items, except for wagons, were generally furnished by the government and eagerly taken over by the Pueblos. Government aid in the construction of irrigation dams and ditches added to agricultural efficiency and increased production. Bourke's observations in the summer and fall of 1881 indicate abundant crops and general prosperity among the Pueblos (Bloom 1935–1938).

Among the Rio Grande pueblos weaving, an important craft (except for sashes), was discontinued sometime during the century. Woven cloth and blankets were the most important items of tribute made to civil authorities by the Pueblo Indians during the seventeenth and eighteenth centuries. Apparently as a technique associated with Spanish oppression, the craft was dropped. The Hopi pueblos, more distant and isolated from the center of Spanish dominance, have continued to weave until the present. For some reason, however, the Hopi gave up pottery-making after Spanish contact but the craft remained among the New Mexico Pueblos and is an important item of sale to tourists today. About the turn of the century, a woman of the Tewa village of Hano (Hopi) brought about a renaissance in pottery-making, but only for First Mesa Hopi. By copying old pottery designs excavated by an archeologist in the nearby ruins of Sikyatki, this woman reactivated pottery manufacture. The craft soon spread to the other two villages, Sichomovi and Walpi (on First Mesa), and is now the basic craft in these villages.

At the end of the nineteenth century, the Pueblos appear not to be any more Christian than in the previous century. Bourke (Bloom 1935–1938:262) describes Pueblo communities as tightly integrated, self-sustaining units, living a full ceremonial life. In all the pueblos, kivas showed signs of recent use, contrasting sharply with the mission churches, many of which were in ruins. Bourke witnessed a lively Corn or Tablita dance at Santo Domingo, where the participants were meticulously costumed and performed with dedication.

By 1900, all the pueblos had been exposed to Protestant missionaries of various sects. None of these new forms of Christianity made an impression on the Indians, although there is no evidence of hostility toward the missionaries. In the beginning, Protestants used little or no coercion nor did they apparently object to the ceremonies of the Pueblos. This attitude was to change, however. In the first two decades of the twentieth century, under the religious crimes code, Indian Service officials were instructed to stop ceremonial rites that, in their opinion, violated Christian standards. In the early days of Protestant missionary work, particularly among the western pueblos, missionaries also held additional positions as teachers. They were thus in a position to influence the Indians considerably, but there is no evidence that very many of the Indians took the religion seriously. Among the Rio Grande pueblos, Protestant missionaries encountered opposition from Catholic priests who resented competition in a field over which they claimed priority. Protestant missionaries claimed that the priests were opposed to education, but the competition between the two religious groups for Pueblo converts was probably the answer to the conflict. The Pueblos remained nominally Catholic throughout the period, but clung as tenaciously as in the past to their indigenous religion.

The fairs at Taos and Abiquiu with Comanches and Utes, respectively, ended during the Mexican period with the development of trade over the Santa Fe Trail. Pueblo Indians retained contacts with Comanches until about 1880. Some of the northern Rio Grande Pueblo Indians made annual trips into the Plains country to camp, visit, and hunt buffalo with Comanches. Individual Pueblo men also occasionally became *Comancheros*. This term was applied primarily to Hispanos who carried on trade with Plains Indians, particularly Comanches. Old men in the Pueblos as recently as two decades ago spoke with nostalgia of these sojourns into the Plains country. Finally, the destruction of the buffalo and the placement of the Plains Indians on reservations ended these contacts.

History 1900–1968

ANGLO-AMERICAN DOMINANCE

Sometime during the 1940s the Anglos surpassed the Hispanos in number and became the dominant population. In 1950, the number of New Mexico residents with Spanish surnames (including most Rio Grande Pueblo Indians as well) comprised only 37 percent of the total population. The Anglos continued to increase and by 1960 the Spanish-surname population represented only 25 percent of New Mexico's 951,023 population (Holmes 1967:9–11). We have noted that the Pueblo population in New Mexico in 1900 was 9026 (Hodge 1912:32). This figure did not include the Hopi Pueblos of Arizona, whose population was about 2000 in that year. In 1900, then, the total number of Pueblo Indians was about 11,000. There was a slow, steady increase to about 15,000 in 1930. Since the 1930s, the Pueblo population has more than doubled: The Rio Grande Pueblos alone numbered 21,525 in 1967; adding an estimated Zuni population of 5000 and 6000 Hopi Indians to the total, Pueblo population is well over 35,000 for 1967. Effective smallpox vaccination programs eventually defeated the big killer of Indians since the early days of European contact. The tremendous spurt in population in the 1930s is the result, however, of better economic conditions associated with improved medical care and the observance of sanitary precautions. The movement of Pueblo Indians into frontier Hispano communities ended during the first or second decade of the present century as free land became unavailable, but also because the direction of acculturative and assimilative lures shifted. Instead of becoming Hispanicized, Pueblo Indians now become Anglicized. Perhaps the term "urbanized" is more appropriate for this process. Pueblo Indians who find communal life untenable, who are evicted by Pueblo authorities, or who simply cannot find the means for economic support at home, move into large western cities: Albuquerque, Denver, Los Angeles, San Francisco, and other large cities. In these urban centers, work opportunities are far greater than in their home communities and for those who seek a new life, the choices are virtually legion. Here Pueblo Indians form a part of a growing Indian population; some marry Indians of other tribes, or they marry Anglos. The large city can become a melting pot for Indians; but so satisfying is Pueblo life that many return periodically for feast days or for any excuse. Typically, the majority live in the city during their early years, but come back to enjoy the pleasures of communal living in the pueblo in later life.

THE LAND PROBLEM

Difficulties over the control of arable land surrounding the Rio Grande Pueblo Indian villages arose in the Mexican period. The movement of Hispanos and Indians into frontier areas of New Mexico, where free land was still available, temporarily eased the situation just prior to and immediately following American occupation. However, as the Anglos bought or otherwise expropriated the old Spanish and Mexican land grants and took up the available unclaimed land (Swadesh 1968:166–167), the problem of squatters on Pueblo lands became a serious problem. Most of the disputes were between Hispanos and Pueblo Indians, although increasing numbers of Anglos became involved as the latter acquired lands formerly held by Hispanos.

Land grants originally given to the Pueblos by the Spanish crown entitled them to their land. The Treaty of Guadalupe Hidalgo bound the United States to respect the land rights of all former citizens of Mexico, including Pueblo Indians. The basis for Pueblo land grants was contained in a royal cedula published on June 4, 1687 authorizing grant of four leagues square, or 17,712 acres, measured from the church. When the United States assumed jurisdiction over the Indians, the land grants of all but the western pueblos of Zuni and Hopi had been invaded and disputes which were not resolved until the mid-1930s began.

The settlement of the Pueblo Indian land disputes was complicated additionally by the undecided legal status of the Pueblo Indian. Under Spanish rule the Pueblos were wards of the crown, but became citizens of Mexico in 1821. The United States considered all Indians wards of the government, but the Pueblos presented a problem. They were a sedentary people and already citizens of Mexico when the United States took over New Mexico. Although the legal status of the Pueblos was not settled until 1913, the United States government began to provide most of the specialized services for these Indians already furnished for other

Indians. Hispanos and Anglos took the position that, since the Pueblos were citizens under Mexican rule, they could sell or otherwise dispose of their land as they saw fit. This argument was upheld by the territorial governments. The courts also exempted the Pueblos from the Nonintercourse Acts of 1834; these acts were designed to protect Indians and Indian land and prohibited settlers from entering or making settlements on Indian reservations. The attorneys for the Indians attempted to change the decisions of the territorial courts without success. The Joseph case, in 1876, in which the United States Supreme Court ruled that the Pueblo Indians had complete title to their lands and could therefore dispose of them to whomsoever they pleased, further complicated the issue. But the friends of the Pueblos and their attorneys continued in their attempt to correct the injustices done to the Pueblos. They, therefore, sought to change the legal status of these Indians. Finally, in 1913, a year after statehood, the United States Supreme Court reversed the position taken by the territorial courts. The Pueblos now had the same legal status as other Indians:

> The people of the Pueblos, although sedentary rather than nomadic in their inclinations and disposed to peace and industry, are nevertheless Indians in race, customs, and domestic government, always living in separate and isolated communities, adhering to primitive modes of life, largely influenced by superstition and fetishism, and chiefly governed according to the crude customs inherited from their ancestors. They are essentially a simple, uninformed, and inferior people (United States vs. Sandoval, 231 U.S. 28).

While this decision was written in the condescending, ethnocentric, and racist language of the times, the memorable decision achieved for the Indians a beachhead from which they could fight for the land appropriated by their neighbors. The Supreme Court ruling made it clear that the Pueblos could not alienate their land and they were entitled to reclaim lands legally sold. Actually few if any Pueblo Indians had ever sold grant lands; non-Pueblo neighbors had simply moved in on grant lands. The descendants of the original squatters later claimed that the land had been acquired by purchase. Since the non-Pueblo settlers on Pueblo grants were mostly Hispanos, the former friendly relations between the two peoples now became severely strained. As a champion of Hispano and Anglo land claimants, Senator Holm O. Bursum of New Mexico introduced into the Senate of the Sixty-seventh Congress a bill to quiet title to lands within the Pueblo land grants. The bill would have given clear title to non-Pueblo Indian landholders on Pueblo grants and thus would have deprived the Indians of land illegally lost. The friends of the Indians launched a concerted fight to defeat the Bursum Bill, which in the end was successful. Primary credit for this effort goes to the New Mexico Association on Indian Affairs and the General Federation of Women's Clubs. Mr. John Collier, who later became Commissioner of Indian Affairs, together with Mrs. Stella M. Atwood and Mr. Francis C. Wilson, legal counsel, worked relentlessly to defeat the bill.

To provide a solution for non-Pueblo Indian claims to land on Pueblo grants a special commission known as the Pueblo Lands Board was established. This commission reviewed the value of both land and improvements and compensated either claimants or Indians for lands lost. The Superintendent of the United Pueblos Agency and a special attorney for the Indians were charged with the task of clearing Pueblo lands. Settlements were eventually completed in 1938 pensated either claimants or Indians for lands lost. The Superintendent of the over (Aberle 1948:10).

The land controversy we have discussed involved only the Rio Grande Pueblos; the pueblos of Acoma, Zia, Zuni, and the Hopi did lose Spanish grant lands. Land losses or severe restriction to lands formerly available to the pueblos affected the Western as well as the Rio Grande pueblos, however. Since the livelihood of most of the pueblos, but particularly the western pueblos, depended on livestock as well as farming, Pueblo grant lands were not sufficient to furnish subsistence needs. Even before the advent of the Anglos, therefore, the Pueblos had acquired additional land either by successful petition to the Spanish crown or by purchase. In addition the Pueblos also used land adjoining the Pueblo grant for grazing stock. During the nineteenth century, non-Pueblo intruders settled on these lands previously acquired by the Pueblos; they also fenced lands over which the Pueblos claimed use rights. Hence the land problem was not one solely of the Pueblo village grants but its alleviation or solution involved the acquisition of additional lands. Moreover, Pueblo community land grants, lands independently acquired, and the lands surrounding Pueblo villages were all heavily grazed and depleted by the middle of the nineteenth century. Even before the end of the land controversy settlement described above, the Pueblos as the result of severe economic deprivations had obtained additional land. Such land was acquired between 1877–1933 by acts of Congress, executive orders, and by community or personal initiative. After 1934, the Pueblos acquired land by permit, lease, exchange, or purchase. The federal government, through the establishment of a Land Acquisition Program, assisted the Indians in these endeavors (Aberle 1948:7–16).

After almost a century of land losses and disputes, the Pueblos finally received sufficient land to struggle through a decade of stock-raising activities and bare subsistence farming. The inhospitable physical environment of the Pueblos, however, cannot bring prosperity to a farming and stock-raising folk, particularly if they must share it with a population which outnumbers them twenty to one. Since World War II, wage work and income derived from tourist enterprises have brought a better life for these Indians and the economic independence of the Pueblos appears to lie in the exploitation of these resources.

PUEBLOS AND HISPANOS

Hispanos continue to be the nearest neighbors of the Rio Grande Pueblos. The conflict over land and the specialized services made available by the United States government to the Indians but not to Hispanos brought a split in the good relations the two peoples had established during the first half of the nineteenth century. Although most Hispanos living on Indian land were given the choice of keeping their land or being compensated in money for lands lost if they moved, the separatist treatment welled up into resentment against the Pueblos. During the 1930s, open range lands acquired for the Pueblos (reservation lands) by the government were fenced, thus preventing the grazing of Hispano livestock on these lands. Hispano livestock owners had permitted their livestock to range freely over this land but were suddenly cut off. Furthermore, when Hispanos used grazing land that necessitated driving their livestock through Indian reservation lands, they were charged "trespass fees." These events aggravated further the widening breach of poor relations between the two peoples. Free schooling, free hospital services, and aid in farming techniques for Pueblos but not for Hispanos were additional irritating factors which mounted the rising resentment against the Pueblos.

We can better understand these changing attitudes if we reconsider briefly a number of historical factors and the nature of Hispano-Pueblo relationships in the past. The status system of the colony as a whole placed the Indians at the bottom. The Pueblos were a notch above the nomadic Indians because they were sedentary and nominally Catholics. The persistence of the Pueblos in continuing with their indigenous religious practices, however, relegated them to a low position on the status ladder. To be Catholic and Hispanic in culture was the inevitable and logical state of affairs. Any people who did not aspire to this natural state of affairs must be inferior or else under the domination of the devil. This is clear in the attitudes, programs, and actions of Spanish civil and church authorities throughout the seventeenth and eighteenth centuries. The Hispanicized population espoused this set of attitudes fully. Those Pueblo Indians who through the years have trickled into the Hispanic settlements have been viewed as enlightened and credited with realizing the obviously superior life offered by Hispanicized culture. Such Pueblo Indians were quickly absorbed, for it must be realized that the attitudes Spaniards and the Hispanicized population held against Indians was primarily cultural and not racial. Once Indians adopted Spanish culture, they became legitimate members of the Hispanicized community. The belief in the superiority of the Hispanic way of life is so strong that even today Hispano neighbors of the Pueblos cannot understand why the Indians have not abandoned their indigenous culture in favor of Catholicism and Hispanic culture. While most Hispanos can appreciate their own cultural and social autonomy, they cannot understand a similar desire on the part of the Pueblos to maintain their own way of life.

Friction in more recent years between the two peoples has also been aggravated by the attitudes and activities of the Anglos. The latter, rather than relegating the Pueblos to a status position below the Hispanos, have tended to assign the same slot to both ethnic groups. Indeed, the curious and effervescent tourist is usually more enthusiastic about the elaborate Pueblo ceremonies than he is about the rather placid life of the Hispanos. As a result, thousands of tourists visit the Pueblos; and they have discovered that handsome profits can be made from arts and crafts and that the recent development of recreational facilities on their reservations can be lucrative. For Hispano neighbors, this change has been a rather disturbing one. The group they have through the years considered pagan and obviously subordinate to their own civilized existence, has been given equal, even superior status by the dominant newcomers. Although both the Hispano and Pueblo populations have shared in the general prosperity brought about by recent wage work opportunities, the Pueblos, through assistance from the government, have forged ahead. The Rio Grande Pueblo homes are now in the process of

Typical interior of Rio Grande Pueblo home—Isleta Pueblo, southern Tiwa.

installing indoor plumbing, toilet and bath facilities, and modern sewage disposal systems. Many of the Pueblos have also developed camping, fishing, and recreational sites near their villages and are attracting large numbers of tourists. These economic activities, plus the communal nature of the Pueblo, particularly working and sharing patterns, have raised the general economic level of the Pueblos above that of their poorer Hispano neighbors. John J. Bodine's characterization of Anglo-Hispano-Pueblo relations in Taos is typical of such relations in virtually all of the Rio Grande Pueblos:

> One would expect, as elsewhere, that the members of the two European derived groups would jockey for first place in the status structure, but there would be little question that the Indians occupied the position at the bottom. However the Taos Anglos in weighing the elements of ethnic attractions have consistently placed the Spanish Americans on the lowest rung of the ladder. The reasons are clear. The Anglo of Taos tenaciously holds the belief that this community is a kind of Utopia. It is transformed into a never-never land by the rather constant employment of a kind of mental gymnastic in which imagination reigns supreme. From the Anglo point of view one can legitimately speak of the "mystique" of Taos. In its creation the Anglos glorified Taos Indian culture and relegated the Spanish American to the bottom of the prestige structure . . . (Bodine 1968:146–147).

> One would suppose that the mysterious nature of *penitente* activity [of the Hispanos] would have been a factor to intrigue and enflame the imaginations of the ethnic-seeking Anglos. Indeed Anglo Americans were fascinated by the macabre possessions and crucifixions that took place each year in the valley. But their fascination was not accompanied by respect for these customs. Catholicism generally and the penitente cult in particular engendered more prejudice than admiration. The majority of Anglos were either Protestants or non-practitioners of religion. Setting themselves in a sea of papists only tended to reify their anti-Catholic feelings. Even Anglo Catholics found the excesses of penitente custom incomprehensible. So this

spectacular ethnic difference figured rather unimportantly in the attractions of the area. On the other hand, Indian religion was lauded by most Anglos as being beautiful in its symbolism and majestic in its performance.

This has been a very hard thing for the Spanish to swallow. Regardless of whether as individuals they were loyal members of the Church, certainly Catholicism or at least Christianity was the only road to salvation. For generations the priests had worked to convert the pagan Indians to the True Faith. Their reluctance to accept this core aspect of civilization was taken as proof of their inferiority. Most Spanish are still very derogatory in their remarks about the nominal adherence to the Church of most Indians. To discover that the Anglos heaped praise on the Indian religion, while either ignoring or belittling their own, increased not only their resentment toward Anglos but toward the Indians as well. Yet the Spanish are forced to pay lip-service to the importance and beauty of Indian culture since they are painfully aware that most tourists come to Taos not to see them but to see the Indians and their famed four and five storied pueblos. Again they are forced into the background and have been unable to convince anyone that their cultural system is more advanced, more respectable and far more worthy of emulation than that of the Taos Indians. I strongly suspect, but have no means of measuring it, that a certain amount of Spanish resistance to acculturation is prompted by their need to demonstrate cultural superiority. Any number display definite signs of social paranoia.

One rather small victory the bearers of Hispanic culture have achieved is to insist on the term "Spanish American". They point out rather vehemently that they are the pure and direct descendants of the Spanish *Conquistadores*. They are Spanish, not Mexican. Use of the term "Mexican" is definitely derogatory in Taos . . . (Bodine 1968:149–150).

Bodine's characterizations would apply to Hispanos who live as neighbors to other Indian pueblos as well. We have noted elsewhere the extreme defensiveness of the Hispanos regarding their racial and cultural ancestry. In recent years, Hispanos themselves are beginning to evaluate their racial and cultural background. They are particularly questioning the designations by which they are called. The following letter by Peter Ribera Ortega, which appeared in the *New Mexican*, Santa Fe, July 23, 1967, is typical of the kind of self-examination going on among Hispanos. Ortega's letter is a reply to an earlier one by a Miss Valentina Valdez:

One thing we have to soon get rid of is our persecution-complex; and, our love for wanting to be labeled "Spanish-Americans." I for one don't relish being called a "hyphenated American," not even by my own santa raza. The term "Spanish-American" is a stinking sociological and political term, that was originated for ulterior motives. This type of bad-thinking assuredly still survives (witness my critic, Srta Valdez!). If we're going to be truthful, we're neither blue blood-Spanish, nor twenty carat "Mexican," nor "Spanish-American"; but only and basically NEO-MEJICANOS, an interesting blend of the "CONQUISTADORES," the "CRIOLLOS" of Mexico, and every once in a while a dash or few drops of good old PUEBLENO. And to be blunt about this touchy subject, I don't mind the admixture, because we still have the moral obligation to "know ourselves," before we can expect to be respected as "someone," quo no, amigos-lectores?

Another aspect of the friction between the Pueblo and the Hispano is the attempt by the latter to protest and to stop if possible activities initiated by or for Indians. Since Hispanos are usually in control of local politics, they are often in a position to work against Pueblo goals. Opposition to giving the Indians the right of franchise came mainly from Hispanos, but a three-judge district court finally broke down constitutional barriers to Indian enfranchisement in 1948 (Trujillo vs. Garley, District Court, New Mexico). At Taos, Bodine reports that local Hispanos try to block the efforts of the Indians to receive special benefits:

> The Spanish-American mayors and their councils have frequently used their positions of authority to try and thwart attempts by the Indians to gain any more prestige within the Taos social milieu. They can always be counted on to oppose the claims of the Indians to grazing, water, a right-of-way or even a cash settlement for past land grabs by either the Spanish or the Anglos. The Spanish Americans are easily aroused over such issues and become the staunchest supporters of the cause against the Indians. I feel there is little question that the Spanish suffer most from the injustices of the past. Naturally their ire is raised when they see the Indians, who have received so many benefits from the Federal government, attempt to obtain even more. However I believe that a good part of their resentment is the result of the discrimination emanating from Anglo-American society. They try to retaliate by any means available and they certainly cannot accept further blessings bestowed on the Taos Indians regardless of whether those blessings will affect them directly or not (Bodine 1968:150-151).

As Bodine notes, Hispanos suffer most from the injustices of the past. The legal status of the Pueblos as Indians brought benefits and protection which sometimes affected their Hispano neighbors adversely. This was particularly true in the case of the land disputes already discussed. Most aggravating to Hispanos, however, are the special services such as those for health, education, and welfare assistance— services which have been provided for Indians for many years but from which Hispanos were excluded. The economic condition of the masses of Hispanos and Pueblo has been virtually identical for two or more centuries. While culturally different, their problems and their goals have meshed at many points. They have defended themselves and on occasion fought the same enemy. They tilled the same soil, irrigated from the same water source, often using the same ditches, and planted the same crops. They lived in the same kind of houses requiring the same skills to build and maintain them. They experienced the same droughts, the same epidemics, and have rejoiced together in gathering the fruits of a bountiful harvest. These shared experiences were drawing the two peoples together during the first half of the nineteenth century. Common grievances were responsible in unifying them in the 1837 rebellion against the regime of Governor Albino Perez and again in 1847 in the attempt to overthrow the newly established American government. The differences between the two peoples might have disappeared altogether, but Anglos and the United States government intervened. The Pueblos became entitled to the special services and protective measures afforded other Indians; but the Hispanos, as Mexican citizens of Spanish descent, were denied such privileges. Had economic conditions been the basis of special treatment, the Hispanos would have qualified. Indeed, they would have qualified in terms of Indian blood as well; but to the Hispano the admission of Indian blood was degrading. Indeed, many of them did not know of their Indian ancestry for the history of Hispano heritage has been so distorted. True, a few Hispanos in the early years attended Indian boarding schools; some even availed themselves of

Indian health services, but such individuals could not justify entitlement to such services and were also censored as "Indians" in their home communities. Thus, the breach between the two groups has widened through the years.

The Pueblos have been quick to pick up negative Anglo-American attitudes toward Hispanos and Mexicans and regard themselves in a superior status position. In some pueblos, Catholicism has been identified with Hispanos; and in recent years, a considerable number of Pueblos have left the church to embrace various Protestant sects. There may be more fundamental reasons for Protestant successes in certain pueblos, however. Since the second decade of the present century, Pueblo Indians have been more fluent in English than in Spanish; indeed, very few of the present generation speak Spanish. Yet Spanish was used in the confessional and in sermons through the 1920s by priests assigned to many of the pueblos. Obviously, for those Pueblo Indians having difficulty understanding the deeper meaning and values of Catholicism, an alien language or a poorly understood one simply complicated matters. Hence, the attraction to a religion presented in a second language, English, which the more recent generations had learned, and learned better than Spanish had ever been learned by most Pueblo Indians. Moreover, the various Protestant sects were the religions of the status dominant Anglos.

Where Hispanicization set in early, intimate Hispano-Pueblo relations appear to be enduring. This is true at San Juan and at Cochiti (Goldfrank 1927:9; Lange 1953:681), where a number of Hispano-Pueblo marriages have taken place. The antagonism between Hispanos and Pueblos may lessen as federal programs are made available to both groups, as public schools receive both Indian and Hispano students, and as better health and welfare services are provided for both ethnic groups without discrimination.

The Pueblos away from the Rio Grande have not experienced the prolonged and intensive relations with Hispanos. Hopi and Zuni know very little about this ethnic group; for these pueblos, the Navaho are the nearest neighbors and quite intimate contacts have developed with specific Navaho individuals and families in recent years. The Zuni exclude Mexicans from viewing their important winter Shalako ceremony and other ceremonies that Indians and Anglos are permitted to attend. Yet it is difficult to know on what basis the exclusion would be made unless the visitors identified themselves as Hispanos. The prohibition may actually apply only to members of the neighboring village of Atarque; most of the adults of this tiny Hispano community are known personally to the Zuni. It would be difficult for either the Hopi or the Zuni to separate Hispano from Rio Grande Pueblo Indians on the basis of physical criteria alone. Separation by reference to behavioral traits is obviously possible, but it is doubtful from the meagre contacts that these Pueblos have with Hispanos that such differentiating criteria are known; this would be particularly true of the Hopi.

PUEBLOS AND ANGLOS

By 1881, two railway lines entered the Pueblo country. The Atchison, Topeka, and Santa Fe line ran within sight of the pueblos south of Santa Fe, near Old Laguna and Acoma, thirty miles north of Zuni, and some seventy-five miles south of the Hopi villages. The narrow gauge Denver and Rio Grande passed near or within a few miles of most of the northern Tanoan pueblos. These railroads brought a steady stream of Anglo tourists and an increasing number of residents. The newcomers complicated the land problems already discussed; and they also upset the traditional economy. Pueblo life was based on subsistence farming with some stock-raising in pre-American times, but the establishment of trading posts in the latter part of the nineteenth century involved the Pueblos in a credit system. Later, with the large influx of tourists and still later, with opportunities for wage work, the Pueblos came into full participation with a cash economy (Aberle 1948:7 and 22).

The initial contacts between Pueblos and Anglos were United States government personnel and Protestant missionaries. With the establishment of reservations and schools toward the end of the nineteenth century, Anglo missionaries and United States Indian Bureau officials concentrated on the eradication of "Un-American" Indian customs and practices. During the first and second decades of the present century, investigators were sent to the pueblos to study reported immoral and anti-Christian practices of the Indians. These investigators brought back reports of customs which violated Anglo-American standards of decency and morality. Under the Religious Crimes Code, Indian Service officials were instructed to prohibit ceremonial practices that might be contrary to accepted Christian standards and to punish those Indian leaders who encouraged or permitted such rites. The boarding schools, purposely located at considerable distances from Indian reservations, were designed to wean Indian youngsters from their traditional culture. Indian children were forcefully recruited and taken to schools without the consent of their parents or relatives. In these schools the use of the Indian language and all other native customs were prohibited. Infractions were dealt with brutally through a variety of physical punishments.

The effect of the policies of the United States and the behavior of Anglo missionaries on Pueblo culture was profound. The Rio Grande Pueblos reintrenched their native ceremonial system much as they had during the seventeenth century when Spanish oppression and attacks on the native religion were particularly severe. The Zuni and Hopi Indians had been effectively neglected after the initial adverse experience with Spanish civil and church authorities. In these pueblos the severity of religious persecution had been forgotten and their initial response to contact with Anglos was friendly and hospitable. As government agents and missionaries began to proselytize and to prohibit some of the sacred rites of the Indians, they went into a shell of secrecy, guarding the more esoteric aspects of their religious system.

Two types of adjustment patterns to white contact continue to characterize the Pueblos at present, despite a more enlightened governmental policy and the extension of religious freedom to American Indians in recent years. The Rio Grande Pueblos exhibit a pattern of compartmentalization (see Spicer 1954:665; Dozier 1961:175–178). Compartmentalization must be understood as a type of adjustment found primarily among the Eastern Pueblos. Not all areas of the socio-ceremonial system have been compartmentalized, but only those aspects or rites that Spanish authorities, as well as later American contact agents, sought to destroy and supplant with a different system. There were borrowings and additions as well as continuity of indigenous patterns and even amalgams of introduced and old patterns in peripheral areas that did not fall in the zone of Eastern Pueblo culture under attack.

The adjustment pattern of Zuni and Hopi Pueblos, on the other hand, was primarily one of "rejection." These Pueblos, except for a negligible number of individuals, responded by rejecting the white man's religion and those patterns of Spanish and Anglo-American culture that appeared to threaten the integrated nature of Pueblo life.

Some explanations for these types of adjustment patterns have been proposed. An explanation proposed by Reed (1944:67) would account for the rejective pattern of the Pueblos by reference to their "well-integrated" communities. Spicer (1954:677), however, calls attention to the fact that the Yaqui Indians of Sonora also lived in well-integrated villages and yet worked out a "fusional" type of adjustment to Spanish contact, at least for the major part of the contact period. Spicer emphasizes explanations based on the "conditions of contact" rather than on one focused on the integrated nature of the recipient culture (Spicer 1954:677). The Yaqui were initially contacted and converted by Jesuits who came by Yaqui invitation and, as stipulated, without military escorts. These missionaries used a minimum of force and coercion and permitted the Indians to rework Spanish cultural and religious forms and meanings with their own. The result was an amalgam where it is not always possible to trace the provenience of the specific traits and complexes.

The Pueblos, particularly the Eastern Pueblos, worked out a different type of integration as a response to Spanish contact. Spanish cultural agents in New Mexico were ruthless Spanish civil authorities and Franciscan priests supported by well-armed soldiers. The Franciscans who came to the Pueblo country were purists and wanted to stamp out completely the indigenous religious system and to replace it with Catholicism. In this endeavor, as we have noted, they were sporadically supported by the civil authorities. Spanish authority and military power were, however, never quite adequate to destroy the native beliefs and customs of the Indians in the frontier post of New Mexico. On the other hand, the Pueblos inhabiting a large number of politically independent villages could not effectively resist the superior organization and better armed Spanish soldiers. The bitter lesson of the Pueblo Revolt of 1680 was constantly before the eyes of the Pueblos. Constantly fearing a forceful attempt to eradicate the native religion and punishment of their religious leaders, the Pueblos took their religion underground and pretended to be devout Catholics toward Spanish civil and church authorities. The Pueblos worked out a surveillance system, watching their own people to make certain that no one revealed any information about the ongoing ceremonial system. The transgressor was whipped, even put to death, depending on the kind of information divulged to outsiders (Hoebel 1962:560). It was a technique born out of necessity to permit the continuity of a cherished religion, but also a precautionary measure to prevent the whipping and execution of native ceremonial leaders by Spanish authorities. Surveillance measures were eased during the period of Spain's waning power in the late eighteenth century and through the period of Mexican rule. Anxiety over religious persecution again became acute in the early 1900s with the attempt by Protestant missionaries and the United States Indian Service officials to stop so-called anti-Christian practices of the Indians. In the pueblos, Pueblo authorities once more tightened their control over their members to insure the secrecy of the ceremonial system. White visitors were closely watched and regarded with suspicion and distrust.

The suppression of Indian customs and ceremonial activities was not focused on the Pueblos alone at this time. This was a general policy of the United States Indian Bureau applied to all American Indian groups. But the Pueblo communities, because of a rich ceremonial life, were more profoundly affected. Dissatisfaction with the policies and programs of the Indian Bureau was building up, however, among influential Indians and non-Indians; and in a momentous Congressional report, the Merriam Report (1928), the unjust and inadequate program of the Bureau of Indian Affairs was exposed. A team of investigators found deplorable conditions in the schools, both on the reservations and in off-reservation boarding schools. The study of the Bureau's administration of Indian health, social welfare, and other programs revealed gross misunderstanding of Indian needs and problems. In addition, many of the Bureau's personnel, some in key positions, were found to be corrupt and incompetent.

As a result of the Merriam study, a new regime came into the Bureau. Since the 1930s, the Indian Bureau's policy toward the Indians has changed radically. The aim of Indian administration at present is not to transform Indian communities into variants of the dominant American culture as quickly as possible, but to help them achieve equality in economy, education, and health with their fellow non-Indian citizens. Indian ways are to be respected and Indian arts and crafts encouraged. There must be no interference with traditional customs; they should be permitted to continue or change at the pace the Indians themselves set. In addition, through the Indian Reorganization Act of 1934, whether formally adopted by an Indian community or not, the Indians are given considerable autonomy over law and order and other internal affairs in their communities.

Not all of the various administrations since the above policy changes were effected have adhered to the advocated policy; indeed, in the early 1950s, a return to the pre-1930 regime appeared imminent, but a subsequent administration reiterated the basic policy established in 1934. Generally, Indians now have a greater voice in the conduct of their own affairs and the interference with and/or prohibition of Indian customs seems to be a thing of the past.

Because Pueblo society, particularly that of the Rio Grande Pueblos, is so highly structured and communal life is emphasized, individual freedom is not always given the expression found in other societies. The emphasis on compulsory participation in the ceremonies has tended to drive out those individuals who are not completely dedicated to Pueblo mores. All of the pueblos resort to force in compelling nonconformists to participate in communal activities. The only alternative open to the recalcitrant individual is to leave the pueblo. The federal government honors the right of Indian communities to run their own internal affairs. Individuals and families who have lost faith in Pueblo religious values and customs tend to leave the pueblo voluntarily, although there are some cases of resistance. This process of dissidents leaving the pueblos has resulted in keeping a population that values communal living and participation in a complex ceremonial life. Formerly, nonconformists were individuals and families who came under the influence of Hispano neighbors and the Catholic church; today, American culture and Protestant sects produce nonconformists. But the number of disaffected Indians alienated from individual pueblos is small, as evidenced by a steadily increasing Pueblo population. Pueblo culture is strong and enduring, and Pueblo Indians value the rewards of community living. Pueblo radicals often choose to conform to the demands of traditional leaders rather than to leave a pueblo.

Nativistic or revivalistic reactions have not arisen in the pueblos. These communities have not experienced the severe cultural loss that seems to be the basis of such reactions; nor have they suffered extreme economic deprivation. The social and religious organizational aspects of their culture are still intact. They have gradually shifted from primary dependence on subsistence farming to a credit and then to a cash system. The change has not been abrupt and the pueblos have not undergone the social disorganization and demoralization that usually accompanies such changes. The pueblos are still founded on traditional institutions that have been modified, but not displaced. Thus, the old institutions and the anxiety-reducing techniques of the traditional culture are still operative and effective. Not having been seriously deprived by Anglo-American contact, the Pueblos have not needed to question the basic adequacy or value of their culture. Indeed, the tremendous appeal their ceremonies have had to whites, as evidenced by the hundreds, even thousands of white tourists that attend the public aspects of these ceremonies, reassures them of the essential "rightness" of their way of life.

Permanent Anglo residents, whether farmers, business people, or professionals, have little association with Pueblo Indians. Contact with Anglos occurs most often with tourists, artists, and United States Bureau of Indian Affairs personnel. Outside the Pueblo communities Pueblo Indians also establish more formal relationships, usually in employer-employee type relationships. A few friendships, particularly those with artists and with college and/or university professors, have grown into intimate and long-enduring friendships. These friends are frequently drawn into siding with their Pueblo friends in disputes within the village, a practice that has often aggravated the situation rather than helped matters. On occasion, however, they have been of real assistance when the Pueblos desperately needed help. This was the case when the Pueblos and their Anglo friends joined forces to defeat the Bursum Bill (see above).

PART THREE

TRADITIONAL SOCIETY
AND CULTURE

Classification, Distribution, and General Characteristics

EARLY SPANISH EXPLORERS called the sedentary Indians in the northern frontier of New Spain, "Pueblos," a designation which distinguished these Indians from their nomadic neighbors. The later Spanish colonists found the twofold division an important sociologic and cultural distinction as well. The Pueblos became Catholics, at least in an official sense, while the nomadic Indians remained pagan and enemy raiders throughout Spanish and Mexican times. The Pueblos, because they lived by producing their own food, lived in compact, well-constructed homes, and soon adopted the externals of Spanish culture, were thought to be a notch above their nomadic neighbors. As Christians living in villages, the Spanish Crown early assigned land grants to the Pueblos, but not to other Indians. Under Mexican rule, the Pueblos became citizens; they could, therefore, sell or otherwise dispose of their land as they saw fit. As we have noted in the previous section, the legal status of the Pueblos remained a problem to early American government administrators. It was not until the second decade of the present century that the status of the Pueblos began to be defined in the same terms as that of other United States Indians.

Basic language distinctions among the Pueblos were recognized by the Spaniards early in the colonial period. Indeed, church and civil administrative districts corresponded closely to language divisions (Hodge, Hammond, and Rey, 1945). Soon after American occupation, Indian languages of the Southwest were classified and the language distinctions of the Pueblos in substantially the form we know them today were established (Powell, 1891). Roughly, from west to east, the languages of the Pueblos are as follows: Hopi, Zuni, Keres (Keresan), Tiwa, Jemez (Towa), Tewa. The last three (Tiwa, Tewa, Towa) are obviously related and have been grouped under a family designated "Tanoan." Notable dialectic differences exist in Keresan between a "Western" and "Eastern" group of Pueblos and among the Tiwa where each of the four Tiwa villages speaks a variant virtually unintelligible to the others.

Early social or cultural classifications of the Indians of the Southwest by anthropologists made a simple division of "Pueblo" and "non-Pueblo" (Goddard 1913; Wissler 1917:224; Kroeber 1928). These classifications implied a general homogeneity of Pueblo society and culture. Since the early intensive works of anthropologists were conducted among the Zuni and Hopi, the characteristics noted for these Pueblos were thought to apply to all the Pueblos. It was not until the studies of Elsie Clews Parsons (see especially Parsons 1939), that basic social and cultural differences between Eastern and Western Pueblos began to be noted. After Parsons' pioneering investigations, other anthropologists have divided the Pueblos into two groups, although those assigned to each of the two divisions have not been the same. A classification made by Florence Hawley Ellis (Hawley 1937) includes Hopi and Zuni in a Western division, while the Tanoan Pueblos and the Eastern Keresan Pueblos comprise her Eastern division—Acoma and Laguna are

TABLE 2
PUEBLO POPULATION 1630–1968

Column groups: **Western Pueblos** (Tewa, Keresan) = Hopi, Hano, Zuni, Acoma, Laguna. **Eastern or Rio Grande Pueblos** — Keresan = San Felipe, Santa Ana, Zia, Santo Domingo, Cochiti; Tamoan: Towa = Pecos, Jemez, Galisteo; Tewa = Tesuque, Nambe, Pojoaque, San Ildefonso, Santa Clara, San Juan; Tiwa = Isleta, Sandia, Picuris, Taos.

Year	Hopi	Hano	Zuni	Acoma	Laguna	San Felipe	Santa Ana	Zia	Santo Domingo	Cochiti	Pecos	Jemez	Galisteo	Tesuque	Nambe	Pojoaque	San Ildefonso	Santa Clara	San Juan	Isleta	Sandia	Picuris	Taos	Totals
1630a			10,000	2000					850		2000	3000	800	200	600		800	300	300	2000	3000	3000	2000	15,850*
1680b			2500	1500		600			150	300	2000	5000												17,805*
1704					330																			
1707c									204			500											700	1734*
1730d			800	600	400	234	209	318	281	372	521	307	188	171	400	130	296	279	300	421	440	247	732	6237*
1750e			824	960	528	453	353	481	300	521	300	383	220	232	199	99	371	188	261	304	291	328	456	8894*
1760f			664	1502	600	458	404	568	424	450	344	373	255		204		484	257	316				505	9062*
1775–/1776g	7494	550	1617	530	699	406	384	416	528	486	269	345	152	194	183	98	387	229	201	454	275	223	427	16,547
1805h	1150		1470	731	940	289	450	254	333	656	104	264		131	143	100	175	186	194	419	314	250	508	9061
1860–/1861i	2500		1150	523	927	360	316	117	261	172	Moved to Jemez 1838	650	Abandoned circa 1800	97	103	37	154	179	341	440	217	143	363	9050
1900–/1905j	2100		1514	739	1384	475	226	125	1000	300		450		100	100	7	250	325	425	989	74	125	425	11,126
1930–/1932k	2842		1991	1073	2192	555	236	183	862	295		641		120	129		123	382	530	1077	115	112	723	14,188
1940–/1942l	3444		2319	1322	2686	697	273	235	1017	346		767		147	144	25	147	528	702	1304	139	115	830	17,187
1948–/1950m	4000	405	2671	1447	2894	784	288	267	1106	497		883		160	155		170	573	768	1470	139	130	907	19,714
1964n	4500	450	5176	2415	4834	1327	431	468	1905	652		1566		222	249	85	296	908	1259	2331	236	181	1457	30,948
1968o	4700	500	4962#	2688	4996	1542	448	517	2248	707		1707		230	266	75	305	769#	1277	2449	248	167	1471	32,272

a. Census figures contained in the Memorial of 1630 by Alonso de Benavides (1916); *b.* Hodge (1912, Pt. 2, p. 325); *c.* Parsons (1939:861–938); *d.* Population figures taken by Bishop Benito Crespo in his visitation of the Pueblos in 1730, Adams (1954:95–99); *e.* 1750 census of the Pueblos, contained as footnote information in Adams (1954:34–71); *f.* Census figures of the Pueblos taken by Bishop Pedro Tamaron y Romeral in his visitation of New Mexico, 1760 (Adams 1954:43–71); *g.* Hopi and Hano population figures reported by Father Silvestre Velez Escalante in 1775 (Thomas 1932:221–245), the other population figures are from Hodge (1912, Pt. 2, p. 325) for 1776; *h.* Hodge (1912, Pt. 2, p. 325); *i.* Hopi and Hano population figures combined, Hodge (1912, Pt. 2, p. 325); *j.* These population figures are from Hodge (1912, Pt. 2, p. 325); *k., l.* These population figures are from Thompson and Joseph (1944:136); *m.* Hopi and Hano figures from Dozier (1954:286–289) and Stubbs (1950:23–94); *n.* Smith (1966:86); *o.* 1968 census. All Pueblo figures are from Council, Albuquerque.

* Figures not representative of total Pueblo population.

\# Large off-reservation population excluded from the 1968 population figures of Zuni and Santa Clara.

listed as transitional. Eggan (1950) groups Hopi, Zuni, Laguna, and Acoma in his Western Pueblos and the Tanoan Pueblos, with the exception of Jemez, as Eastern Pueblos. The Rio Grande (or Eastern) Keresan and Jemez are transitional in Eggan's classification. Finally, a classification by Kirchhoff (1954:549) places all Tanoan Pueblos, except Jemez, in one division, and Hopi, Zuni, the Keresan Pueblos, and Jemez in a second division.

The early classifications were set up primarily on descriptive criteria. Later classifications offered a historical explanation as the provenience of the traits used to group the Pueblos (Strong 1927; Spier 1929; Hawley 1937). In setting up a twofold division of the Pueblos—into a Western and Eastern division—Eggan (1950, 1966:112–141) combined sociological and historical explanations. Eggan used kinship types and other correlated social factors as the basis of his classification. My own classification will follow Eggan's, but I intend to expand on some of

Jemez Pueblo—The only Towa-speaking pueblo, about fifty miles west of Santa Fe, New Mexico.

Eggan's ideas for social and cultural differentiation. I want particularly to develop the irrigation hypotheses first proposed by Wittfogel and Goldfrank (1943), but also suggested by Eggan as an explanation for the East-West difference in social organization.

The hypotheses, perhaps more properly "hunches and speculations" regarding the immediate prehistoric origins of the Pueblos either as physical or cultural groups are legion. None of the evidence provided by archeology, linguistics, ethnology, or physical anthropology for the many ideas about the prehistory of the Pueblos is conclusive, however. The advocates of these disciplines disagree among themselves and often offer hypotheses directly opposed to those espoused by colleagues of their own subdiscipline. Indeed, an explanation defended with considerable heat by one scholar at one time is later abandoned in favor of another. Each hypothesis in its time is argued with considerable vigor and plausibility. Much of this controversy has arisen with the development of glottochronology or lexicostatistics. Archeologists and ethnologists have given the technique more credence than it has been accorded by linguists. As new glottochronological dates have appeared, archeologists and ethnologists have sorted out their data to conform with the new time depths. Actually differences among the linguistic chronologies are fantastic (Fox 1967:27; Trager 1967:336). As the result of these diverse reports, equally improbable and incomparable hypotheses have been proposed about the immediate prehistory of the Pueblos and as carriers of distinct cultures. Fox (1967:23–47) has performed a yeoman's job of summarizing the most plausible of these hypotheses, although he falls into the trap of engaging in some wild speculations.

It is not possible at present to identify the immediate prehistoric antecedents of the Pueblos, but the following statements are generally accepted. The present Pueblos are the genetic and cultural descendants of the widespread prehistoric traditions of the Mogollon and Anasazi. Abandonment of former sites and movement into historic locations occurred as a result primarily of drought and general climatic changes, but not because of disease or invasion by nomads (Kelley, J. C. 1952; Schwartz, 1957; and Woodbury 1961). Hopi, Zuni, and Acoma pueblos go back at least 700 years in the sites they now occupy (Ellis 1967). It is also generally agreed that occupation of the northern and central Rio Grande area occurred later—at least in terms of relatively large villages—by peoples from two different prehistoric traditions: the Keresans and the Tanoans (Dutton 1966; Ellis 1967; Wendorf and Reed 1955). From the distribution of Tanoan pueblos at the time of Spanish entry and from the greater diversification of the Tanoan languages, it would appear that settlement of the Rio Grande by Tanoan speakers antedated occupation of the area by Keresans. The archeological record would also appear to be in agreement with this statement. Archeological evidence of settlement by sedentary peoples of the area occupied during historic times by Tanoan speakers goes back prior to 1000 A.D. (Wendorf 1954; Wendorf and Reed 1955; Wetherington 1968). Glottochronological dates, as we have noted, vary atrociously; but since they are restricted to splits within the Tanoan (or dialectical divisions among the Keresan), they are not relevant in establishing the primacy of the two distinct language groups in the Rio Grande area. The ethnological data suggest more pronounced differences between the two in the immediate prehistoric period but with continuous adjustments leveling off differences as we approach the contemporary period. The primary difference between the major groups of Pueblo languages is linguistic. Hopi, Zuni, Keresan, and the subfamilies of the Tanoan are distinct languages. Other important differences occur in political, social, and ceremonial organization, but these are only partially correlated with linguistic differences. The linguistic-sociocultural fit is least apparent among the Pueblos of the Rio Grande area. It is clear that considerable borrowing has taken place among the major language groups and that adjustment to a different ecological environment has brought other differences. The determination of the core culture of each pueblo prior to settlement in the area where they were found by Spanish explorers is likely to prove unrewarding at this time. Even if we were to demonstrate that certain Pueblos came from a specific archeological region, such knowledge alone would not tell us very much about their cultural characteristics at present or in the recent past. Cultures change rapidly and adjust to new social and ecological environments quickly. Witness, for example, the Hano (Hopi-Tewa). We know that the ancestors of this pueblo came from the Rio Grande area; that they were formerly Tewa speakers and members of the *Thanu* (Tano) pueblos of the Galisteo Basin region in New Mexico. The Tewa language has survived, but only an extremely detailed analysis of its society will reveal putative structural survivals from its past. Hano in its general cultural and social characteristics is a Hopi pueblo. What we have to do is attempt to understand the kinds of cultural and social adaptations which were needed and how the various pueblos have made such adjustments in the areas in which they now live. We also need, insofar as this is possible, to determine the kind and amount of borrowing which has taken place within recent historic times. We will attempt to consider these factors in this section in order to provide a view of Pueblo life in its unity and diversity and to gain some knowledge of the processes underlying Pueblo society and culture.

Population and Settlement Pattern

The first census figures were reported in 1630 by Father Alonso de Benavides as 60,000 native Pueblo converts living in ninety villages, each of which had its own church (Hodge, Hammond and Rey 1945). This figure may be an exaggeration as Benavides was suspected by historians of padding population figures to emphasize the zealous work of the friars. Father Benavides served as custodian of the custodia of New Mexico from 1625 to 1629. The number of villages and churches was probably correct since it was important to specify the actual number of chapels in order to draw the needed supplies and furnishings from Royal and Church storehouses. A more realistic estimate of the population in 1630 was probably about 40,000. Benavides' estimate of 60,000 may have been realistic, however, for the initial contact period in 1598; but by 1630, the Pueblos were experiencing the brunt of Spanish oppression and refugees were leaving their villages to join the nomadic tribes.

At the time of Benavides' tenure as custodian, population figures for the individual pueblos varied from 2000 for Pecos and Taos to as low as fifty for the others, the average probably being around 400. The Pueblo villages along the Rio Grande began about the location of present San Marcial, Socorro county, with a village at intervals of every three or five miles as far as Taos in the north. On the east side of the mountains, paralleling the Piro and Tiwa villages along the Rio Grande was another group of villages. These latter pueblos were abandoned by the time of the Pueblo Revolt of 1680, the Indians joining their Tiwa and Piro relatives along the Rio Grande and others establishing settlements below El Paso. To the west were Acoma, a single large village, and Zuni, which consisted of several villages until about the middle of the seventeenth century when the Indians congregated into one village. Laguna, Acoma's neighbor, was founded after the revolt by refugees from the Rio Grande Keresan pueblos (Hodge, Hammond and Rey 1945:258; 287–288). Far to the west were the Hopi, living in some five main villages. Hano, like Laguna, was not established until after the revolt by predominantly Tano refugees (Tewa speaking) from the Galisteo Basin in New Mexico (see population charts and maps).

A general village settlement pattern appears to be roughly correlated to the

Circular kiva, partly underground—San Felipe Pueblo.

language groups. There is also a rather distinctive pattern in the number and arrangement of the ceremonial structures or *kivas*. Contemporary Keresan village settlement plans are predominantly of the parallel alignment type, like Acoma, Zuni, and the Hopi villages. The settlement pattern appears to be old and undoubtedly characterized Keresan pueblos at the time of Spanish contact. Among the Tanoans the single- or multiple-plaza type is typical and predominant in the archeological sites reckoned to be Tanoan (Reed 1956:14–15).

The distribution of *kivas* in the individual pueblos has obvious socioceremonial significance. The importance of the moiety and sodality in religion and social organization among the Tanoans is reflected in the distribution of its ceremonial structures. The Tewa have one large *kiva* and two smaller structures; the large one is used by the whole village where factionalism has not seriously disrupted communal activity. The Southern Tiwa, Isleta and Sandia, have two *kivas*, one being larger than the other (Hawley 1950). In addition, Isleta has ceremonial house structures used by the moiety associations (Parsons 1932b:209). Espejo (Bolton 1916:177) reported two *estufas* (*kivas*) among the Piro and Southern Tiwa in villages which were abandoned after the Pueblo revolt. Taos and Picuris, the Northern Tiwa, have multiple *kivas*, yet a geographical grouping consisting of a north and south clustering of *kivas* is evident. The Keresans have two *kivas* of approximately equal size which function primarily as gathering places and as rehearsal and costuming centers for dual drama-dance groups. These villages are the only pueblos at present with a consistent two-*kiva* system. Multiple *kivas* are characteristic of the Acoma, Zuni, and Hopi pueblos where such structures are definitely associated with clan and sodality (association) organizations. Acoma and Zuni *kivas* form a part of the residential house structures, but elsewhere they are isolated structures, separated from residential units. Laguna does not appear to have *kivas*, but ceremonial activities may be simply conducted in what appear to be ordinary residential rooms.

Of primary importance to the Pueblos are the rooms in which the clan (west) and the sodality (east) altar and fetishes are stored and set up. Although these are indistinguishable from ordinary rooms, they are the most sacred structures of the Pueblos. More will be said about this structure later.

Common characteristics of all Pueblo homes are the contiguous alignment of rooms, and until recently, multistoried terraced rooms, rising to four and five stories in some pueblos. Along the Rio Grande, houses are almost all of adobe; although away from the river valley where other materials are available, they are frequently of sandstone slabs or pumice blocks. Acoma, Laguna, Zuni, and the Hopi pueblos have not used adobe as much as have the Rio Grande pueblos. Although adobe brick was apparently known among the prehistoric Rio Grande pueblos (Schroeder and Matson 1965:120), the pre-Spanish homes were primarily of coursed adobe construction. Adobe brick house construction has replaced most other forms of house building since Spanish times. The walls of Pueblo houses receive a fresh coating of mud plaster every year in order to protect them from torrential rains common in the summer time.

Environment, Economy, Technology

The land of the Pueblos is the high arid plateau country of northern Arizona and of northwestern and central New Mexico. There are no permanently flowing streams in the Hopi country. A small stream serves Zuni village, but there is no extensive use of spring or stream water in either the Hopi or Zuni villages for farming. These Pueblos rely almost exclusively on rainfall and wash-offs for a successful harvest. The Eastern Pueblos have located their villages either on the banks of the Rio Grande or its tributaries. These Indians are not dependent solely on rainfall for the successful growth of crops, but have constructed irrigation canals to divert the waters of streams and rivers to planted fields. Conclusive evidence for the use of irrigation in pre-Spanish times has been validated by archeologists, but is also contained in the accounts of the early Spanish explorers (Bolton 1916:177–179; Schroeder and Matson 1965:117–120).

Among the Hopi, Acoma, Zuni, and probably among many of the pre-historic Indians, irrigation for crops may have been done by small families or kin groups, perhaps lineage and clan members. Farming based on rainfall and flooding does not require the investment of prodigious labor. But water brought to fields, located sometimes at considerable distance from permanently flowing waters, necessitates a larger manpower output. The complex tasks of clearing, terracing, breaking, damming, and ditching requires greater communal effort in a society based on irrigation. The need for a large labor force to maintain an irrigation society is particularly evident where technological achievements are simple. Pre-historic farming was carried on primarily with the simple digging stick, wooden shovels, stone axes, and woven fiber baskets for moving dirt and debris. Pueblo workers involved in farming and other communal tasks included adult men and women. Rio Grande pueblo village enterprises thus typically involved the whole adult population; this is not true of the western pueblos where work tasks are usually family or clan affairs.

The aboriginal crops of the Pueblos were maize, beans, gourds (squash) cotton, and tobacco. Since Spanish times, wheat, alfalfa, and chili have been added as well as fruit trees such as peach, apple, plum, and cherry. The latter were never grown abundantly, however. Chili, a New World crop grown extensively in Mexico in aboriginal times, was unknown among the Pueblos before the advent of the Spaniards. The Western Pueblos still restrict farming crops to the aboriginal maize, squash, and beans, although cotton and tobacco are rarely grown at present. Because of the absence of irrigation, wheat, alfalfa, and chili have not become important in the West; but, in the Rio Grande area until recently, they have competed successfully with the prehistoric triumvirate of plants in terms of acreage planted and harvested. Farming among the Western Pueblos is a hazardous occupation. Only by ingenious and arduous methods of planting and caring for their growing crops have these Indians garnered a living from the land. The rainfall is scant, averaging only about 10 inches per year. The altitude of over 6000 feet brings early and late frosts which limit the growing season. During late summer, sudden torrential rains cause considerable damage. To insure a crop against these odds, the Western Pueblo farmers plant two or three fields distributed so that full advantage is taken of the type of soil and the kind of terrain in which the seeds are sown. Alluvial fans, flood plains, and flat sandy areas are preferred. By planting in all of these areas, it is hoped that despite inclement weather, one of the plots will produce a harvestable crop. The observation made by Kirk Bryan of Hopi-planted fields is applicable generally to all the Western Pueblos:

> The areas utilized are variable in size and location, but each is chosen so that the local rainfall may be reinforced by the overflow of water derived from higher ground. The selection of a field involves an intimate knowledge of local conditions. The field must be flooded, but the sheet of water must not attain such velocity as to wash out the crop nor carry such a load of detritus as to bury the growing plants. Such conditions require a nice balance of forces that occur only under special conditions. Shrewd observation and good judgment are necessary in the selection of fields (Bryan 1929:445).

In addition to taking practical precautionary measures to achieve a bountiful harvest, the Western Pueblos also observed magical rites for the same reason. Indeed, we will see that the two groups of Pueblos contrast rather sharply in the amount of supernatural aid sought to assist them in their farming activities. The Rio Grande Pueblos can do more in a practical way to regulate needed moisture for their crops, hence their ingenuity appears to have been directed toward attaining and maintaining a social organization adequate to cope with the needs of an incipient water works society. While the Rio Grande Pueblos appear to have "dry farmed" to a limited extent, their primary dependence has been on crops grown on irrigated fields (Lange 1959:5). These Indians have, therefore, expended considerable time and labor in leveling land for garden plots. Such plots are located at lower elevations from the source of canals and ditches emanating from the Rio Grande or its tributaries. Thus, irrigation water is brought by gravitational flow to planted fields. While the construction and maintenance of the main irrigation canals are communal tasks, work on lateral ditches and ditches within garden plots are family or extended family activities.

Ownership of house sites and garden plots in the west are by clan or lineage; among Tanoans in the east, by extended family or by larger units which are essentially minimal bilateral descent groups. The work in the fields—planting, weeding and harvest—was similarly a task of these kinship units. Pueblo Indians added to their diet by gathering wild, edible plants and by organizing periodic tribal hunts to gather rabbits and other small game. Other delicacies were a special species of wood rat, deer, and antelope. When the Spaniards first encountered the Pueblos, most of the villages kept vast flocks of turkeys, both for food and feathers (Schroeder and Matson 1965:115). Periodic trips to the Plains country to hunt buffalo are also well-remembered activities among old Pueblo residents. It is likely, however, that buffalo meat and skins were obtained primarily by trade or gift exchanges with friendly nomadic tribes.

Women assisted men in communal type tasks, but in other activities there was a fairly rigid division of labor. Men planted and tilled the fields and cut and hauled firewood. Men also hunted, dressed the skins of animals they killed, made their own bows, arrows, shields, and war clubs, and wove baskets, blankets, and sashes. Women cared for the children, prepared and cooked the meals, made pottery, and performed other duties around the house. Whereas men constructed houses, both the living quarters and ceremonial chambers, women did the plastering.

Craft specializations either by village, by families, or by individuals within the village, had not taken place. There is also no evidence of intravillage markets nor even of extensive trading between villages. Nor was the pueblo divided into a pronounced class structure either in the west or the east. Among the Rio Grande pueblos, however, members of nonkinship sodalities or associations were in charge of governmental functions; whereas in the west, governmental duties were the prerogatives of clan members. The village chief among the Rio Grande Pueblos was exempt from the ordinary duties required of all members of the pueblo. He was the recognized chief ceremonial and secular officer and as such was respected and considered the primary authority in all matters—sacred and profane. This individual, known as the *cacique* during Spanish times, was the member of a socioreligious sodality which ruled the village with authoritarian power. The *cacique* and the priests associated with him compelled village members to perform communal duties, both secular and ceremonial, under threat of physical punishment or banishment from the village with attendant confiscation of houses and land. The Rio Grande pueblos, therefore, possessed far greater political centralization than their Western Pueblo counterparts.

Pueblo Neighbors

The Pueblos did not live in isolation in prehistoric times nor in the recent past. There were nomadic tribes with whom they interacted, on friendly, symbiotic-type relationships before European contact; and after the establishment of Spanish rule, more frequently on hostile relations. As we have indicated earlier, however, the abandonment of former pueblo sites and migration into historic sites need not be attributed to troubles with hostile tribes. A people escaping from predatory enemies would hardly locate in open sites, less easily defensible than the communities they left. Even the Hopi were found by early explorers living at the foot

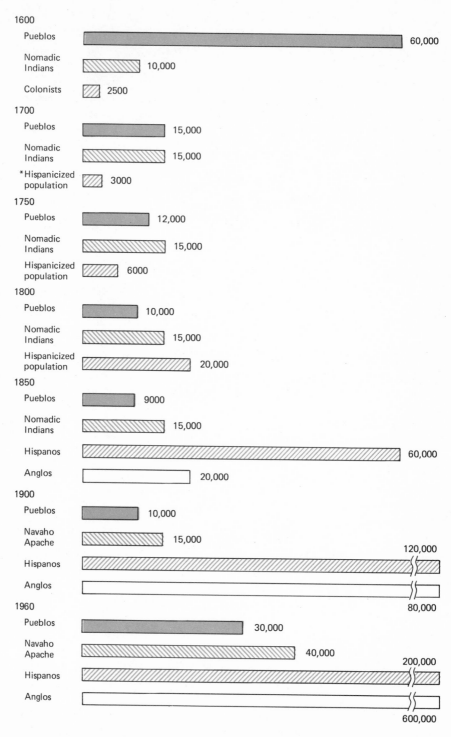

Figure 9. Population: Pueblo and neighbors.

of the mesas, for the most part, rather than on top where they might better defend themselves against enemy attacks. Trouble under Spanish rule made these Indians move to the top of the mesas where most of them still live today. The factors of drought and arroyo cutting, for which there is abundant evidence (Hack 1942; O'Bryan 1952; Woodbury 1961), seems sufficient reason for migration to historic locations. This is underscored when we note that the movement in all cases was to areas of permanent or more dependable water supply.

Coronado's chronicler, Pedro de Castaneda, reported in 1541 contacts between the Pueblos and a nomadic tribe called the Teya, perhaps an Apache tribe:

> These people (the Teya) knew the people in the settlements and were friendly with them, and they went there to spend the winter under the wings of the settlements. The inhabitants did not dare to let them come inside, because they cannot trust them. Although they are received as friends, and trade with them, they do not stay in the village over night, but outside under the wings (Hodge 1907:356–357).

Shoshonean-speaking nomadic Indians also were in the northern peripheries of the Pueblo country in Spanish times. Marvin Opler (Linton (Ed.), 1940:123) places the ancestral Utes north of the Pueblo area in prehorse days. The Espejo expedition in 1582 found the Pueblos wearing shoes and boots made from buffalo hides and deerskin, which suggests trade relations between the settled villagers and nomadic Indians. The simplicity of life among hunters and gatherers undoubtedly made them adhere to the Pueblos, whose economy was more dependable and their culture generally richer.

The Irrigation Hypothesis

We have indicated that at the time the Spanish entered the Southwest, the Rio Grande Pueblos were at the threshold of a more complex society. Following some interesting ideas advanced by Wittfogel and Goldfrank (1943) and Wittfogel (1957), I believe that intensive irrigation practices utilizing water from permanently flowing streams have brought about the centralized orientation of the Eastern or Rio Grande Pueblos (compare Eggan 1966:138–139). This hypothesis needs to be expanded at this point, although data on specific details of Pueblo social and ceremonial organization will be presented later.

In providing support for the irrigation hypothesis, certain premises about the nature of social structures are pertinent. Professor Fred Eggan has presented these premises admirably for the Pueblos:

> If we are to understand the differences between the social structures of the eastern and western Pueblos, we need to know, first, whether they derive from a common basic type or from different types. There is some economy in assuming a single earlier type, but we also need to keep alternative hypotheses in mind. Second, social structures have tasks to perform in maintaining social continuity and in meeting the needs of the community. For these purposes some structures are more efficient than others. Third, social structures change more often from internal readjustments than from external contacts. Borrowing may take place, but innovation and re-

modeling of existing structures are more common. And, last, we need to remember that different structures may perform similar functions (Eggan 1966:135).

The continuing day-to-day tasks that must be performed in a simple farming economy like that of the Pueblos was probably similar in all Pueblo communities, east or west. Only when there is need for work requiring the mobilization of fairly large numbers of adults does there appear to be a necessity for structures of a different kind. Irrigation, we believe, is one of these tasks and it is our belief that the kind of small corporate lineages or clans found in the Southwest are incapable of accomplishing the work required in a waterwork society. The Western pueblos —Hopi, Hano, Zuni, Acoma, and Laguna—could carry on a subsistence economy based on "dry" and "flood" farming techniques with lineages and clans. In the Rio Grande area, however, the complex demands of irrigation made such organizations inefficient and our data appear to indicate that nonkinship units (sodalities or associations) were the organizations which could and did mobilize the large numbers of people needed to operate an irrigation society. It is interesting that whereas the irrigation-based Keresan pueblos along the Rio Grande possessed lineages and clans, governmental duties (unlike the Western Pueblos) were in the hands of sodality and association members. Indeed, there appears to be evidence of an interesting historical shift from clan involvement in government to the assumption of sociopolitical tasks by nonkinship units—the so-called "medicine associations" of the Keresans. The Tanoan pueblos apparently already had nonkinship based units to perform governmental tasks or else invested political authority in sodalities (associations) previously organized for other purposes. The concentration of political authority in one or two village sodalities is only one way to achieve village centralization. Any one of the following possibilities might have been employed: a council of clan heads, a council of elders, a council of elected individuals, the creation of an organization specifically delegated to direct governmental and religious functions on the community level. This latter course was apparently followed by the Tewa. The selection of an organization to perform integrative functions in the village is, of course, influenced by structures available in the society or in neighboring ones; it is probably rare that wholly new structures are created. In this respect, it is interesting that none of the pueblos substituted the Spanish-imposed civil administrative system to provide village integration and centralization. The reason may have been that there was a need to control the religious functions of the village as well; the Spanish civil government system was essentially a secular one and its religious officers were associated with an alien religion. Perhaps the Pueblos were merely displaying their general antipathy toward Spanish-introduced items; hence, the civil governmental system never displaced the native sociopolitical and governmental order.

It seems clear that clan organizations were inadequate for the intricate demands of an irrigation society, particularly where technology remained on a simple level. The development of a sodality-type organization appears to be a method for achieving village centralization and for mobilizing and directing the communities' total or at least minimum manpower resources. Such an organization was soon put to the direction of other village-wide operations: religion, hunting, warfare, and curing—actually the exorcism of evil from the pueblo, a communal task in the Rio Grande pueblos. The initial impetus for the organization, we believe however, was irrigation. We will return again to our central hypothesis after presenting a review of the peoples surrounding the Pueblos and after laying the basic foundation of traditional Pueblo society and culture.

Pueblo Sociocultural Imperatives and Pueblo Pattern of Organization

While the individual pueblos and linguistic subgroups show considerable variation in details, there is a basic similarity in the overall pattern of Pueblo political and ceremonial organization. Pueblo society revolves around five basic concerns: (1) weather, (2) illness, (3) warfare, (4) control of flora and fauna, and (5) village harmony. These imperatives are perhaps the concerns of all peoples, but the approaches in dealing with them differ among the various societies of the world. Even among the Pueblos there are differences—differences which distinguish the Western Pueblos from the Eastern, and in the Rio Grande area, the Keresan from the Tanoan. Indeed, there are differences from pueblo to pueblo. Generally, for example, the western pueblos attempt to cope with these basic concerns by magical practices; the Rio Grande Pueblos, particularly the Tanoans, by more practical ones. We suggest that the opportunity of the Rio Grande Pueblos to deal directly with weather control through irrigation has brought about this basic difference. Magical rites are by no means absent among the Rio Grande Pueblos, although they do not receive the emphasis accorded them by the Western Pueblos. In the west, all activities are subordinated to religion. The subsistence economy receives the full concentration of religious devotion and ritual. In an environment that is fraught with uncertainty regarding the success or failure of the basic means of livelihood, religious activity attempts to force nature to be more bountiful. Lean and good years are explained in terms of faulty or successful observance of religious retreats and rituals. Activities marginal or unrelated to the basic subsistence economy receive little attention. Warfare and hunting, for example, are comparatively unimportant. Indeed, warfare may have been virtually absent among these pueblos before the neighboring nomadic tribes became mobile through the acquisition of the horse. The Western Pueblos have traditionally emphasized the sacred over the secular (compare Gillin 1948:509–514).

Among all of the pueblos the sociocultural imperatives listed above are handled by specific institutions. We will discuss these institutions in more detail shortly, but at present it is appropriate to present the dominant features of western and eastern pueblo social organization. The western pueblos—Hopi, Hano, Zuni, Acoma, and Laguna—emphasize matrilineal exogamous clans, female ownership of house and garden plots, matrilocal residence, and the Katcina cult. Major religious emphasis is on weather control: rain production (by magical means) to make crops grow. The eastern Tanoan pueblos have a dual division of the society: bilateral extended families which appear to be minimal bilateral descent groups; male ownership of houses and land; matrilineal clans are absent; the Katcina cult while present is weak, and indeed the cult is absent among the Tiwa pueblos. Finally, there are a number of esoteric sodalities that crosscut the dual division organizations in membership. The major religious orientation revolves around government, which in the past was particularly concerned with regulating the tasks associated with irrigation and community work. Warfare and hunting also formerly received greater attention among these pueblos. Curing or exorcism rites are likewise important, but these two preoccupations were highlighted far more among the neighboring Keresan pueblos. The Keresans are intermediate in their social organization and religious preoccupation. Dr. Florence Hawley Ellis characterizes the Keresans as follows:

> We might hazard the hypothesis that in general the Keresans appear to have clanship as a native trait, originally of importance in government, religion, and marriage control and that the patrilineal concept for membership in "moiety" was superimposed on their own dual kiva-kachina system. More important to the majority of Keresans at present than either are their "medicine societies," whose duties cover not only curing, but also weather control and selection of religious and secular officers, or approval of the choice of all or part of such officers by the cacique whom they have put into power. Membership in these societies is by curing, trespass, or choice, and is independent of membership in other organizations (Hawley 1950b:511).

In this section we will present what appears to be the traditional indigenous social and cultural characteristics of the Pueblos. To a certain extent what we describe here may be a reconstruction; but because of the general conservative nature of Pueblo society and culture, many of the customs and institutions we describe are still operating today. The tendency of the Pueblos, particularly the Rio Grande Pueblos, to compartmentalize, that is, to keep indigenous patterns separated from recently introduced patterns, also gives us assurance that what is presented here is still viable and persisting. It is, of course, important to emphasize that undoubtedly much change has taken place as the result of contact with Euro-American society and culture; some of these changes were explicitly noted in the historic section and other changes will be indicated in the final section. The general features of Pueblo society and culture presented here have been taken from the ethnographic literature on the Pueblos and integrated with my own published and unpublished research materials. No attempt has been made to acknowledge the sources of general aspects of Pueblo social organization known to most ethnographers; where new or controversial data are presented, acknowledgment is made where the information is cited or quoted. Interpretation of the data is my own, except as otherwise indicated.

THE WESTERN PUEBLOS

Hopi, Hano, Zuni, Acoma are not only western geographically, but they form a unit in terms of a number of shared social characteristics. These characteristics contrast rather sharply with the Tanoan pueblos on the eastern periphery of the Pueblo area. The Rio Grande Keresan pueblos (including the Towa pueblo of Jemez) occupy a somewhat intermediate position. Yet in terms of basic social organization, these pueblos lean more closely to the Tanoans; hence the dichotomy: Western versus Eastern (or Rio Grande) Pueblos.

The key features of the social organization of the Western Pueblos have already been noted: matrilineal exogamous clans, matrilocal residence, importance of women in the ownership of houses and land, emphasis of the Katcina cult, and religious preoccupation with weather control (compare Eggan 1966:114). For the Hopi, less true for Hano, Zuni, and Acoma, we may also indicate as characteristic the rather weak development of village integration. The socially and ceremonially important units in the village are the clans, or more properly, lineages —the living segments of the clans represented in each village. Indeed, the dominant role of these lineages in government, religion, subsistence, and community affairs provides the major contrast between the Western and Eastern Pueblos. Among the latter, as we shall see, involvement in essentially similar functions is the prerogative of nonkinship associations (societies or sodalities). A lineage or lineage segment in a village has a ceremonial room and its female head (usually the oldest woman of the lineage) looks after the ritual paraphernalia which are stored in that room. Ceremonial associations are clan or lineage controlled, although membership is drawn without regard to clan affiliation. Each association has at least one ceremony which is staged and directed by the lineage in the village. When a

Traditional Western Pueblo men's attire—Zuni Pueblo men.

ceremony is being conducted in the village, the male head of the lineage (usually the female head's brother) erects the lineage's altar in the lineage ceremonial room. Members of the lineage and clan members from the village as well as those from other villages are invited to visit the ceremonial room, smoke the ceremonial pipe and offer prayers. The altar itself contains the ritual paraphernalia of the lineage. Occupying a central position within the altar and its array of ceremonial objects is the clan (actually lineage) fetish—an ear of corn wrapped in cloth and feathers. Each ceremonial association has in addition a similar fetish—the association's sacred symbol—which, on the occasion of a ceremony, is also displayed on the altar, along with the clan fetish and other ritual clan possessions.

From the above outline, it is clear that Western Pueblo social organization is based on unilateral descent, and the social structures given prominence in Hano life are also unilateral organizations. The nuclear or elementary family, which is the basic family type in American society, is a temporary unit among the Western Pueblos and the result of acculturation to white American influences. The Western Pueblo family organization is an extended type where relatives related along the maternal line live in rooms and houses adjacent to one another. Married men live with their wives, but look upon the households of their mothers and sisters as their "real" homes. These men return frequently to their natal households to participate

Traditional Western Pueblo married woman's attire—Zuni Pueblo.

in ceremonial life and to exercise their authority over junior members of their own lineages. Western Pueblo households are the terminal structures of a number of matrilineal lineages which, in turn, form the important clan structures. One household, putatively the oldest household of the lineage in the clan in a given village, is the custodian of ceremonial lore and the ritual possessions of the clan. The oldest woman in this household is the head of the clan, but the "real" clan leader is her brother or perhaps a maternal uncle. This man is held in high esteem. He stages and directs the ceremonies of the ritual associations owned by the clan and is acquainted with all of the ceremonial lore and the uses and significance of the religious paraphernalia of the clan.

Kinship

The kinship sytem of the Western Pueblos has been characterized by Eggan (1950:291–292; 1966:114) as "Crow type" organized in terms of the lineage principle. Eggan proposed the classification on the basis of the terminological arrangement of kin terms. The classification has been criticized by Schneider and Roberts (1956) and more recently by Fox (1967) as not conforming exactly to a Crow system among the Zuni and Keresans respectively. Nevertheless, the terms are organized primarily in terms of the lineage principle and kinship behavior is consonant with and emphasizes the solidarity and unity of the lineage groups. These distinctions are similar among all the pueblos designated as Western and they contrast sharply from the Tanoan kinship system as we will see. The Keresans are an intermediate group, their kinship system leaning more toward the Western Pueblo type; but in behavior and in the orientation of their social institutions definitely closer to the Tanoans.

Kinship behavior among the Western Pueblos may be comprehended most easily by a discussion of the extended matrilineal household where an individual receives his first and lasting cultural orientation. The household normally consists of a woman and her husband, married daughters and their husbands, unmarried sons, and children of the daughters. The women are the important members of the unit; they own the house, are responsible for the preparation and distribution of food, make all the important decisions, and care for the ritual possessions of the family. The oldest woman of the household enjoys the most respect, and the members of the unit look to her for instructions and seek her advice in times of trouble. Next in importance is her oldest daughter, who assumes the duties and responsibilities of the household when her mother is away. Men born into the household and lineage leave the house when they marry, although they return frequently, exercise considerable authority in religious matters, and may discipline their sister's children when asked. The husbands contribute to the economic support of the household, teach their children the techniques of making a livelihood, and provide warmth and affection toward their children; but in disciplinary matters and economic decisions, they defer to their wives and their wives' brothers and uncles.

Interaction with the father's relatives goes on almost simultaneously with

Pueblo homes—Zuni Pueblo, Zunian linguistic stock. A Western Pueblo.

those of the matrilineal household. These relatives, particularly father's mother and father's sisters, are frequent visitors and the child, in turn, frequently visits the home of his paternal grandparents and sisters. These relatives exert little authority and do not discipline, but they provide love, comfort, and aid during crucial and anxious periods of his life.

The Western Pueblo matrilineal extended household in the past occupied a series of adjacent rooms. With the increasing importance of wage work and livestock activities in recent years, this situation has changed. Families living on farms and ranches during the summer are now essentially of the elementary type: husband, wife, and children, and in some cases a widowed grandmother, a divorced daughter, or other relative. Off-reservation employment restricts the size of the household even more drastically. Although it is not uncommon to have one or even both parents of the wife living with a nuclear family on a farm or ranch, older people refuse to make their home with children who live in government quarters or rented houses in towns and cities. The large extended household of the Pueblos generally has thus tended to become a smaller and less integrated unit in recent years; nevertheless, there is keen awareness of all the relatives that comprise the household group. Modern forms of transportation afford resumptions of extended-household living. Frequent ceremonies draw members back to the village enabling close relatives to interact with one another and thus renew and strengthen the bonds of relationship.

Lineage and Clan

The household described above and the lineage to be briefly discussed here have no names anywhere among the Western Pueblos; nevertheless, they are basic social units among these Indians. Eggan (1950:299–300) reports as follows about the Western Pueblo lineage organization:

> The clan is the major grouping in western Pueblo thinking. It has a name, frequently a central residence known as *the* clan-house, relations with sacred symbols, often control of agricultural lands or other territories. Where the clan and the lineage coincide—as they do in perhaps half of the Hopi instances and undoubtedly elsewhere as well—there is no confusion, and either term may be used. But, where the clan is composed of multiple lineages, the distinction is important, since lineages within a clan may vary greatly in status and prestige. The specific mechanisms for inheritance and transmission normally reside in the lineage; the clan is normally the corporate group which holds ritual knowledge and economic goods in trust for future generations.
>
> It is probable that an equivalence of clan and lineage is the earlier pattern, if our reconstruction of Hopi development is reasonably correct and is found to hold for other villages, as well. But with the growth of populations and the widespread migrations of the thirteenth and fourteenth—and later—centuries, the development of multi-lineage clans was almost inevitable in the western Pueblos. Multiple-lineage clans are more stable and organize a larger population, other things being equal, than do single lineages. Where there are several lineages, one of them usually controls the major functions associated with the clan, and the others are subordinate; any tendency to specific allocations of clan functions among the various lineages is made difficult by the variations which occur over even a short period of time.

Additional remarks about the nature of the Western Pueblo lineage and clan are necessary to complete the above description. The lineage is the living and functional representation of a particular clan; its members are in intimate contact with one another and bound together by deep loyalties. Marriages remove the men to the various households of their wives, but they renew lineage ties frequently to visit with maternal relatives and attend to ritual duties. Women of the lineage never permanently leave the village and constantly interact fulfilling household and clan responsibilities. An older woman of one of the lineages is the head of the clan and her brother or maternal uncle usually performs the necessary rituals for the clan. Upon the death of the female head, the position goes to the next senior woman of the same household and lineage, but prominent members of the clan in the village may decide to designate as her successor a mature woman from another household and lineage. This is unlikely, however, for Pueblo custom tends to favor procedures deeply rooted in time and tradition. Among the Western Pueblos succession of important offices ordinarily remains within one household and lineage except where lineages have become extinct. The custom of having one household and/or lineage acting as the custodian of ritual paraphernalia and of providing the clan heads, both male and female, has tended to give a status ranking to lineages and clans. The village or town chief, an important official in all of these pueblos, although without the authority of his counterpart among the Eastern Pueblos, comes from a specific clan in most of the Western Pueblos: Bear clan, Hopi and Hano; Dogwood clan, Zuni; Antelope clan, Acoma, and perhaps Laguna (Eggan 1950:303).

Formerly, households of the lineage occupied a block of contiguous rooms, a pattern that has broken down in recent years, but the intimate bond of kinship remains even though the member households may be dispersed. Since each pueblo recognizes affiliation with other pueblo clans having the same name, lineages of equivalent clans in other pueblo villages are also considered lineal kinfolk and the ordinary clan relations are extended to members of such lineages. Clans are land-holding units, each one having lands set aside for the use of its members. The control of ceremonies and their ritual paraphernalia are in the keeping of certain lineages. Adopted children retain the clan of their mothers; in most cases, however, children are adopted by members of their own clan. Marriage between members of the same clan is forbidden, as is marriage with a member of an equivalent Pueblo clan. In addition, marriage is disapproved with a member of father's clan. Violations of these latter restrictions occur, however, especially in recent years; but the rule that forbids marriage with a member of one's own clan is rarely violated.

Ceremonial Organization

The clan or lineage, as we have noted, is the repository of ceremonial lore and ritual paraphernalia. Religious life is carried out separately by the Katcina cult and a series of religious sodalities or associations. The Katcina cult is tribal-wide in all of the Western Pueblos, joined by all children regardless of sex at ages six to ten at Hopi, Hano, Acoma, and Laguna, but restricted to males at Zuni. In all groups, the cult is associated with the *kivas*—the ceremonial structures which among all the Pueblos serve as theaters, dormitories for unmarried males, and men's workshops. The Katcina cult involves the representation of supernatural beings, vaguely considered to be ancestral spirits. These supernaturals are believed to have the power of bringing rain and general well-being to Pueblo communities if properly petitioned through ceremonies made as dramatic as possible and given cheerfully without ill feelings toward anyone or toward any aspect of the universe. There are many types of Katcina, some of animals and birds such as the owl, eagle, bear, and mountain sheep; others are identified by some characteristic aspect of their appearance: the Long-Beard Katcina, the Left-Handed Katcina, and so on; still others are called by the sounds they emit. Only men impersonate the Katcina in the ceremonies; women are not permitted to don such masks and costumes. Katcina dancers may be all of one kind, paired, or of mixed types. The number of dancers usually varies with the number of men in a particular kiva; among the Western Pueblos they typically range between twenty and thirty.

In addition to the Katcina cult, each of the Western Pueblos has a series of ceremonial associations. These consist of curing or medicine associations and associations for hunt, war, social control (clown), rain-making, and so forth. While men dominate Pueblo ceremonial life, there are a few ceremonial associations strictly for women. At Hopi, Hano, and Laguna ceremonial associations are clan "owned" and managed. At Zuni, they are under the control of a group of priests; some of the priests are associated with clans, but Zuni associations have greater independence than those of other Western Pueblos. At Acoma the curing or medicine associations play a dominant role, but are subordinate to the town chief and the Antelope clan. In all the Western Pueblos there is a close relationship between clans, the Katcina cult, associations, and ceremonies; this relationship is, however, most marked at Hopi, Hano, and Laguna.

Some Katcina and association rites occur at fixed times during the year; others may take place at a time specified by the leaders who control and manage the associations. These performances have both public and private (or secret) aspects. The private portion of a ceremony involves the periodic prayer retreats, the erection of an altar prior to a public ceremony, and the costuming of the dancers and participants. The public feature of the ceremony is held either in the village courtyard or in the kiva and is open to townspeople; at Zuni, Hopi, and Hano, most of these public performances are also open to view by whites, but not at Acoma and Laguna.

Generally, two initiations are imperative on all men and those women who wish to become deeply involved in the religious life of their pueblo. The first is induction into a kiva group or the Katcina cult; the second, either a mandatory assignment to a specific ceremonial association or the voluntary selection of one from among a number of alternative associations. Membership into a ceremonial association is by a "ceremonial father" at Hopi and Zuni, but ordinarily by vow during illness and subsequent recovery, or trespass into a sacred area set up by specific associations, at Hano, Acoma, and Laguna. In all the pueblos a ceremonial sponsor (a ceremonial "father" or "mother") guides the child through the initial phases of the initiation.

Ceremonies for rain are emphasized at Hopi; curing and rain-making rituals receive equal attention at Hano and Zuni; and at Acoma and Laguna curing ceremonies predominate. These emphases contrast rather dramatically from west to east. The rain-making purpose of ceremonial rites in the west gives way to a concern for attaining health and well-being in the east. In addition, among the Tanoans, there are governmental concerns and direct, nonmagical procedures employed in hunting and in warfare.

While unilineal kinship structures appear to be organized on the same structural principles among all the Western Pueblos, the emphases these structures receive in the different pueblos vary. At Hopi, Hano, and Laguna lineage and clan organizations are more involved in the social and ceremonial affairs of the respective villages than in the other Western Pueblos. At Zuni a high level of village integration has been achieved by vesting more power and authority in the priesthoods at the expense of lineage and/or clan leaders. The following observation by Eggan is pertinent here:

> With the greater emphasis on tribal as against clan organization, there is in Zuni a greater specialization in social and ceremonial control. The ultimate control of the village is in the keeping of a hierarchy of priesthoods who are responsible for community welfare. The Bow priesthood acts as an executive arm for this body in matters affecting the spiritual welfare of the group; the governor and his assistants take care of secular matters under the direction of the hierarchy. That this control is relatively efficient is evidenced by the degree of social and ceremonial integration

maintained in the face of all the modern influences toward disintegration and dismemberment (Eggan 1950:218).

Acoma has also achieved greater village integration by empowering the Antelope clan with centralized control of the village. The town chief comes from this clan and he and leaders of the clan exercise virtually absolute control over lineage and clan heads, the Katcina cult, and the ceremonial associations. Despite these differences, however, unilineal kinship structures play a much more important role in these villages than among the Eastern Pueblos.

THE EASTERN OR RIO GRANDE PUEBLOS

The Pueblos living in the villages along the banks of the Rio Grande or its tributaries speak two unrelated language stocks: (1) Keresan, more properly the Eastern Keresan, since Acoma and Laguna are also Keresan-speaking, and (2) Tanoan. The latter is again divided into Tiwa, Tewa, and the pueblo of Jemez (Towa). Formerly the Tanoan linguistic group also included the Piro, south of the Tiwa pueblos. The population map lists the individual pueblos and their language affiliations as well as population changes through the years. The Pueblo maps indicate successively the distribution of language groups at the time they were first contacted by Spanish explorers, after the Pueblo Revolt of 1680 (circa 1750), and at present.

As we have noted earlier, the sources of Rio Grande pueblo population is imperfectly known and the reports and statements about their derivation falls within the designation, "conjectural history" (compare Fox 1967:23–47). The following hypotheses are offered as another bit of carefully "reasoned conjectural history." The only virtue of these suggestions, perhaps, is that they are the last words on the subject as of this date; but there will be others!

San Felipe Pueblo—Rio Grande Keresan pueblo, forty miles south of Santa Fe, New Mexico.

Most anthropologists are agreed on a broad, general statement, such as the following: The Rio Grande region received a large influx of peoples shortly after A.D. 1000. The work of the archeologists is perhaps the strongest support for this suggestion (Mera 1934, 1940; Wendorf and Reed 1955; Wetherington 1968). There are, however, ethnological data to support the suggestion as well. Legends of the Pueblos all indicate migration into the area from former habitations outside of the Rio Grande Valley. In the ceremonies depicting the ancestral rain-making supernaturals, the Katcina, the songs sung in connection with these spirits derive them from outside of the area. Keresans believe that after death they become rain spirits and return to their original home in the West (White 1935:94, 114–115; 1942:210). The songs that accompany animal dances among the Rio Grande Pueblos also report the arrival of these animals from a long

Typical costuming of Rio Grande Pueblo Tablita ("Corn") dancers—Jemez Pueblo.

journey beginning in the ancestral home. The Indians, themselves, believe that formerly they lived far away, indicating a northern origin. Thus, while the Rio Grande Pueblos consider the area their home at present and believe that their ancestors have lived there for many centuries, they do not consider it their ancient homeland.

While there is general agreement that extensive settlement of the central and northern Rio Grande areas in New Mexico took place in the last 1000 years, there is no such agreement on the priority of arrival. Our suggestion is that the Tanoans preceded the Keresans into the Rio Grande area by several hundred years. If this suggestion is true, then it means that the Tanoan Pueblos made the initial adjustment to life in the Rio Grande Valley. Specifically, these Pueblos first experimented with large stream irrigation and adjusted their social and cultural institutions to cope with the demands of the new environment. If such adaptations were made initially by the Tanoans, then we would expect the Keresans as later arrivals to borrow whatever institutions might be considered adaptive to the new ecological area. But first let us present the evidence for our suggestion that the Tanoans arrived in the Rio Grande area before the Keresans: Linguistic diversity is generally attributed to long residence in a region and to the isolation of the population units with little or no contacts between the separated groups. The Tanoans fulfill both of these conditions. The Pueblos that speak, and spoke, Tanoan languages were spread out over a larger area than the Keresans; indeed, the Tanoan pueblos surround the Keresans on three sides—north, east, and south. The Keresan pueblos in the Rio Grande area appear like a wedge driven into the central Tanoan Pueblo-speaking area. The differences among the languages of the Tanoan group are not extreme, however, and would fit the general hypothesis that the major divergencies occurred in the Rio Grande area, at least if we follow the linguists who have worked extensively with classifying Tanoan languages (Trager 1967: 335–350; Whorf and Trager 1937:609–624). The Keresan languages, despite dialectical differences, are comparatively more uniform—a condition we would expect for a group which has remained over a period of 600 to 800 years in a limited geographical region with many opportunities for intimate contacts.

The hypothesis arguing for the priority of the Tanoans in the Rio Grande area and the suggestion that the major social structural features were borrowed by Keresans from Tanoans, we believe, are demonstrated in our discussion below of the socioceremonial patterns of the two Pueblo groups.

The Rio Grande Keresan Pueblos

The Eastern or Rio Grande Keresan Pueblos consist of the following: on the Rio Grande proper, Santa Ana (agricultural community), San Felipe, Santo Domingo, and Cochiti; and on the Jemez River, Zia and Santa Ana (ceremonial village). Jemez pueblo, although linguistically Tanoan, fits in with the Eastern Keresan Pueblos in terms of social and ceremonial structural patterns of organization (see maps for location of these pueblos).

These pueblos lived as neighbors for many years before the arrival of the Spaniards; for almost 400 years they also have been in close contact with Spanish-

Mexican culture, and for the last 100 years with Anglo-American culture. Despite the extensive mutual association of Keresan and Tanoan-speaking peoples—both of these groups with the European cultures involved—the social and ceremonial organizations of these two Pueblo groups have remained essentially distinct. Influences are apparent, but the systems have not merged and the important characteristics of each system have remained. Spanish-Mexican and Anglo-American influences have been strong, but the Rio Grande Pueblos have retained much of their indigenous social and ceremonial patterns, while fitting into an external system a significant amount of introduced elements, both material and nonmaterial.

THE KINSHIP SYSTEM

Keresan kinship terms are arranged in a pattern that suggest affinity with the general Western Pueblo system (Hopi, Hano, Zuni, Acoma, and Laguna). Eggan (1950:313) considers the Keresan kinship system as of the "western lineage type," while White (1942:139; 1962:193–196) suggests that it was originally of the Crow type, but changing. Fox (1957:32–47) has recently argued as to whether or not the Keresan kinship system has any relationship to the western lineage type or Crow type and whether or not it is changing to anything else. Fox may be right that the Keresan kinship system developed independently, yet it does bear undeniable resemblance to the Western Pueblo type described by Eggan (1950). The fact that both systems are fitted to a matrilineage or matriclan system may be the reason for the similarity. From the terms and kinship behavior, we see no reason why the system should not be considered of the western lineage type. There is, however, considerable evidence of "inconsistencies," whether or not one considered only the terms collected in the conventional method, or took into consideration the terms used in different social contexts as well. Moreover, the inconsistencies appear related or correspond to inconsistencies in kinship behavior as well. While the kinship terms may have been collected and analyzed by an ego-centered method, the Keresan specialists (Parsons, Hawley Ellis, Goldfrank, Lange, and Leslie White) also had opportunity to observe kinship behavior in various social situations. We believe that a number of the alternate uses of terms or of alternate behavior instead of being random and "inconsistent" are patterned and indicate a response to changes going on in other areas of the Keresan social structure. Specifically, we suggest that the kinship system adjusted to a lineage or clan system is changing because of the decreasing importance of the clan in religion and government. Evidence for the decline or "breakdown" of the clan comes from other data, although it is to be expected that such change would be registered in both the kinship terminology and kinship behavior. The following outline of the kinship system is provided to call attention to inconsistencies, more properly "changes," in both the terminology and kinship behavior. Later we will present our irrigation hypothesis to explain these changes.

TERMINOLOGY

Classificatory terminology is important in the system, as well as the use of separate terms (in most but not all cases) by men and women for the same relative. Inconsistencies appear in all areas that we believe can be explained, at least in part, on Tanoan influence and the resultant breakdown of clan importance. It is important here to remark that "Tanoan influence" does not mean that the Keresans took over the Tanoan kinship system or any portion of it. What we suggest is that the Tanoans (probably the Tewa) operated as a catalyst to produce the changes needed to adjust to the demands of a new ecological area.

To continue with our characterization of Keresan terminological structure: Ego distinguishes brother and sister; parallel and cross-cousins are classified as siblings in most of the groups.

Ego's own son is classified with brother's son, mother's sister's son's son, father's brother's son's son, and father's sister's son's son. Daughter terms parallel those for son in usage. Here some effort to equalize maternal and parental kin appear to be operating.

Grandparent-grandchild terms are reciprocals, suggestive of the Tewa system, although in the latter, as we will note, they are not true reciprocals; rather it is the application of one term to the senior relative and the addition of a diminutive suffix when the junior member is addressed. Grandparent-grandchild terms are used for grandparents, their siblings, and the children of anyone designated as "son" or "daughter."

Mother is classified with her sisters, father's brother's wives, and with father's

Traditional Keresan Pueblo woman's attire—Acoma Pueblo.

sisters. The grouping of mother with father's sisters is a departure from the Western Pueblo pattern and suggests again the tendency to equalize the relationship between maternal and paternal relatives.

Father is grouped with father's brother, father's sister's husband, and, in some groups, with mother's brother. The classification of father with mother's brother seems not too well established, but exists as an alternate pattern in Santa Ana, Santo Domingo, and Cochiti. The attempt to achieve a symmetrical arrangement is again apparent here.

The term for "mother's brother" is applied to mother's brothers generally, and at Zia a diminutive term for uncle is used for cross-cousins (Hawley 1950: 505). In some of the Keresan villages, notably at Santa Ana, two patterns are evident. Leslie White (1942a:159) characterizes these patterns for Santa Ana:

> We note that we have two patterns: (1) mother's brother is called "uncle" and his children "son" and "daughter," and (2) mother's brother is called "father" and his children are "brother" and "sister." We believe that the presence and use of these two patterns at Santa Ana today indicate a transition from one type of kinship system or pattern, to another. It is our considered opinion that the pattern in which mother's brother is called "uncle" and his children "son" and "daughter," which is characteristic of the Crow type of terminology, is the earlier of the two patterns. We believe that this pattern is breaking down and giving way to the pattern in which mother's brother is called "father" and his children "brother" and "sister."

A separate term for mother's brother, indicative of the role of this relative in the household is typical of the Western Pueblo terminological system. The alternate pattern suggests the loss of the specialized functions of mother's brother, as appears to be reflected in kinship behavior as well. Fox (1967:162–163) found the two patterns at Cochiti as well, and Lange (1957:389), reporting alternate kinship usages in Cochiti, attributes such inconsistencies to acculturative influences and the declining importance of the clans:

> Still another result of acculturative influences [nonsocial environmental influences as well] accompanying the decline in the clan structure has been the retraction of kinship terms referring to more distant relatives. Another shift, again reflecting the diminishing emphasis upon matrilineal clans and the corresponding elevation in the importance of patrilineal aspects, is the extension of terminology applicable to the mother's clan members to include those of the father's clan as well. . . . Finally, a characteristic most apparent at present and presumably absent or at least much less prominent in times past is the widespread confusion and disagreement regarding the proper application and range of inclusion of specific terms.

White, in his study of the Keresan Pueblo of Sia (Zia) in 1962, again, as in other Keresan pueblos, found a change in the kinship system from one pattern to another:

> As in the case of Santa Ana (White 1942a:159) and Acoma (Eggan, 1950:237–238; Mickey 1956), there appears definitely to be a trend from [the terminology of] the Crow type to a bilateral and generational system: father's sister is classed with mother and mother's sister; both maternal and paternal cross-cousins are called

"brother" and "sister" by some informants. Of the features of the Crow terminology, only the relationship between mother's brother and sister's son, m. sp., remains and even it is giving way in the usage of some informants. The terminology has undergone more change in ego's father's matrilineage than in his own.

The reasons for believing that the change is in the direction toward a bilateral system and away from Crow-type terminology, rather than the reverse, are: (1) Some of the earliest observations of kinship terminology among the Keres give terms of the Crow type rather than of bilateral system. (2) The change from a Crow terminology to one of bilateral type would be the result of a breakdown rather than of development, and the culture in general is tending to break down. (3) There are indications that the influence of clan and lineage organization upon kinship terminology, which would tend to produce Crow features, is diminishing. (4) The influence of Spanish usage has been in the direction of bilaterality (White 1962: 193–196).

The last sentence needs qualification. Spanish and American usage, as well as Tanoan influence (specifically Tewa) has been in the direction of bilaterality. It is not so much the influence of these alien societies and cultures, which is crucial in understanding the changes which are taking place, but the adjustment to a new ecological environment, particularly to irrigation farming, which favors a society managed by nonkinship units; hence the assumption of social, governmental, and ceremonial powers by the esoteric associations at the expense of lineage and/or clans.

We may summarize the evidence for changes we believe are reflected in the Keresan kinship system. It is not only the terminology that exhibits change, but kinship behavior does too. In addition, there is the shift of religious and governmental responsibilities from clan to medicine associations, evidence for which comes from data independent of kinship. Further, we have the archeological evidence of movement into the Rio Grande from areas that were obviously more arid. Hence the need to adapt to a new ecological region. Finally, the Keresan Pueblos have experienced more constant and prolonged contacts with sedentary, farming people, speaking different languages and possessing radically different kinship systems. Initial contact in the new environment was with Tanoans, resulting in intermarriages and considerable cultural exchange. Then came fairly intensive contact with Spanish civil and church authorities, the imposition of new cultural patterns, and prolonged and continuing contact with Hispanicized neighbors. All three groups influenced and reoriented the Keresan kinship system without displacing it. The inconsistencies evident in the Keresan kinship system we therefore propose are the result of this complex of influences.

KINSHIP BEHAVIOR

Although our data on kinship behavior among the Keresan pueblos are meagre, the materials show similarities to western pueblo patterns and also tendencies to equalize the relationship between maternal and paternal relatives; hence a shift away from the overriding importance of matrilineal kin among the Rio Grande Keresan pueblos. Matrilineal relatives do not receive the special attention, nor play the dominant role they do among the western Keresan pueblos of Laguna and Acoma or of the pueblos of Zuni and Hopi. Our description of kinship behavior also demonstrates that kinship behavior is consonant with terminology.

We may describe the behavior of kin in terms of the matrilineal, extended family which appears to be an important unit of Keresan social organization. Mother, mother's sisters, and mother's brothers are most important in the socialization of the individual. The child is reared within the context of the maternal kin and until he is married spends the greater part of his life with them. Father and father's relatives have different relations to Ego. They are concerned, particularly, that Ego is properly guided along the life cycle. One of father's sisters is especially important in this respect and sees to it that her niece or nephew is properly launched from one crisis period to another in his or her development.

The behavioral patterns sketched above show inconsistencies. In some households, notably at Cochiti, the father exercises disciplinary powers, while the mother's brother and father's brother are respected relatives but without specialized functions to Ego. In general, however, Keresan kinship behavior patterns follow basic western pueblo practices, that is, the greater importance of the maternal relatives, the importance of mother's brother, and the specialized functions of father's relatives, particularly of father's sister.

Another change is evident: The nuclear family appears to be emerging as the important social unit while the extended matrilineal family loses ground. This trend is noted for Cochiti by Lange:

> While the family may be correctly considered as the base of social organization, it is rivaled in many instances by the household. Reflecting the matrilineal clan system, Cochiti households have been traditionally matrilocal. However, with patrilineal moieties (kiva organizations) and Spanish and Anglo influences, this traditional dominance has been much less pronounced in recent decades. As of 1880, Bandelier (September 23, 1880) was told there were 60 to 70 *escaleras* at Cochiti. This term, translated literally as "ladders," referred to families in the sense of households, often including grandparents and grandchildren. . . .

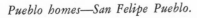

Pueblo homes—San Felipe Pueblo.

... Accounts of the clan are essentially unanimous in pointing out the declining significance of the clan structure at Cochiti. It is evident that as this decline has continued, the family [Lange means the conjugal or nuclear family] has become increasingly important. With a steadily-growing proportion of the Cochiti being educated away from the pueblo, finding employment away from the village, and marrying individuals who have no kinship affiliation which fits into the traditional structure of the tribe, it is not surprising that this change in emphasis has occurred (Lange 1959:367 and 373–374).

While modern pressures have undoubtedly reduced the family to its nuclear components from the former matrilineal and matrilocal extended unit, we suspect that the decline of clan importance occurred much earlier; in pre-Spanish times, we suggest. We will discuss Keresan clan breakdown below and in our summary of Pueblo social and cultural institutions.

KERESAN CLANS

The former importance of the Keresan clan in government, control of property, religion, and ceremonies is evident in a comparative analysis. For the most part these functions have been assumed by the so-called medicine associations (see below), whose membership cuts across the pueblo. Nevertheless, there are still hints of clan roles and functions. At present, Keresan clans are most typically concerned with marriage control; but in specific villages, there are indications of other responsibilities. Thus, in Acoma and Zia, the *cacique* (the village chief, a word of Arawakan origin applied by Spaniards to New World native religious and political leaders) must come from a specific clan. In these pueblos and at Laguna, as well, certain ceremonies are in the possession of clans. According to Parsons (1923:212–214):

Within the memory of living persons, Laguna clans had heads who owned fetishes, who settled disputes between members who successively went into a series of summer retreats for rain, assisted the medicine societies at the winter solstice ceremony and performed certain ceremonies in connection with supernatural beings associated with clans.

Other Keresan pueblos, too, appear to have retained clan functions that are religious in character. Thus, at Santa Ana, White (1942a:155) discovered that the Siyana clan was the "father" of a group of Shiwana or katcina dancers; while at Zia, certain clans conduct initiation ceremonies and the leaders of certain religious societies must come from particular clans (Hawley 1950b:506–507). Only exogamy remains a consistent clan function today, but there are enough vestigial clan responsibilities in Keresan pueblos to suggest that the clan at one time possessed corporate characteristics as among the Hopi. Keresan clans are no longer important governmental and religious units today and almost all of such functions have been taken over by the "medicine associations." The result of these changes has been the consolidation of authority in a small powerful group of officers who coordinate all communal projects and give the village a centralized direction.

The following statement about Santa Ana clans by Leslie White (1942a:

157) would seem to apply to the Eastern or Rio Grande Keresans generally (with the possible exception of Zia):

> Clans of Santa Ana are matrilineal, exogamous, "nontotemic," kinship groups. They have nothing to do with ceremonialism (except the one instance of the *Siyana* clan [see above]), nothing to do with officers or societies of the pueblo. There are no clan properties, either in land or in houses. The functions of the clan are: (1) the classification of relatives, (2) the regulation of marriage (in so far as clan exogamy operates), and (3) a certain degree of cooperation, solidarity, sharing of experience, among clansmen. Thus, the clan is a kinship group almost exclusively; its functions in the fields of religion and ceremonialism, and in pueblo political or ceremonial organization, are virtually nonexistent.

KERESAN CEREMONIAL AND SOCIOPOLITICAL ORGANIZATION

The basic concerns or anxieties which the Keresans face and attempt to resolve are the same among all the Pueblos (see p. 133). The principal cults and associations and the rituals have been built around these concerns. In the development of these institutions there has been obvious interpueblo borrowing for the organizations are remarkably similar. The concerns and major organizations to deal with them are coupled in the following list: (1) coordination of communal activities—medicine associations; (2) weather control, primarily the production of rainfall—Katcina cult; (3) illness—specifically medicine associations, but membership in cults and associations generally; (4) warfare—war association; (5) maintenance of flora and fauna—hunt association and fertility rites of *koshare* and *kwirena* (clown associations); (6) village harmony—*koshare* and *kwirena* (clown associations). While it is evident among the Keresans and in most of the pueblos that a specific organization—an association or sodality—was developed to deal with a pressing anxiety, for major concerns one or more organizations and virtually all the rituals will attempt to control, minimize or dissipate the fear, suffering or unhappiness arising from that source. Thus, plant, animal, and human fertility is an objective of all ceremonies because fertility is so basic to Pueblo culture.

We may restate briefly the basic principles of Pueblo world view and its underlying concepts in order to understand the Pueblo way of resolving conflict and trouble. To the traditional Pueblo Indian, life is interrelated, balanced, and interdependent. Man is a partner with nature; the two bear a reciprocal relationship. Man performs rites and ceremonies and nature responds with the essentials of life, withholding the bad. Ceremonies must be performed joyfully and faithfully; nature will respond in kind. Man alone can disrupt universal equilibrium by thought, word or deed. The consequences of imbalance are illness, disasters, drought —any misfortune. Rites and ceremonies properly performed keep the seasons moving, allow the sun to rise and set properly, bring rain and snow, quell the winds, and insure a well-ordered physical environment and society.

Special motifs or themes may be accentuated in different pueblos or groups of pueblos. Weather control, for example, pervades the institutions and ceremonies of the Western Pueblos. The Keresan pueblos are less concerned about this problem—but more than their rather pragmatic Tanoan neighbors. We have suggested that the arid, inhospitable environment of the Western Pueblos may account for this all-encompassing preoccupation with the weather. Dorothy Eggan's characterization of the Hopi country helps us to understand why these Indians have made weather control the dominant theme of their culture:

> [The Hopi country] is a land of violent moods, of eternal thirst and sudden devastating rains, of searing heat and slow, aching cold. . . .
> Here the seasons marched by with scant regard for man's trampled ego. The Hopi could only sit and wait while sandstorms cut to ruin the young plants that meant "life for the people." Through long hot summer afternoons they daily scanned the sky, where thunderheads piled high in promise and were dispersed by "bad winds." When at last the rain fell, it often came in destructive torrents which gutted the fields and drained away into arroyos. Of course these sedentary people, lacking even the relief through action with which their nomadic foes responded to these conditions, worked out a religion resigned to control the unappeasable elements . . . (Eggan 1953:278).

In the Rio Grande area where practical and technological efforts may be used with a high degree of success in reaping a good harvest, magical efforts have been turned to another basic anxiety: illness. Few people deal with illness pragmatically; magical rites pervade every act that deals with this anxiety. Among the Rio Grande Keresans, institutions and rituals for curing became the focal point of their religious preoccupation. Most Keresan pueblos have two or more curing or medicine associations. In some pueblos there are two or more orders in each association, the medicine men of these orders being specialists empowered to treat only specific kinds of illnesses. It is important to point out that Keresan medicine associations do not only cure but have other functions as well. This is clear from White's statement about Keresan medicine associations:

> In 1928, after a relatively brief study of the Keres, I wrote: ". . . [the] chief function [of the medicine societies] is the curing of disease," [Comparative Study of Keresan Medicine Societies, p. 604; see also pp. 617–619]. Other students of the pueblos have sometimes taken the same view. I am now convinced that this statement is not warranted. The medicine societies have numerous and important ceremonies whose function is to bring rain, control the sun, the seasons, and the weather. These ceremonies are communal in character; all of the curing ceremonies except the communal purge of the pueblo are primarily private affairs. The question of the principal function of medicine societies has been discussed by the writer with a number of good Keresan informants who unhesitatingly placed rain-making (control of sun, etc.) before the curing of disease (White 1942a:124, footnote 62).

White's statement indicates the importance of the magical control of weather, but equally emphasized is the communal nature of the ceremonies performed by the medicine associations. Weather control, that is, rain, control of sun, the seasons, and so forth is a communal or governmental function among all the pueblos—east or west. The social units or agencies responsible for this function change, however. In the west, lineage and clan heads are charged with these responsibilities; among the Tanoans they are tasks handled by special "cosmological" associations. The Tewa have two such associations, one in each moiety—a "Summer" and "Winter" moiety association, each forming a small nucleus of the total moiety membership. In these pueblos, the head of each moiety association governs for half a year and then transfers governing responsibilities for the pueblo to the other moiety chief. Among the Tiwa, kiva associations assume these "controlling" or "governmental" responsibilities.

We suggest that lineages and/or clans also formerly controlled communal activities among the Keresan, both religious and secular. It is our belief that as the demands of an incipient irrigation society made its impression on Keresan pueblos, medicine associations took over responsibility for communal tasks. This may have happened by equating Keresan medicine associations with the special cosmological associations of the Tewa moieties. These Tewa associations also have curing functions, but such functions are marginal to the communal and governing functions. In time, we propose Keresan pueblos became highly centralized communities, probably even more highly integrated than Tewa pueblos.

Within the ceremonial sphere, the greater preoccupation of the Keresans with rain-making ceremonies appears to indicate a recent migration from a region where growing and maturing of crops depended primarily or wholly on the exigencies of the weather. The Katcina cult, which is strongly represented among the Keresans, is concerned almost exclusively with rainmaking functions. Even the important Keresan medicine associations have the additional function of inducing rainfall. Such preoccupations and emphases upon institutions to deal with the environment appear justified in an area where insufficient rainfall and the absence of an adequate technology often prevent a bountiful harvest. They are incongruous, however, in an environment where more direct efforts could be used to insure the maturing of planted crops, namely through irrigation. The observations of Wittfogel and Goldfrank (1943:26) seem appropriate:

> Even in a saturated waterwork society, magic may be used to support man's action, but the main effort is directed toward the construction of canals, dikes, and sluices. The deficient waterwork society depends more fervently upon magic for what it cannot achieve technically. The Havasupai, northern neighbors of the Hopi, enjoy an adequate water supply. They declare realistically, "We have a creek to irrigate with: the Hopi plant prayer plumes in their fields because they have none and have to pray for rain all the time" (The quotation is from Spier 1928:286).

But customs relevant for events in the past often linger on in the present even though they no longer serve a direct purpose. If it were possible to analyze the "weather control" aspect of Keresan ceremonies in detail, the vestigial character of the weather control function may become obvious. Indeed, we suspect that the term "weather control" as a designation for one of the functions of Keresan medicine associations more properly refers to "keeping the universe moving"—the general and typical Pueblo concept of relatedness in the universe and reciprocity between man and nature. A shift has taken place in the medicine associations, a change from specific functions to one of coordinating communal tasks. In a number of Keresan pueblos this coordinating role of the principle medicine associations is shared with the clown associations, particularly with Koshare and Kwirena (Goldfrank 1927:37ff; Lange 1959:298; White 1935:54, and footnote 43).

As the directors or coordinators of communal tasks, the members of the medicine associations attempt to foster good relations among all the villagers. White comments about the role of medicine men:

> The medicine societies, or perhaps it would be better to say medicine men, have another important function in pueblo life: that of maintaining morale and of preserving "old time ways." In a purely unofficial way the medicine men do much to foster and sustain a certain esprit de corps in the pueblo. Because of their position and status as medicine men they exercise a great deal of influence over other people. And the medicine men are, apparently, almost without exception, ardent champions of the old ways, the ancient customs, and deplore modern innovations. They thus exert a powerful influence in the pueblo on the side of conservatism if not of reaction (White 1942:124).

Keresan medicine men who coordinate communal activities are priests, just like their counterparts among other Rio Grande pueblos. White sees the Pueblos as a kind of embryo of feudal society:

> In the medicine men we see the beginnings of a full-fledged priesthood. Although we may justly speak of the pueblos as primarily democratic, we may see among them in embryo a feudal system which we find almost fully developed among their neighbors to the south, the Aztecs. . . . The culture of the pueblos is significant . . . in that it has preserved the essentially free and democratic character of the simpler societies, but reveals in embryo the characteristics of a feudal society (White 1942:187).

White calls attention to the stratified nature of Aztec society: a ruling class, priests, a professional warrior class, commoners, and landless serfs. He reports that the Keresan pueblos had the germ of a ruling class in the medicine men, war priests, and a warrior's association. The Keresans did not, however, have hereditary offices, nor was land owned by a special group but by the people in general; the resources of the land were generally available to all. Yet, as we will note later on, despotic rule by the religious-political hierarchy did take place in virtually all the pueblos and across the years some Indians lost houses, property and land, and were evicted from their pueblos. Thus, considerable power was held by a central authority— the medicine men and war priests.

KERESAN CEREMONIAL UNITS

Keresan ceremonial organizations (see Table 3), methods of recruitment, and the primary functions of these groups are discussed below:

Medicine Associations

Keresan medicine associations recruit as follows: (1) by vow during illness and subsequent recovery (the vow may be made by the prospective member or he may have been "given" to the association by his parents); (2) by trespass, that is by entering, either purposely or accidentally a sacred area set or defined by the association when the latter is performing a ceremony; (3) medicine associations may also be joined voluntarily, although this method was apparently not employed often. Membership in Keresan medicine associations is small. White (1935:63) believed that these associations had the right to reject applicants unless they fulfilled the rigid standards set by the associations and as a consequence restricted membership. Lange (1959:257) found that Cochiti medicine associations typically contained no more than two or three members.

The *cacique*, or village chief, and his assistants in the Keresan pueblos are invariably medicine men. The Flint medicine association ordinarily provides the *cacique*, but in most villages he is also a member of the Koshare clown association. Thus, the clown and medicine associations are closely allied in forming the sociopolitical and ceremonial authority structure of the Keresan pueblos. This group of priests, and formerly with the help of the war association priests, coordinate and manage the communal enterprises of the pueblo.

Dual Division or Moiety Organization

The dual divisions of the Rio Grande Keresan pueblos are associated with two kivas. Every one in the village is a member of one of the divisions. Kiva or moiety affiliation is not along kin lines, except at Santa Ana where of nine clans in the pueblo, six are affiliated with the Squash Kiva and three with Turquoise Kiva (White 1942a:142). Zia's dual organization is also associated with the two kivas, but in this pueblo the basis of membership in the two divisions is directional and in terms of residence. "Those who live north of an imaginary east-and-west line, drawn through the village between the north and south plazas, belong to the Wren kiva; those who live south of this line belong to Turquoise" (White 1962:183). Zia's dual division is like Taos and Picuris where north and south side residential units form one kind of a dual division. The Tewa who appear to have made dual divisions a central feature of their ceremonial organization also have a north and south side division. This binary cut divides and groups a Tewa pueblo's population into a different set than the division into summer and winter people (Ortiz 1965).

Keresan dual organizations, like Tanoan ones, are properly ceremonial groupings rather than kinship organizations, but there are other important differences in the dual organizations of the two groups of pueblos which we will discuss in the next section. Lange's description of Cochiti pueblo moiety organization is generally valid for Keresans with the exception of Santa Ana pueblo, as noted above:

> . . . present-day clans are represented in both kivas, and if kiva membership was ever strictly endogamous, it must have been quite some time ago. A person does receive his kiva designation from his father, and a wife normally joins the kiva of her husband if she is not already a member, but present-day kiva membership can hardly be compared with clan membership. Unlike a clan affiliation, a kiva membership can be shifted at virtually any time. Permission to change must be obtained from the two kiva heads and the war captains, but since there is no record of such a request's being refused, it can be seen that kiva affiliation is flexible. Hence more and more emphasis is being put upon the ceremonial aspects, at the expense of kinship or social considerations (Lange 1959:309–310).

The Katcina Cult

Some notion of a cult of supernatural beings is found among all the pueblos. The cult is most complex among the Western Pueblos and secondarily among the Rio Grande Keresans. In these pueblos these supernatural beings are represented by elaborately costumed and masked dancers in ceremonials given at specific times during the year. The cult is less important among the Tewa and Katcina supernaturals are not impersonated in the Tiwa pueblos, except at Isleta where the cult was introduced by Laguna ceremonial refugees in the late nineteenth century. Among the Keresans, the mythical home of the Katcina supernaturals are said to be in the West, at a place called Wenima. The following statements by White (1962:236) regarding the origin of Zia Katcina dances and ceremonies would probably be acceptable to most Keresans:

> In the mythical past, when the people were still living at White House, the katsina used to come to the pueblo in person to dance, but because of some incident, . . . they no longer come in person. The people were told, however, that they might impersonate the katsina by wearing masks and that the katsina would then come in spirit. This is how the masked dances and ceremonies originated.

Everywhere among the pueblos, small children are led to believe that the Katcina are real supernatural beings. In some pueblos this deception is extended to women; indeed, in all pueblos women have very little to do with the cult and are usually excluded from membership. The cult then is essentially a men's organization. Rain and fertility are the functions associated with the cult, although Katcina ceremonies are believed to bring about general well-being to the pueblo as well.

The word "Katcina" is a close approximation of the Keresan and Hopi designation for these supernaturals. The Keresan Pueblos also use an alternative term, "Shiwana," and the other Pueblos have other names, but all recognize the term, "Katcina." Rio Grande Pueblo Indians are very secretive about the cult and masked rites and may deny that they exist. Katcina ceremonies are closely guarded; only those Pueblo Indians who know and revere the Katcina may see them. Hispanos, Anglos, and even Indians from other tribes are barred from attending the rites which are held in secluded places away from the village, in the plaza or in the kiva at night. The Western Pueblos do not guard Katcina ceremonies like the Rio Grande Pueblos. Laguna, Acoma, and Zuni prohibit Hispanos from viewing the public performances of masked dancers, but Hano and the Hopi villages admit all visitors to Katcina ceremonies. The concern of the Eastern Pueblos to protect and guard the identity of the cult and its rites is obviously a carryover from the past. Spanish attempts to suppress Pueblo Indian religion focused on the masked rites and the repressive acts of United States government officials to Pueblo ceremonial rites during the second and third decades of this century also singled out Katcina activities. The Western Pueblos, because of distance and isolation from Spanish and Anglo population centers, did not experience the full brunt of the repressive measures. It is understandable, therefore, that the Rio Grande Pueblos are more cautious in guarding ceremonial activities, particularly the esoteric rites of the Katcina cult than the pueblos to the west.

In most of the Keresan pueblos, the Katcina cult is associated with the kivas as a dual organization. Zia and Santa Ana pueblos depart from this pattern, however. In Zia, some seven medicine associations, including one of the clown associations have masks and each may conduct its own ceremony. Participants are drawn from males who are inducted into the cult on a village-wide basis. Santa Ana's Katcina cult is divided into five groups, each managed by a medicine association. In all the Keresan pueblos medicine associations and the clown organizations (Koshare and Kwirena) control and manage the cult and its activities. The *cacique* and his assistants (who are associated with the mythical war gods) take prominent leadership roles in Katcina ceremonies. Among the Keresans the *cacique*'s assistants are designated by reference to the origin myth as the war gods—Masewi and Oyoyewi, who are considered older and younger brothers, respectively.

Katcina ceremonies are undoubtedly the most spectacular and colorful of Pueblo ceremonies. Whereas some deviation in staging, dressing and costuming is permitted in other types of Pueblo dances and performances, the Pueblos observe strict attention to detail in Katcina performances. While Zuni and Hopi masks may outnumber Keresan ones in sheer quantity, it is doubtful that the masks of these pueblos are more cleverly executed or more colorful than Keresan masks. White (1962:238–249) provides information on Zia masks and thirty drawings of ingeniously designed masks, while Lange (1959:470–508) has sketches and detailed information on more than fifty Cochiti masks which are equally elaborate. It is remarkable that, despite periodic destruction of Katcina masks and paraphernalia during Spanish times and attempts by both Spanish and, later, American government authorities to suppress the cult and its activities, the organization persists today and appears to be strong and meaningful to the Pueblos.

Associations with Special Functions

In addition to the medicine associations, the dual division organizations, and the Katcina cult, the Keresan pueblos have other associations with special functions. The clown associations—Koshare and Kwirena—have already been noted. These organizations are closely associated with the medicine associations and its members assist the *cacique* and his assistants in the management and conduct of communal activities. Recruitment, as with other associations, is by dedication, vow, or trespass. The first two means of entering a society both involve cure from a serious illness before joining. Trespass or trapping involves walking into a sacred area (either by design or accident) set off by the association in its regular meeting room, kiva, or pueblo courtyard. Membership is open to both males and females. In all associations open to both sexes, however, men take the prominent roles; women members serve in the capacity of preparing and carrying food to members. They rarely participate in the prayer retreats and in the semipublic dances or other rites conducted by the association. The clown organizations, beyond their roles as coordinators of communal projects, also perform social control functions. Deviant behavior of the pueblo in general or of specific individuals is brought to the attention of townspeople by public ridicule at the time of communal activities. Clowns everywhere, of course, serve the function of comic relief: Pueblo clown activity can be hilariously funny. Undoubtedly too, townspeople find release of emotions by watching clowns perform acts denied them by Pueblo mores or authorities. Clowns may also, at times, perform the work of the pueblo gestapo by exposing individuals suspected of discrediting Pueblo culture or by drawing attention to individuals who actually defy the authority of the village. This latter activity falls more properly within the domain of the *cacique*'s assistants (often called "war captains"); but they may be assisted by the clown organization. Virtually in all the Rio Grande pueblos the clown organization is a member of the authority system.

THE WARRIORS' ASSOCIATION The prominence of the warriors' association among the Pueblos has declined with the cessation of warfare; although, in some pueblos, the association has remained an important organization with modified functions. In the Keresan pueblos the real warriors' association known as Opi is now extinct, but there is still considerable knowledge about the organization in the individual pueblos (see White 1932a, 1932b, 1935, 1942, 1962; Lange 1959). Membership in the past was restricted to men who had either killed or participated in the killing and taking of an enemy scalp. At Zia only a man who had killed an enemy warrior and taken his scalp could become a member. White (1965:176) reports that the Zia Warriors' Association ought properly to be called a "scalptakers" association since the taking of a scalp was essential for membership. Although the warriors' association has been extinct for some time, in three of the Keresan pueblos—Zia, Santa Ana, and Cochiti—men may become Opi by killing a bear or lion, and at Santa Ana by killing an eagle as well. White (1942:177) suggests that the "animal 'Opi' have been instituted to take the place of man killers and scalpers." It thus seems that with the passing of warfare as a constant and demanding activity, the association has sought another method of recruiting members and does not require, in these pueblos, a scalp as the fee for membership.

There is no evidence of a women's scalp association as a companion organization to the men's warriors' association among the Keresan pueblos. Such organizations occur among the Tewa and at Isleta, where women members "feed" or "fed" the pueblo's store of enemy scalps by sprinkling corn meal and pollen, and by otherwise caring for them. The women's scalp association held its own retreats and conducted separate ceremonies periodically. Somewhat closer to nomadic Indian enemies—especially the Comanches—the Tanoan Pueblos may have elaborated the war theme more than the Keresans and Western Pueblos generally.

The extent to which Pueblo warfare was tied in with Spanish attempts to control the raiding and plundering of New Mexico settlements by nomadic tribes was not realized until recently. The discovery and translation of Spanish documents dealing with the eighteenth century reveal the large number of auxiliary Pueblo warriors who served under overall Spanish control, but who were led by their own Captains of War. The following quotation from Jones (1966:176 and 178) indicates the intricate partnership the Pueblos has established with Spanish authorities and settlers:

> Pueblo Indian auxiliaries performed a major role in the Spanish reconquest and pacification of New Mexico in the late seventeenth and most of the eighteenth century. As the constant allies of the Spaniards, these loyal mercenaries contributed to the defense of the province in many ways. They served repeatedly on campaigns against the hostile tribes which surrounded the province. Also, they accompanied missionaries and Spanish officials on expeditions to aboriginal groups not yet con-

verted to the Iberian way of life. They served as interpreters and informants, demonstrating both their knowledge of Castilian and their fidelity to the Europeans. In addition, they contributed to the sustenance of campaign forces, providing food, horses, and other livestock as needed. . . . This constructive contribution of the Pueblos has largely been ignored by historians and the general public. Instead, interest has been devoted to the destructive acts of the Pueblos in overcoming the Spaniards during the great rebellion of 1680. The loyalty, courage, constancy, and organizational ability of the Pueblo auxiliaries in the century following the reconquest are more notable aspects of their character, however, than their destructive tendencies in the expulsion of the Spaniards. Indeed, their aid was invaluable to the Spanish soldiers and settlers of the eighteenth century, and was a positive contribution to the defense and pacification of New Mexico.

Spanish authorities permitted the Indians to adjust or otherwise organize their military units in keeping with traditional Pueblo organizations, customs, and beliefs. They set up quotas of warriors for each village, but pueblo authorities were to pick their own commanders or "war captains." Pueblo mythology already sanctioned the warrior roles of the *cacique's* assistants, the "war gods," and these became the *capitánes de la guerra* in virtually all pueblos. Some Spanish authorities were disturbed by the rather brutal and gory behavior of Pueblo warriors, particularly the practice of painting themselves before encountering the enemy, the taking of enemy scalps, and the scalp dances following the return of a successful war party. The Pueblos were such superb warriors, however, that these practices were tolerated, although they were never fully condoned (Jones 1966:87–90; Adams and Chavez 1956:257–258).

The warriors' association must have antedated the time of extensive warfare with nomadic Indians, but recruitment of members was undoubtedly facilitated and the popularity of the organization enhanced during Spanish times. It is clear that the association was an extremely important part of the social and ceremonial organization of all the Rio Grande Pueblos. War rituals were especially highlighted among the Tanoans, where we have noted that a Women's Scalp Association and a Men's Warriors' Association exist or existed until recently (see also Adams and Chavez 1956:258; Dozier 1961:143). While the association is now extinct among the Keresan pueblos, the members of the organization were formerly a part of the sociopolitical and religious hierarchy. At Cochiti the Warriors' Association chief stood second in the priestly hierarchy, subordinate only to the *cacique* (Dumarest 1919:198–199; Goldfrank 1927:38–49; Lange 1959:276–277). In the Keresan pueblos the position of the war chief and his functions have been absorbed by the *cacique*. The Flint medicine association, the group of which the *cacique* is usually a member, keeps the scalps and supervises the ceremonies formerly performed by the Opi or "Scalptakers" (Warriors') Association (White 1935:60, 1962:177; Lange 1959:277).

THE HUNTERS' ASSOCIATION Wild game, animals, and fowl were formerly an important part of Pueblo life. As we have noted, when first contacted by Spanish exploratory expeditions, large numbers of turkeys were kept in the villages. In addition, the Pueblos also kept a few captive eagles, parrots, and macaws (still to be found in some pueblos today) for their feathers. Turkeys, of course, supplied both meat and feathers. Large game animals such as deer, antelope, and buffalo, furnished a considerable portion of the food supply in the old days. These animals also provided hides and skins for robes, ceremonial paraphernalia, and much of the wearing apparel. In the past, the bow and arrow, the lance, and for smaller game, the throwing stick were the only weapons used; but in recent years, firearms have been added. Pueblo Indians occasionally hunted as individuals, especially in the quest for larger game animals. The hunting of smaller game was, however, a communal activity. Communal hunts were carried out under the direction of the war captains, the assistants or executives of the *cacique*, the living counterparts of the mythological "war gods."

The importance of game animals and fowl among the Pueblos is also evident by a hunters' association, still active in most of the pueblos, by a host of ceremonies and a rich mythology. In all of the pueblos, the hunters' organization is associated symbolically with the mountain lion, and in some of the pueblos the association itself is designated by the actual or ceremonial name applied to this animal. The Pueblos have special names, used only in a ceremonial context, for ritually important birds and animals. In all the pueblos, coyote, eagle, bear, and lion are accorded special attention; all are regarded in a ritual context as essentially human. As among southwestern Indian tribes, generally, the coyote is a trickster and is a popular figure in the mythology. Eagles are revered for their swiftness, flight endurance, and their penetration of tremendous heights. Their feathers are probably the most prized and the most ritually important. The bear is the special curing companion of the medicine man and the skin of the forelegs made into a kind of glove is used in curing ritual. Finally, the lion is thought to possess special magical powers in attracting game animals and fowl as perhaps the most successful of the predatory animals. Animal dances depicting the game animals used for food—buffalo, deer, and antelope—are an important part of Pueblo ceremonialism. Just as Katcina dances are believed to induce rain, so the game animal dances are believed to bring about an increase in these animals and also to enhance the skills of man to acquire them. There is a rich mythology of hunting, the essence of which is expressed in the following quotation from White:

> Certain animals are designed to be used by man; these are the game animals. Other animals live by "killing their food" [the predators]; they are the ones who "have the power" to kill the game animals. If human beings wish to be successful hunters, they must secure power from the beasts of prey. The Caiyaik, the hunting shamans [the Keresan Hunters' Association], are the only ones who can do this. They are able to secure power from the (supernatural) animal hunters [like the bear, eagle, mountain lion] because they "know how" (i.e., possess the secrets which were given to them in the beginning and have been handed down since that time), and because they have the necessary paraphernalia. It is the business of the Caiyaik to secure power from the spirit hunters and bestow it upon Indian hunters, or otherwise employ it so that game may be secured (White 1942:283).

The hunters' association's head is a priest, as are the heads of other Pueblo ceremonial associations. As a priest, his functions are to pray for the success of all hunting ventures, either those of individual hunters or communal hunts. The role of recruiting hunters, directing their hunting activities, dividing and distributing the kill—all of this falls within the province of the war captains and their assistants who, as executive officers of the priests, carry out their orders. Priests do not engage in the actual supervision of townspeople; their responsibilities are sacred and involve the manipulation of supernatural power by the observation of traditional formulae and rites. The private activities of the hunters' association and the public rites (such as animal dances), which they order to be performed, result in the magical increase of game and insure the success of individual and communal hunts.

Membership in the Keresan Hunters' Association is open only to men. Although it is not clear who may join, it may be ventured that men who have been cured of an illness or accident received while on the hunt form most of the association's membership. Some may have joined by trespassing (trapping), which is another method of recruiting members (compare White 1962:171–173). These methods, along with the dedication of a child by parents or by other close relatives, are the usual ways of joining Keresan ceremonial associations. Actually these procedures are the same among the Tanoans as well, except of course for joining the warriors' association.

Eagle dance—Cochiti Pueblo, Rio Grande Keresan pueblo.

In concluding our Keresan section, we may point out some of the important aspects of Keresan social and ceremonial organization. Loss of clan functions appears to be the most important characteristic of Keresan social organization. Only exogamy remains a consistent clan function today, but there are enough vestigial clan responsibilities in Keresan pueblos to suggest that the clan at one time possessed corporate characteristics like the Hopi. Keresan clans are no longer important governmental and religious units today; almost all such functions have been taken over by the medicine associations. The result of these changes has been the consolidation of authority in a small, powerful group of officers who coordinate all communal projects and give the village a centralized direction.

Keresan ceremonial organization reveals that, whereas the Katcina cult is important, it does not hold the crucial position the cult maintains among the Western Pueblos of Zuni and Hopi. Actually within the Keresan area itself it is an organization of far greater importance at Acoma, where environmental conditions are more like the west. Medicine associations appear, indeed, to be the strongest institutions in Keresan society; but while we feel that the curing of disease and rites of exorcism originally were the main functions of these associations, among the Rio Grande Keresans, the medicine associations have assumed governmental and other ceremonial functions as well. More precisely, one or two medicine associations have become more important and the one to which the town chief or *cacique* must belong appears to be the most important.

The Tanoan Pueblos

The Tanoan Pueblos represent three linguistic families: Tiwa, Tewa, and Towa. Taos, the most northern and eastern pueblo, is Tiwa; a few miles south of Taos is Picuris. Both of these pueblos are members of the northern branch of the Tiwa language family. The southern branch of Tiwa is also represented by two pueblos: Sandia, about twelve miles north of Albuquerque, and Isleta, about the same distance south. There is only one Towa pueblo, Jemez, on the border of the tributary to the Rio Grande which bears its name, Jemez. Between Santa Fe and Picuris are the Tewa pueblos: Tesuque, Nambe, Pojoaque, San Ildefonso, Santa Clara, and San Juan (see Map 9).

While the individual pueblos and the linguistic subgroups show considerable variation in details, there is a basic similarity in the overall pattern of Tanoan political and ceremonial organization. Tanoan pueblos revolve around the same basic concerns as the other pueblos: weather control, curing, warfare, the propitiation and control of wild game animals and fowl, and the maintenance

San Juan Pueblo—Tewa-speaking pueblo, about twenty-five miles north of Santa Fe, New Mexico.

of intrapueblo harmony. While these basic concerns also occupy Keresans, there is a difference in emphasis and in the approach toward the minimization of anxieties and difficulties which ensue from these concerns. Ceremonial life is richer among Keresans. Pueblo concerns are more likely to be treated and resolved by magical practices in Keresan pueblos; Tanoans, on the other hand, deal more directly with these concerns; and whereas magical rites are not absent, they are frequently subordinated to secular activity. As we have noted, Jemez, although linguistically Tanoan, is closer to the Keresan pueblos in its patterns of social organization. This pueblo is thus included in the description of Keresan pueblos and excluded in the description which follows.

Generally, in concepts, attitudes, dedication to traditional customs, and in a host of other things, Pueblo society and culture from Taos to Hopi are remarkably similar. For this reason, much that has been presented will not be repeated. The

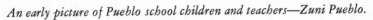

An early picture of Pueblo school children and teachers—Zuni Pueblo.

foregoing presentation of Tanoan social and cultural characteristics is thus given in abbreviated form, noting differences rather than similarities.

The Tanoan Kinship System

Tanoan kinship terms are descriptive and thoroughly bilateral. Parallel and cross-cousins are treated similarly, either raised one generation or lowered one, depending on whether they are older or younger than Ego. In Ego's generation and below, sex distinctions are not indicated. Reciprocals are employed with various sets of relatives in virtually all Tanoan pueblos, but are particularly characteristic of the Tewa. Jemez is an exception to many of these generalizations, as also to other features of social and ceremonial organization (see Parsons 1925; Ellis 1953).

Behavior of kin appears to reflect terminology rather faithfully. The basic social and economic unit of the Tanoan Pueblos before recent economic changes was the bilateral extended family—a kind of minimal descent group. The size of this unit is variable; at Taos and Picuris the number of individuals in the unit may include only members of the nuclear family. The unit in its most extended form, as among the Tewa, comprises a man and his wife, one or more married daughters and their husbands, and all unmarried sons and daughters of the married members of the household. Some daughters of the old couple and their children may align themselves with the households of their husbands, and occasionally one or more sons of the old couple may join his wife's extended household. Initially a newly married couple may shift household allegiances; but once mutual work, food-sharing, and visiting patterns are established, the bilateral kin group takes on remarkable cohesiveness. Generally changes in household affiliation or the beginning of a new household arise from changes in factional affiliation or the occasional creation of a new faction by one of its members. In the recent past, when farming was the main economic occupation, household members planted, tilled, and harvested their fields together. At present, with the greater importance of wage labor, farms lie idle, but frequent mutual-assistance patterns continue among members, even though residence is ambilocal or neolocal. The household unit is thus a bilateral descent group, although perhaps not as large nor as corporate as similar cognatic groups elsewhere (compare Murdock 1960:9–11).

*Traditional Tanoan Pueblo men's attire—
San Juan Pueblo.*

Age is important in discipline and training. Disciplinary cases are handled by the oldest man in the household who may be a father or a paternal or maternal grandfather. In the absence of a father or grandfather, the oldest uncle (bilaterally reckoned) may perform these functions. These male relatives also exercise the task of training a male child or youth, while a mother or a paternal or maternal grandmother assumes responsibilities for training female children. In the absence of such female relatives, the oldest aunt (bilaterally traced) may instruct, advise, and guide the vocational and avocational destinies of a girl. Serious cases of discipline, as well as family troubles of an extreme kind, are handled at the village level by duly appointed authorities or disciplinarians. Controversy over land, house property, and the like are also problems presented to village authorities, usually the governor or war captains.

Land tenure contrasts rather sharply from that of the clan or lineage dominated Western Pueblos. The Keresan pueblos tend to fall in with the Tanoans in land ownership and land use, despite the presence of clans in these pueblos. Land is, in theory, owned by the village and families have only use rights. This is universal among the Pueblos; but among the Tanoans, land use rights are passed on to both daughters and sons. The rights to use of land and property are usually transferred by the oldest surviving member of the household when he or she is no longer economically productive. Older members of the household are favored with choice plots of land and property, but younger married members also receive an inheritance. It is true, however, that younger members of the family often get poorer land and less property; they may, however, appeal to the war captains or the governor for additional land.

The above sketch of the terminological structure and behavior can be expanded by further data to indicate that unilineal organizations appear not to have been important in the past and certainly not at present. These statements are not true of Jemez. This pueblo, because of its proximity to Keresan pueblos and frequent intermarriage with Keresans, has exogamous clans, although there are many indications in its kinship terminology and social institutions that clanship is new at Jemez (Parsons 1925:24–25). Clans or other unilineal organizations are likewise absent among the Tiwa. There is no awareness of clan concepts or practices at Taos, much less any evidence of unilineal organizations in the social structure of this pueblo (Parsons 1936:38–39). The "corn" groups among the Southern Tiwa (Isleta and Sandia), often called "clans," are religious associations whose members are drawn through the mother's side, but function primarily in crisis rites for the individual (Ellis 1951a:149). The Tewa "clan names" have nothing to do with clans. These names are inherited variously from the father or the mother. As with other property, a clan name seems to be the possession of the bilateral kin group already described. (For data on Tanoan kinship organizations, see Harrington 1912; Parsons 1925:19–25, 1932a:219–232, 1936:28–39; Trager 1943:557–571; Dozier 1955, 1960b.)

In summary, Tanoan Pueblos classify kin bilaterally on a principle of generation, emphasize age, and generally ignore sex distinctions. There is no evidence of a former lineage or clan system in the kinship terms or in the network of social relations among the kin group. Clan names do exist in some pueblos, but such names appear to be applied to the esoteric associations or are terms applied to bilateral descent groups, since one family may derive it from the father, another from the mother. As with property, food, and work patterns, we may say that the name is the possession of the bilateral extended kinship unit. The Tewa clan names have nothing to do with government, ceremonies, or the regulation of property or marriage. They are uttered as a litany along with other esoteric terms by ceremonial leaders on such solemn occasions as association retreats and masked dance ceremonies. We suggest that Tewa clan names are an imperfect and undigested diffusion of the clan concept from Keresan neighbors. The fact that the Northern Tiwa, farthest removed from the Keresans, do not have such clan names would tend to support this hypothesis.

Kinship behavior reflects the basic terminological structure. Functions pertaining to government, land ownership, religion, and ceremonies are vested in associations whose membership is drawn from the village without regard to

Chorus and drummers. San Ildefonso Pueblo— a Tanoan, Tewa-speaking Pueblo.

kinship relations. The result is a tight village integration and centralization of authority.

Social and Ceremonial Organization

The important unit of social and ceremonial organization among Tanoans generally is a dual division of the society usually referred to as "moieties." Tanoan pueblos tend to dichotomize in a variety of other ways. The Tewa, particularly, employ dual contrasting sets together with associated symbols and concepts in an interesting manner (Ortiz 1965:389–396). In all of these pueblos there is a dominant dual organization of the society which is of overwhelming importance. This has been recognized for some time as the moiety organization without kinship significance (Parsons 1924:336, 1929:278). Actually, Tanoan moieties are more properly governmental divisions both for the management and conduct of practical tasks and ceremonial activities.

In addition to moieties, Tanoans have three specialized types of social and ceremonial associations: (1) those with governmental and religious functions associated with the dual divisions; (2) medicine associations that conduct curing and exorcising rituals; (3) associations with special functions, such as war, clowning, and hunting. In addition, Tanoan pueblos have a Katcina cult or some vestige of an organization concerned with supernatural beings connected with ancestral spirits which we have noted among the Western Pueblos and Keresans as well.

The relationship of ceremonial structures to the social and ceremonial organization of the various Keresan and Tanoan Pueblo groups has been clarified by Florence Hawley Ellis (Hawley 1950a). We have discussed the kivas of the Keresan pueblos. Tanoan pueblos appear to have one communal kiva and either one or more associated with the dual divisions of the society. The Tewa pueblos have one large kiva and either a smaller one or the complete absence of a second one. The Tewa, therefore, do not have a two-kiva system as formerly reported (Parsons 1929:99). Until recently among the Tewa, and still true at Nambe and San Juan, masked performances were held in the large kiva. Tesuque performs its masked dances in the plaza, but rehearsals are held by both moieties in one kiva. Likewise, large group dances, such as the so-called "Corn" or "Tablita" dances, are rehearsed by both moieties in the large kiva and performed together in the plaza by San Juan, Nambe, and Tesuque. San Ildefonso and Santa Clara dropped the practice of intermoiety cooperation and participation because of factional disputes about the turn of the century. These disputes took the form of a dual split along moiety lines in both villages. In Santa Clara, one moiety, the Summer, went so far as to build its own kiva, thus giving the pueblo a two-kiva pattern. Tewa ceremonial associations do not have special structures as those of Taos and Picuris; in the Tewa pueblos, either separate houselike structures or the homes of association heads are used as meeting rooms.

Picuris and Taos each have six kivas, divided equally into a north- and southside division, but each pueblo until recently also used a communal structure (Hawley 1950a:287). The kivas at Taos and Picuris represent association structures, the moiety division asserting itself in terms of a spatial division, double chieftainship, and rival relay races. Isleta has only one large round kiva; members of its six ceremonial associations (like those of the Northern Tiwa) meet in separate houses or rooms. There is in this pueblo a dual or moiety system associated with Summer and Winter with double chieftainship and, above this, a town chief more important as a single chief than in any of the other Tanoan pueblos (see Parsons 1932:254–258). Sandia, the other southern Tiwa village, is also reported to have but a single round kiva like Isleta, but the absence of ethnographic materials makes it impossible for us to report social organizational relationships.

THE DUAL DIVISION ORGANIZATION OR MOIETY The moiety is all-inclusive among the Tewa and at Isleta. A Tewa inherits his moiety affiliation from his father, but membership may be changed later. Thus, a woman upon marriage may shift to her husband's moiety; or a man might, as an adult, undergo initiation into the opposite moiety to which his father belongs. The particular extended kin alignments and factional disputes seem to bring about changes in moiety membership. At Isleta, children take the moiety of parents; but if the parents belong to different moieties, their children are assigned alternately to one moiety and then the other. No information is available on the nature of the dual organization in Sandia pueblo, the other southern Tiwa village. As we have noted, at Taos and Picuris, dual division affiliation is by north- and southside kiva divisions. Male and female children are assigned by parents to Taos kivas, but only men are formally initiated. Assignment to kiva group or ceremonial association membership is entirely optional with parents at Taos, while in Picuris apparently all (male and female) join the kiva group of their fathers (Parsons 1936:45–47, 114–116).

Tewa men and women undergo an initiation to validate moiety membership.

"Zuni" Corn dance—Santa Clara Pueblo.

Initiation ceremonies occur about every four years and the ages of the initiates vary from six to ten, but an occasional adult changing moiety affiliations may also undergo the rite. The initiates are under various kinds of taboos and food restrictions during this period. At Taos, initiates are about the same ages, but in other respects, Taos kiva groups appear to be more like Tewa ceremonial associations (see below). Isleta corn groups are similar to Tewa ceremonial associations; membership is through mothers and apparently involves life crisis rituals (Ellis 1951b:149).

MOIETY CEREMONIAL ASSOCIATIONS Among all Tanoans a special type of ceremonial association, different from those discussed below under "Village Ceremonial Associations," is related to each moiety. Although these associations serve a curing function by virtue of the fact that members are dedicated to it to be cured, their more obvious and primary functions are governmental and ceremonial. Among all Tanoans one or more of these associations, either singly or collectively, have the following tasks to perform: (1) the maintenance of an annual solar calendar and the announcement of dates for fixed ceremonials during the year; (2) the organization and direction of large communal dances and ceremonies; (3) the coordination of purificatory and cleansing rites for the village conducted by the medicine associations; (4) the coordination of communal hunts conducted by hunt associations; (5) the coordination of warfare ceremonies conducted by the war association, aided in some pueblos by a companion women's scalp association; (6) the organization and direction of planting harvesting activities; (7) the tasks for cleansing and constructing irrigation ditches; (8) the repair and construction of the communal kiva and the cleaning of the plaza for communal ceremonies; (9) the nomination and installation of secular officials.

Among the Tewa, women may become members of the moiety associations; but as in other esoteric associations where they are permitted to become members along with men, their roles are as preparers of meals and food carriers for the men when the association is in retreat. With the Tewa, one woman member does have a rather important ceremonial duty. She is the "pathmaker" for the Katcina impersonators in the night kiva ceremonies. She leads the file of Katcina dancers into the kiva by sprinkling a path of corn meal ahead of them.

The dual chieftainship among the Tanoans is the result of the, moiety organization. Each of the Tewa moiety chiefs is a member of the moiety sociopolitical association. With the Northern Tiwa, Taos and Picuris, the moiety chiefs are the chiefs of the two most important associations of the northside and southside divisions. The chief of the northside division at Taos is considered town chief. At Isleta, there is a double chieftainship, but in addition a town chief above the moiety chiefs. The two Tewa moiety association heads, Poetunyo (Summer) and Oyike (Winter) are equal in power and each rules the pueblo for half a year. In actuality, the Tewa have the only true double chieftainship.

The assistants to the town chiefs in virtually all pueblos are the war captains; sometimes also referred to as war chiefs. The use of "war chief" for these officers is unfortunate; the term "war captain" ought to be applied to the town chief's assistants if they are the annually appointed officers authorized by Spanish officials after the Pueblo revolt. This term is a proper translation of the position as used by Spanish authorities: *capitán de la guerra*. Properly, the term "war chief" refers to the head of the warriors' association, formerly an important position in the native ceremonial system and, with modified functions, still important where the office exists today. When Spanish military authorities authorized the use of Pueblo warriors in expeditions against nomadic Indian enemies after the reconquest, *capitánes de la guerra* were created. Each pueblo was permitted to choose its own military leaders, the number apparently determined by the size of the population in the pueblo (Jones 1966:54–55). The Pueblos appear to have filled positions of war captains from offices already in the native social and ceremonial system. Thus, the traditional assistants of the town chiefs were the mythological war gods, hence the position of war captains was logically assigned to the assistants of the town chief. If additional war captains were authorized in a particular pueblo, assistants were simply added to the *cacique's* assistants. It is interesting that the town chief's assistants in every pueblo had warrior characteristics, probably because of the mythological importance of the war gods who were thought of as twins or as a pair of younger and older brothers. This was true among the Hopi and Zuni, as well as among the Rio Grande Pueblos. The function of the war captains, besides their military duties in the past in warfare, has been executive and disciplinary with respect to both ceremonial and secular affairs. For the latter duties, these officers have been designated as "Outside Chiefs" by the Indians themselves. Disciplinary action in internal affairs has been taken against pueblo members who may have transgressed against any of the following: harvesting and planting out of season, refusal to work on cleaning irrigation ditches, or the refusal to participate in communal ceremonial activities.

The communal duties of the moiety associations enumerated above are the responsibilities of the kiva associations at Taos and Picuris and of similar associations at Isleta. Among the Tewa, the two moiety associations alternate seasonally in assuming these responsibilities. The Winter moiety association directs governmental and ceremonial affairs from the fall to the spring equinox, while the Summer moiety is in charge for the remaining half of the year. All members of the village, whether they are members of the moiety in power or not, are required to obey and conform to the governmental and ceremonial orders of the town chief in office at any given time.

VILLAGE ASSOCIATIONS   Village ceremonial associations are esoteric associations with special functions. The Tanoan pueblos have at least four such associations, although in some pueblos, a few of them have become extinct in recent years. These associations are as follows: a hunters' association, a warriors' association, and one or two clown associations. In addition, Isleta and some of the Tewa have a women's warrior or scalp association whose activities are closely connected with the men's warrior association. Each of these associations holds separate retreats and conducts independent ceremonies periodically. Each one of them also conducts at least one major ceremony or directs an activity which in one way or another concerns and involves the whole community.

The hunters' association performs or directs small group animal dances and, before important kiva ceremonials, is responsible for a communal rabbit hunt into which the whole population is drawn. This activity is in cooperation with the moiety associations. The mountain lion, as in virtually all the pueblos, is the general protector of the hunters' association and members believe that their power and hunting magic is derived from this animal. The chief of the hunters' association has a major role in installing a new town chief into office; this custom contrasts with Keresans, where medicine association leaders are charged with this function.

The warriors' association also directs small group war dances of various kinds, but also has communal rituals. The latter are the relay and conditioning races formerly important to keep fit and be successful in warfare. The women's scalp association has its own ceremonies, but it also cooperates with the warrior association in the latter's rites. The scalp association members feed and care for the scalps brought back from campaigns against enemy Indian tribes. Scalp associations occur among the Tewa and at Isleta and apparently among all Tanoan (and some Keresan pueblos) in the past. In Santa Clara pueblo, the Women's Scalp Association is validated by the tale of the Blue Corn Girls. The Blue Corn Girls are mythical Pueblo twin sisters (or younger and older sisters). They are the counterpart of the twin war gods, (see above). According to the tale, the Blue Corn Girls receive the disapproval and ire of the pueblo's officers by their egotistical behavior, especially for blatantly ignoring the attentions of the Pueblo youths who sought to court them. As punishment for their unbecoming behavior, Pueblo authorities sent them to the Navaho country with instructions not to return until they have secured the scalp of a Navaho chief. Painted and dressed as male warriors, armed with bows, quivers and shields, the girls journey to enemy territory. On the way, they are assisted by mythological beings: coyote, grandmother spider, and others. As a result of supernatural help, they are successful in their quest, and return with the scalp of a Navaho chief. They are joyously received by the women of the pueblo and the day is turned into a feast and celebration. The event has been commemorated until recently by a general celebration whenever a new member is inducted into the association. During the day's festivities, sex roles are reversed: men grind corn, bake bread, and perform women's activities, while women dance in warrior's dress, carrying the scalp pole with the pueblo's collection of enemy scalps dangling from it.

A greater emphasis on hunting and war is characteristic of the Tanoans generally. Such emphasis may be due to the marginal position of these pueblos, both geographically and culturally. They are the closest to buffalo and Plains Indians and there is evidence that in the past these Pueblos sojourned frequently with Plains Indians while trading with the latter and hunting buffalo (see Florence Hawley Ellis 1951a:187–188). The Northern Tanoans are also in an area of more abundant game, the region of the southern Rockies and its eastern flanks, where grass is more plentiful.

The clown associations of the Tanoans may have been borrowed from the Keresans along with the Katcina cult. The clowns among the Tewa are particularly similar to Keresan clowns, both in appearance and function. The very names, Kosa and Kwirena, are related to those of Keresan clown associations. As among the Keresans, Tewa clowns are intimately connected with the Katcina cult and with kiva ceremonials. The Kosa "bring" the Katcinas from the mythological lake of emergence in the north.

Medicine associations, where they exist among Tanoans, appear to be borrowed from Keresan pueblos. Among the latter, they are more numerous and more elaborately developed. Actually, one of the names of the medicine associations among the Tewa and at Isleta clearly indicates its Keresan origin. Medicine associations at Isleta are the Laguna and Isleta Fathers, the former clearly borrowed from the Keresan pueblo of Laguna—actually from the colony of Laguna Indians now located on the Isleta reservation. Among the Tewa, the Tema Kè, or Cochiti Bear curing association was derived from the Keresan pueblo of Cochiti. There is also a medicine association among the Tewa called the Tewa Bear, whose name, like that of Isleta Fathers, implies a medicine association with deeper roots in the pueblo; but its origin may also have been Keresan. Jemez pueblo has medicine associations patterned along Keresan models and virtually all Tewa pueblos have a curing association borrowed from this pueblo. Two kiva ceremonial associations at Taos perform curing rituals, but apparently there are no Keresan-type curing associations in this pueblo (Parsons 1936:59–60). There is no evidence that Picuris has curing associations either. The absence of medicine associations in these pueblos suggests strongly that these curing organizations were borrowed from the Keresan pueblos. In all pueblos there are, of course, individual curers in addition to organized priests or shamans belonging to specific medicine associations. Where specific curing associations are absent, the Indians go to individual curers, although there is an increasing dependence on modern medicine and modern medical facilities to treat injuries and illnesses formerly taken to native curers and priests.

Membership in pueblo ceremonial associations is lifelong. Formerly, most Indians belonged to one or more ceremonial organizations, but the attraction of these cults has diminished in recent years. There is a distinction between association people and nonassociation people in all the pueblos. Conceptually, the distinction is between those who are "aware" and "know" and those who do not. Adults who do not belong to a ceremonial association are considered like children, whereas association members are "men" and "women." The recruitment of association members follows a similar pattern in all Rio Grande pueblos. Parents may dedicate a sick child, believing that by so doing the child will get well. An individual who has recovered from an illness as the result of being dedicated to a ceremonial association waits until puberty to enter the association. At Taos, children ages six to ten are formally inducted; these ages correspond to Tewa moiety initiations which everybody enters. An adult who becomes ill may likewise dedicate himself to a ceremonial association and upon recovery join the association. Trapping, already described among Keresan pueblos, is another manner by which members are recruited. During the period of training or apprenticeship, the novitiate is confined to the pueblo for one or two years. This is a period of ritual taboos and food restrictions. Men must let their hair grow long and have it braided (Tewa and Northern Tiwa) or tied in a club in back (Southern Tiwa, Jemez, and Keresans).

Moiety associations and village associations are joined in the same way. Parents of a child select the association which they want the child to join after having consulted with "association" people; usually the association selected is one to which one of the parents belong. An adult may also select an association of his own, but commonly adults are "called" to a specific association. Persistent thoughts or dreams about an association when one is ill are believed to be summonses to join that specific ceremonial association.

The Tewa conceive of an esoteric association as a human being: the head is the chief, the arms are his right and left arm assistants, and the body is made up of the members of the association. When a leader dies, the right arm becomes the head, the left arm moves to right, and a new member is chosen from the body to fill the left arm vacancy. Should the right arm assistant die before the head, the left moves to right and a new member is chosen as above to fill the left arm position. The Tewa conception of an association and the manner of succession apparently applies for Jemez and Isleta, but not for Taos. Taos associations do not have right and left arm assistants; a successor is therefore selected directly from the members. Parsons discovered that the chiefs of the northside and southside kivas had been succeeded by their own sons; but in association groups within the kivas, the chief was selected by a counsel of older men of the kiva acting with the chief of the moiety to which the kiva belonged. Parsons explains that the former system which appears to be hereditary may arise from the fact that chiefs give one or more of their sons to their own kiva in the hope of training a successor within the family (Parsons 1936:77–79).

THE KATCINA CULT The cult of masked gods so popular in the west and among the Keresans may have been borrowed by the Tanoans. Frank G. Anderson (1955, 1956, 1960), who has made an exhaustive study of the cult, is of the opinion that Zuni is the primary source of diffusion of the cult:

A Katcina dance—Zuni Pueblo.

Zuni remains . . . the most important source for much of the cult, originating many basic features as well as details. This widely held opinion is based on the obvious complexity of all aspects of the cult here, and its thorough integration with the general socioceremonial organization. However, Zuni has borrowed as well, particularly, of course, from its nearest neighbors, the Western Keres and Hopi. . . . Probably no town, however, has so well integrated the items borrowed as has Zuni, giving many traits and complexes an appearance which has in some cases probably misled investigators into assuming for them a native origin (Anderson 1960:377).

Anderson summarizes the position of the cult among the Tanoans in admirable fashion:

The history of the kachina cult among the Tanoans has been almost entirely one of borrowing. Jemez has clearly taken the most—the Jemez cult is very nearly as full as that of the Eastern Keres, on which, for the most part, it is based (Parsons 1939:985). Moiety here may be original or may have been derived from the Tewa. Their principal contribution—one might say their only one—is the so called "Jemez" kachina, now very widespread and popular.
The Tewa have borrowed less fully, again almost entirely from Eastern Keres (Parsons 1939:985; 1929:280). Their contribution has been a plan of organization, based on the moiety, which has spread, I believe, to Jemez and Eastern Keres. Hawley sees both the cult and the big kiva as prehistoric borrowings from Keres (Hawley 1950a:297). . . .
The Tiwa, except perhaps Sandia, have borrowed less of the kachina cult than any of the other tribes. They hold a fairly typical series of beliefs concerning kachinas, but the objective features are very meager. Such as they are, the latter seems to be due to Keresan influence, either direct or through the Tewa (Parsons 1939:984–5). It is clear, for example, that the maskless dances of Isleta and the Turtle Dance of Taos are connected historically with the kachina cult (Parsons 1930b:347; 1936:91, 115), but they may not be so connected conceptually by the performers (Anderson 1960:379–380).

Isleta and Taos do have a series of beliefs and traditions about "kachinas," although meager, which correspond with those of other Rio Grande pueblos (Parsons 1932b:347; 1936:114–115). Thus it would seem that the Tiwa were ripe for borrowing the cult. Spanish suppression of masked performances may have impeded full diffusion.

The Tewa Katcina organization is a dual one—organized along moiety lines, but, now and in the past at San Juan and Nambe, the large kiva is used by both groups, while Tesuque uses the courtyard. Formerly the other villages also employed the courtyard, but the large kiva has been most frequently used, at least in the recent past. Thus, the cult is in some respects considered a communal ceremony, despite its dual organization. The number of Katcina participants is small—about five or six "line" dancers and as many side dancers. The cult is closely associated with the moiety associations, but is under an independent supervisor, the Katcina Father, who cooperates closely with the moiety association head when engaged in cult activities. The Katcina Father is a lifelong position, but apparently he is appointed by the moiety chief. The clowns, either Koshare or Kwirena, or both, appear with the dancers, and "bring" the Katcina from underneath a lake in the north, apparently the mythological emergence lake (see Parsons 1936:112).

The "bringing" of the Katcina among the Tewa is an impressive, dramatic performance (see Laski 1959; Ortiz 1969).

All males are eligible for membership in the cult among the Tewa. One woman who acts as pathmaker for the Katcinas is the only woman who participates in the activities of the cult. This woman is not, however, a member of the cult, but a member of the moiety ceremonial association. The Katcina organization is distinguished from other cults in that members are not recruited in the usual way by vow, dedication, or trespass. This is also true among Keresans, except at Santa Ana, where the cult is similar to a medicine association and both men and women join by vow or trespass or by being dedicated to it by parents as the result of illness in early childhood and subsequent recovery (White 1942:138–142). Among the Tewa all males automatically become members, although a postpuberty initiation ceremony formalizes membership. The Katcinas are believed to be the bearers of rain; this is their primary role. They are also believed to be bearers of good health and general well-being.

Of all Tanoan pueblos, Jemez has borrowed the most from its non-Tanoan neighbors. This is understandable since Jemez is very close to Keresan pueblos and considerable intermarriage with Keresans has taken place. Jemez has borrowed many Keresan elements, among them the clan and medicine associations. The clan has not been taken over by the other Tanoan pueblos as a functional unit, however. Medicine associations exist at Tewa and Isleta; but in both groups, these associations have been borrowed, clearly, from Keresan neighbors. At Isleta and among the Tewa, medicine associations have either retained the name of the Keresan pueblo from which the association was borrowed or its members must go to a Keresan village to be initiated. It is significant that where these associations exist among Tanoans they have no rain-making functions or coordinating communal responsi-

Deer dance—San Juan Pueblo.

bilities; they exist purely for curing and exorcism. Moieties, particularly the moiety associations, appear to be fundamentally Tanoan. Clown associations may have been borrowed also—perhaps along with the Katcina cult. The other village associations are compatible with the emphasis of Tanoan life on warfare and hunting, but perhaps the idea of the ceremonial organization was borrowed from Keresans. The Katcina cult is obviously marginal among Tanoans; it has become firmly established only at Jemez and among the Tewa. The cult is absent among the Tiwa; Sandia may have it, but only additional ethnographic data will demonstrate its importance or lack of importance in this pueblo.

PART FOUR

GENERAL PUEBLO CHARACTERISTICS

Becoming a Pueblo

WHILE THERE ARE DIFFERENCES in the socialization techniques employed among the Pueblos, the similarities outweigh the differences. As a result of these similarities, the finished product—the Pueblo adult personality—is remarkably uniform. Socialization techniques may be described, therefore, for the Pueblos as a whole, noting differences only where they appear significant.

The first two years of Pueblo life are highly permissive. Toilet training and weaning are, and were, gradual processes. Yet while the child is rarely disciplined, the environment was pervaded with anxiety. Until recently, the cradle board was common in every village and virtually every adult above the age of forty has been brought up on one. The cradle board was a convenience for parents, but it was also rationalized as a training or educational device for the child. Thus the child was put into the cradle board when it cried and when it became difficult to manage. The cradle board became, in fact, a device that meant discomfort and confinement rather than an object of warmth and comfort. Other factors of anxiety in the atmosphere consisted of constant angry admonitions meted out to older siblings in the presence of the infant. Such scoldings were often accompanied by threats of dire misfortune befalling a disobedient older sibling, which filled the infant child with anxiety (compare Goldfrank 1945:519).

At about the age of two, the external permissive pattern takes on a sudden change. This is about the time the child has begun to walk. Parental admonition is directed to industry, to enduring discomfort without crying, working hard, not wasting food, and the like. Such admonitions may also be coupled with threats of ogres and giants who are said to visit the pueblo to carry away nagging, crying, and disobedient children. As the child grows older, he is made to see the village disciplinarians, a pair attired in buckskin clothes, wearing hideous masks and carrying whips. Although children under the age of puberty are made to hide indoors, parents permit them to steal a glimpse of the bogey men through an open door or window. Parents who feel that their child or children are especially prone to mischief and who are difficult to manage may ask the disciplinarians to visit their homes and discipline their children. Among the Tewa, the disciplinarians make the child or children dance while they crack whips at their heels. Regular village disciplinarians are perhaps more characteristic of the eastern pueblos, but periodic or seasonal visits of bogey or ogre Katcina are also common in the western pueblos (Parsons 1939:203–204).

Between approximately the ages of six and nine, girls and boys are initiated into a kiva group or moiety and undergo ritual training involving rigid physical and dietary restrictions. For boys, entrance into the Katcina cult requires the observance of additional ordeals and in certain pueblos, a whipping ritual. Membership into other esoteric associations after puberty involves further disciplinary measures and restrictions.

The approved personality type is formed by the disciplines regularly carried out through the life cycle from early childhood through puberty and the ceremonial associations which the individual joins. The compact life in the pueblos where there is little opportunity for privacy allows for a minimum of deviation. The clown organizations single out the occasional rebel and enforce conformance to the rigid Pueblo pattern of behavior by public and semipublic acts of ridicule. In the eastern pueblos, the war captains see to it that an individual observes all the orders and the demands made upon the population by the religious hierarchy. The war captains have the authority (in the past, at least) to depose a town chief and to execute him (Hoebel 1962:560). Finally, there is ever present the threat of damaging gossip when an individual does not conform to approved Pueblo behavioral patterns. If misfortunes occur, disease epidemics break out, crops fail, hunts prove unrewarding, or the enemy wreaks destruction, the deviant is hunted out, whipped, or even killed as a "witch" (compare Leighton and Adair 1966: 46–47). Bunzel's description of the approved Zuni personality type may be applied, at least in the recent past, to all the Pueblos:

> In all social relations, whether within the family group or outside, the most honored personality traits are a pleasing address, a yielding disposition, and a generous heart. All the sterner virtues—initiative, ambition, an uncompromising sense of honor and justice, intense personal loyalties—not only are not admired but are heartily deplored. The woman who cleaves to her husband through misfortune and family quarrels, the man who speaks his mind where flattery would be much more comfortable, the man, above all, who thirsts for power or knowledge, who wishes to be, as they scornfully phrase it, "a leader of his people," receives nothing but censure and will very likely be persecuted for sorcery (Bunzel 1932:480).

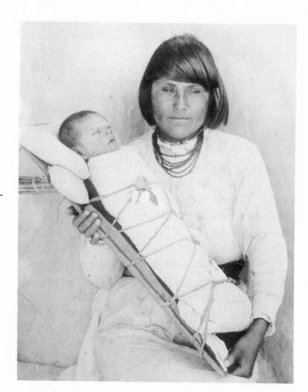

A Pueblo mother and infant in typical Pueblo cradle board—Acoma Pueblo, New Mexico.

Bunzel, of course, is describing the ideal personality type. What is remarkable is that despite the penalties, every pueblo has or has had individuals who have challenged the rigid behavioral standards of their village. In the past, Pueblo officials have executed many witches; they have also evicted others, but the pueblos continue to produce outspoken and rebellious individuals. At present, some pueblos are tolerating their deviant members, but nonconformists tend to escape periodically to the freer life in urban areas, returning to their pueblos only to renew kinship ties and to enjoy the frequent ceremonials. It is possible today for the Pueblo deviant to enjoy the best of two worlds—the communal and ceremonially rich life of the pueblo and the unrestrained pleasures of the city. The number of nonconforming Pueblo Indians is small; there is no reason to believe that the number was ever very large. As a result, traditional Pueblo life has persisted and continues to move into the future as a rather unique communal society, adapting and adjusting, but retaining its social and cultural autonomy.

Language

Pueblo languages are highly diverse; they contain three completely unrelated languages: Zunian, Keresan, and Tanoan. The three subgroups of the Tanoan: Tiwa, Tewa, and Towa, although obviously related, are mutually unintelligible; hence separate languages. There are, additionally, dialectical differences from pueblo to pueblo, within each language group. Hopi and Tanoan have linguistic relatives outside the Pueblos; Hopi with Uto-Aztecan and Tanoan with Kowan. Hopi and Tanoan both are also linked by some linguists into Uto-Aztecan Tanoan. Zuni may also be distantly related to California Penutian. These latter connections, however, indicate extremely distant relationships. See Trager (1967:335–350) for the most recent statement about language relationships among the New Mexico Pueblos.

Although the Pueblo languages have indisputably diverse origins, the response of the Rio Grande Pueblos to language contact has been remarkably similar. We may briefly summarize the effect of Spanish on three of the Pueblo languages on which we have some data: Tewa, Taos, and Keresan.

Tewa morphology and syntax seem not to have been affected strongly by Spanish. The influence on Tewa phonology also appears to be minimal. Loanwords have undergone phonetic changes, but for the most part they are still incompatible with Tewa phonological structure. The number of outright loans in Tewa is less than 10 percent; for Keresan and Taos it is only about 5 percent (Dozier 1956; Spencer 1954; Trager 1944). The percentages for the Tewa may be reduced to virtually zero in certain situations, however. Since many Tewa speakers are bilingual, they recognize Spanish-derived words and when they wish to mask the subject of their conversation, they immediately find native substitutes for the loanwords. Spanish loanwords are also deleted in ceremonial contexts where there is desire to keep the purity of the native language.

Despite the few direct Spanish loanwords, Spanish contact has had a profound effect on Pueblo vocabulary. Introduced items and concepts had to be incorporated into the language. Tewa and Taos responded by two primary processes: (1) coinage of new words, mainly descriptive of the introduced item and concept; and (2) the extension of the meanings of words already in the language to cover the new acquisitions.

Keresan speakers, like those of the Tewa and Taos pueblos, resisted direct borrowing from Spanish vocabulary. The specific techniques used by Keresans to incorporate Spanish-introduced items and concepts into the language appear to differ from the above, however. The Keresan language avoided the technique of coining new words in favor of loan translations and the extension of the meaning of words already in the language (Spencer 1947:133). The result was the same; however, only a minimal number of direct Spanish word loans are found in Keresan.

The resistance to borrowing Spanish loanwords, as well as the custom of deleting Spanish loanwords in certain situations, are paralleled by the reluctance of these Indians to give out information about their way of life. This phenomenon is undoubtedly associated with the suppression of native religious ceremonies and customs by Spanish missionaries and civil authorities experienced by their forefathers and handed down by word of mouth to the present generation. The Pueblos are highly conscious of language and careful not to reveal inadvertently any information that might be a cause for the renewed suppression of indigenous customs and the discipline of native religious leaders.

Ceremonies

Pueblo ceremonies, particularly those of the Rio Grande pueblos, run in a continuum from sacred to profane. Keresan and Tanoan pueblos share this pattern of presenting ceremonies, although the particular rites and dances may differ considerably. The western pueblo ceremonies also run in a pattern that is similar to those of the Rio Grande pueblos, but Zuni and the Hopi pueblos are not so secretive about the sacred rites of the esoteric cults. Some of the early anthropologists, for example, were either initiated into the most secret of Zuni and Hopi cults or else were permitted to witness the ceremonies conducted by these religious associations. No white person has ever been permitted to become a member of the esoteric cults of the Rio Grande pueblos or to see the rites of these ceremonial organizations.

The most sacred of Rio Grande pueblo ceremonies are the rites of the medicine associations and the clown associations. Equally guarded against view by whites are the ceremonial activities of the Katcina cult. Even Pueblo Indians who are not members are barred from observing the ritualistic practices of the religious cults held in private; but the Katcina cult and all the other associations conduct courtyard performances as well, which are open to townspeople. These are partially religious and partially entertainment rites for Pueblo Indians; only no whites may view them. Katcina dances are held almost always inside the kiva; although formerly hill or mountain retreats, or even the pueblo courtyard, if properly guarded from observation by outsiders, was used. Masked performances are the most secret of Rio Grande Pueblo Indian ceremonials, and the most careful precautions are taken so that they are not seen by whites. For curing ceremonies, the house of the association leader or the special house of the association may be used for ritualistic performance. Exorcising or purificatory ceremonies of a communal nature are, however, held outdoors, but are strictly guarded from observation by outsiders. Other association ceremonies are held in the courtyard, but may be viewed only by townspeople.

Also considered within the sacred area of ceremonialism is a second set of ritualistic performances. These are the communal ceremonies, the public portion of which is a dance given in the pueblo courtyard. The courtyard dance is open to the view of Hispano and Anglo visitors, although photographs are strictly prohibited by all Keresan pueblos. In these communal ceremonial activities, all able-bodied individuals are required to take part. Members of the village who have a legitimate excuse for not participating in the dance itself are required to assist as kiva guards, help with staging, costuming, and the like. The preparations for the dances which take place in the kiva are guarded and not open to observation by

Rio Grande Keresan Tablita or "Corn" dances photographed by the kiva—Cochiti Pueblo.

outsiders. The most popularly known of the communal dances are the *tablita* or "corn" dances, as Hispanos and Anglos generally refer to these ceremonies. These dances have become the standard saint's day dance in virtually all the Keresan pueblos. Among the latter, the two kiva groups alternate in performing the dance, but among the Tewa, the dual divisions (moieties) formerly united and presented a dance composed of members of both divisions. Besides the *tablita* dances, there are a number of other dances that belong to this group. Formerly these dances may have been given in conjunction with masked Katcina performances; that is, the Katcina dances may have been performed at night, followed by a daytime performance of the dances just described. The reason for this conjecture is that these dances and songs are similar to those in Katcina performances, except that masks are not worn. One may conjecture that masks were removed to appease Spanish civil and church officials who were especially offended by the masked dances of the Pueblo Indians. Dances of the *tablita* type were observed by Father Dominguez in 1776 (Adams and Chavez 1956:256–257) and have been recently described by Lange (1957:59–74).

A third group of ceremonies associated with the sacred area of Pueblo ceremonialism are the activities of the special ceremonial associations, particularly those of the warriors' and hunters'. The rites of these ceremonial organizations that take place in the association houses are secret; but there are public performances that are open to the public, townspeople, as well as tourists. The courtyard presentations consist primarily of "war dances" or the imitation of game animals important for food and skins: buffalo, deer, antelope, and so forth. The dances and the songs that go with them frequently have Plains Indian aspects. Both Pueblo and Plains Indians have animal and war dances and the two peoples have maintained constant contact through the centuries. It is not possible, therefore, to determine the provenience of these rites and such ceremonies should not be referred to as "Plains Indian dances" or said to have been derived from the Plains Indians. Periodically in the past specific Plains tribes and the Pueblo Indians have maintained friendly relationships; the borrowing of customs must have gone in both directions.

The three sets of ceremonies mentioned above form the core of Rio Grande Pueblo ceremonialism; they express in dance, song, and costuming the propitiatory rites of the people. They are the outward manifestations of the periodic retreats of the esoteric associations, priests, and Katcina leaders. They are examples of imitative magic on a grand scale designed to induce the environment to favor all people, not only Indians, with the good things of life. These ceremonies appear to be almost entirely free of Spanish or Euro-American influences, except insofar as costuming now contains fabrics and ornaments of non-Pueblo manufacture.

A fourth set of ceremonies is essentially secular and is performed primarily for amusement or entertainment. These ceremonies differ from those previously described in that novel forms are permitted and improvisations are constantly made. Often these dances burlesque the whites, especially tourists, and their purpose is obviously for amusement and entertainment rather than to serve religious purposes. They are typically performed during the winter, especially in the Christmas season. Troupes of dancers make a round of the pueblo, going from house to house and giving brief performances in each house. Typical of this set of ceremonies is the "Round Dance," popular among Plains Indians as well as in the pueblos. In recent years, some of the pueblos have permitted visitors to photograph these dances; and in a few pueblos, the prohibition on photographs has also been lifted for the animal and war dances. Pueblo Indians are beginning to discover that fees charged for taking photographs of these dances are a convenient way to bring revenue into the pueblo. This set of dances exhibits numerous innovations. Traditional Pueblo dress and costuming are violated by the use of mirrors, sleigh bells, colored feathers, and so on; although the dance patterns and songs reveal essentially Pueblo or Pan-Indian elements rather than borrowed elements from Euro-American society and culture.

A number of native Pueblo ritual observances coexist along with Spanish or Catholic rites. Thus, there are customs observed at birth, puberty, marriage, and death that have no resemblance to another set of rites performed on these same occasions according to procedures established by Spanish and Catholic custom. Information about the native customs associated with these life crises rites are carefully guarded evidence that these customs belong to the sacred core of Pueblo religion. The customs associated with Catholicism involve baptism, confirmation, marriage, and death and differ little from similar practices observed by neighboring Hispanos.

All Rio Grande Pueblo Indians have Christian names given them in a Catholic baptism rite. These names are freely revealed to outsiders, quite in contrast to names acquired in cult initiations which are carefully guarded so that even the careful ethnographer may have difficulty learning about them. Practices associated with puberty, marriage, and death have similar open and secret aspects and the secret features are those of native or indigenous provenience. At marriage and at death, the Catholic Mass is often said, in the former to bless the union and in the latter for the soul of the deceased. The *velorio*, a Catholic ceremony for the dead, is clearly of Spanish derivation; it is actually a "watch" or "wake." After death, for one or two nights, the body of the deceased is "watched" in a special room. The corpse is dressed in his best clothes by relatives and laid on a table in a room reserved for the purpose. Lighted candles are placed around the body on the table and a small bowl for coin contributions to aid in meeting the expenses of the funeral is placed at the end of the table. In the evening, both Hispanos and Indians come, and when enough of them have assembled, Spanish chants for the dead are sung. A wake may last one, two, or even three nights; burial usually takes place in the morning. If the relatives of the deceased can afford it, a mass is sometimes said before the body is interred. At midnight, a feast is set for the visitors in an adjoining room. The term, *velorio*, is also applied to a night or two of respect and petition for blessings made to a particular saint. In this case, a table is placed in a room with the image or figurine of the saint, on top of the table. Townspeople and neighboring Hispanos are invited to recite prayers and sing hymns throughout the night. The purpose of this ceremony is to obtain the blessing of the saint upon the household of the host. As at a wake, visitors partake of a feast beginning about midnight.

Customs associated with this set of introduced practices are the Mass, the procession, and the erection of a bower in the pueblo courtyard in connection with the pueblo's celebration of the saint for whom the pueblo is named. The bower contains the saint figurines or *santos* of the village church, with the *santo* of the pueblo occupying a prominent and central location among the others. Other events associated with Catholic religious practices occur on All Souls' Day on November 2, and during the Christmas and Lenten seasons. The officers responsible for this system of ceremonies are from the Spanish-imposed civil government organization and comprise primariliy the *fiscales* and *sacristanes*; although the governor and the war captains may also assist, and in some pueblos may actually provide the primary leadership.

In the events associated with the Catholic and Spanish derived customs, Hispano neighbors are not only permitted to participate, but the persistence of this complex among the pueblos may be due largely to their participation. Thus, Hispanos come to Mass, take part in the procession that takes the village *santo* and other saint images to the bower in the morning and which returns them to the church in the evening. They sit in the bower along with the Indians, where they usually outnumber the latter. The two groups chant Spanish hymns, honoring and invoking the blessing of the saints. Hispanos take little interest in the Indian ceremonies, but do participate in those areas of Pueblo ceremonialism to which Spanish-Catholic features have been grafted.

Another set of ceremonies among the Rio Grande Pueblos are also of Spanish and/or Mexican Indian derivation. The most popular of these ceremonies is the *Matachina* danced in virtually every Rio Grande pueblo, but also in a number of Hispano villages. The dance was obviously introduced into Mexico from Europe and from there brought to New Mexico. Gertrude P. Kurath has traced the origin of the Matachina pageant to Europe and in a significant article describes the main features of the dance and notes its distribution among the Pueblos and in Mexico (Kurath 1949:259–264). Other dances or ceremonies bearing European themes and popular among the pueblos are the Horse or Sandaro dance and the Pecos Bull ceremony. Associated with some of these dances, particularly the Matachina pageant, are masked clowns, called *Chapio* (also *Kapio, Tsabiyo*), who speak Spanish and Indian in falsetto. The masks have no resemblance to Katcina masks and are obviously not derived from the latter; furthermore, they are worn in these ceremonies which are open to Hispano and Anglo tourists. These masks have a striking resemblance to masks worn by the Chapaiyeka in Mayo-Yaqui ceremonies. The behavior of both sets of clowns is also similar. The Matachina pageant itself, in variant form, is danced by Tarahumara, Huicholes, and Mayo-Yaqui (Parsons 1939:852, 1005–1007). The Matachina and other ceremonies of obvious Spanish or Mexican Indian derivation are believed to "belong" or to have been "brought" by a mythological god from the South, an Indian god who wore European clothes, foretold the coming of the whites, suggested cooperation with them, but also advised the Pueblos to retain their customs and ceremonies. The god is often identified with Montezuma and called variously: *Bocaiyani* (Santa Ana), *Poshaiyanki* (Zuni), and *Poseyemu* (Tewa). Parsons identifies the Pueblo's

Montezuma with Jesus, but it is obvious that his behavior in the tales depict Indian characteristics as well. She suggests that, "the Pueblos heard a good deal about Montezuma, a 'god' that might be mentioned conveniently to White people [thus to divert attention away from their own carefully guarded religion]" (Parsons 1939:1078–1079).

Ceremonies attributed to Montezuma have been more integrated into Pueblo ceremonialism, although they are not a part of the sacred religious core. We suggest that these ceremonies were introduced by Mexican Indians who accompanied the early Spanish exploring expeditions and also came with the colonists. These Indians held no positions of authority and hence provided no threat to the Pueblos. If these Indians presented the ceremonies to the Pueblos, then it is easy to understand why the Pueblos accepted them. It is possible that the ceremonies already contained reinterpreted Spanish-Indian elements which would make them more palatable to the Pueblos. Whatever the reason, it is remarkable that these ceremonies, although of European tradition, became popular among the Indians; indeed, they appear to have become more important than significant aspects of Catholic doctrine and ritual.

Government Organization

The governmental or political organization of the Rio Grande pueblos consists of two systems: one native and indigenous, the other imposed by Spanish civil and church officials. The latter, according to Bandelier (1890–1892:200), was established in 1620. All Indian groups in the New World under Spanish rule furnished civil officers required by the colonial government. Hence, Gasper Castano de Sosa appointed governors, *alcaldes*, and *alguaciles* among some of the pueblos he visited as early as 1591 (Schroeder and Matson 1965:156). It is doubtful, however, that these appointments made much of an impression on the pueblos until Juan de Oñate reestablished them after the Spanish colony was founded in New Mexico during the first or second decade of the seventeenth century.

THE NATIVE SYSTEM

The native governmental system is involved primarily with religious affairs, but its officers select the secular officials in most pueblos. Moreover, despite the fact that priests do not involve themselves in secular affairs, they have in most pueblos the final authority in all matters—sacred or profane. In the traditional villages, the secular officials merely perform the ordinary and routine responsibilities of the pueblo, but defer to the priests in all important decisions.

The supreme priest or officer in all the villages is the town or village chief. The position is for life, although checks on the village chief's power are provided by the war captains and a council of priests and he may be removed from office if incompetent. Among the Hopi, this officer is called *Kikmongwi*; Zuni, *Pekwin*;

Keresan, *Traikatse* or *Tiamuny*; Jemez, *Whivela*. The Tewa and Tiwa have a double chieftainship. Among the Tewa the two chiefs are equal in status and authority; a seasonal transfer of ruling the village is the traditional form of government in these pueblos. The Summer Chief (*Poetunyo*) rules from spring to fall, the Winter Chief (*Oyike*) from fall to spring. At Taos, dual chieftainship is associated with the heads of the north- and southside kivas, the heads of which are called *tunena*. The northside chief is town chief (Parsons 1939:131). Picuris ceremonial town chieftainship was also associated with northside and southside divisions; one of these chiefs was accorded the title of townchief in the past. The meagre ethnographic data on Picuris does not permit us to reconstruct any further information on its townchief. Isleta, like the Tewa and northern Tiwa, has a double chieftainship, but with a single head above the chiefs as a paramount townchief. According to Parsons (1932b:254–258) this chief is called *Taikabede* and apparently his position rotated among the four Isleta Corn associations. No information is available on the ceremonial organization of Sandia, the remaining southern Tiwa pueblo.

In the west (Hopi, Hano, Zuni, Acoma) and also at Jemez pueblo, the town or village chief is selected from a specific clan by a council of association heads. These, together with the war chief at Hopi, Bow priest at Zuni, war captains elsewhere, install the town chief into office, serve as his assistants, and also check his power (see above). Among the Rio Grande Keresans, town chiefs are appointed from a specific medicine association in each village without regard to clan affiliation. Zia is a partial exception to this statement; in this pueblo, in addition to medicine association membership, the town chief had to be chosen from one of five important clans in the pueblo (White 1962:127). Medicine association membership is crucial and in virtually all villages the town chief is a member of a specific medicine association, the Flint. The war captains, representing the mythological war gods install the town chief into office and serve as his assistants, although they themselves are appointed by the town chief. The war captains are appointed to serve for a year, at the same time that the other officers of the Spanish civil government system are named. (See White [1942:96 footnotes 4–6] for comparative note on Keresan town chiefs.)

In New Mexico the term *cacique* is used by non-Indians to designate the highest ranking priest or chief in the ceremonial organization of an Indian pueblo. The term is also used by Rio Grande Pueblo Indians themselves when speaking about their town chief to non-Indians. The word is of Arawakan (Indians of the Caribbean area) origin applied by Spaniards to New World native religious and political leaders.

The following description of the behavior expected of Keresan pueblo town chiefs noted by White would apply to all Pueblo town chiefs:

> The cacique should hold himself somewhat aloof from the daily and mundane affairs of the pueblo; he is supposed to concentrate on spiritual affairs. He should take no part in any quarrels that may occur; in fact, such things should be excluded from his notice. Everyone should always treat the cacique with kindness and respect. One should always be careful never to do anything that would offend him or say anything that would hurt his feelings. On rare occasions when he attends a meeting

of the council one should be careful not to use any rough language that might offend him. On the other hand, the Tiamunyi should have only kindly and solicitous feelings toward his people; "he should never be hateful toward them." Should the cacique be remiss in his duties, or conduct himself in a manner unbecoming to his high office, he could be disciplined or punished. It would be the war captain's duty to do this, but he would undoubtedly consult the heads of important societies, such as Flint, Giant, and Fire societies, and be guided by their advice (White 1962:125–126).

The Keresan town chief and his assistants, as we have noted, coordinate all communal activities and ceremonies. Alone or with the assistance of a council of association heads, the town chief names the secular officers each year or else asks the officers of a given year to serve another term. Secular officers must come from men who are not heads of any ceremonial organizations. Properly, the association heads are priests and, together with the town chief, they constitute a priestly hierarchy which manages the religious affairs of the pueblo. By virtue of designating the secular officials, they ultimately control both the sacred and secular domains of pueblo life. As priests, they do not act openly; the war captains and the secular officers are their go-betweens and mouthpieces with the people and with the outside world.

THE SPANISH CIVIL GOVERNMENT SYSTEM
AND RECENT PUEBLO COUNCILS

As we have noted above, Spanish authorities, in order to facilitate civil administration and the missionary program, required the appointment of a set of officers in each pueblo. These officers were usually a governor, a lieutenant governor, an *alguacil* or sheriff, a *sacristan, mayordomos* (ditch bosses), and *fiscales* (church wardens). After the Pueblo Revolt of 1680 and the reconquest in 1694, *capitánes de la guerra*, or war captains, were added. During the first century of Spanish rule, the Pueblos were denied horses and prohibited from possessing firearms; after the revolt, however, they were brought into partnership with the Spanish military organization in the defense of both Pueblo and Hispano settlements from nomadic Indians. Throughout the remainder of Spanish control in New Mexico, Pueblo Indians served as auxiliary troops under the command of their own captains of war, although they were subject to the overall supervision of Spanish officers.

The functions of the civil government officers were defined as follows: The governor was to represent the village in all important dealings with outside authorities. The lieutenant governor was to serve as assistant to the governor and represent him when absent, and in the event of the governor's death, succeed him. The sheriff was to maintain law and order within the pueblo. The *sacristan* was church assistant and aid to the priests. The *fiscales* were responsible for mission discipline, while the *mayordomos* were ditch superintendents. The war captains served (and serve) functions in both the traditional governmental system and relations with the outside world. Formerly their primary duty was to provide the quotas of warriors needed against retaliatory attacks against enemy Indians and to take command of their own troops in the field. In addition, however, the war captains carried out the orders of the *caciques* and compelled members of the pueblo to follow the traditional customs.

The Spanish authorities intended to displace the native governmental and ceremonial system by the introduction of a new set of officers, but such a displacement never took place in any of the pueblos. To this day, the native sociopolitical system remains the *de facto* governmental and ceremonial organization. Not only do the native officers remain important, but the village chief appoints the civil government officers annually, the latter holding office for only one year. Moreover, the appointment of some of the civil government officers, such as the war captains, is merely the confirmation of officers already in the native ceremonial and political system (compare Goldfrank 1952:76). Thus the war captains represent the traditional war gods of the Pueblos and owe primary allegiance to native governmental organization. In the event of conflict between Pueblo rule and orders from the outside world, the war captains support the dictates of the *cacique*.

While the Spanish civil government system must have been introduced among the Hopi, there is no vestige of the organization in any of the villages today. At Zuni, throughout Spanish, Mexican and recent Anglo-American times, the governors and lieutenant governors have been important officers in secular affairs. Indeed, the positions of governor and lieutenant governor remain important officers at present in the new pueblo council (see Pandey 1968:71–85).

Secular officers of the introduced type exist in all the Rio Grande pueblos, but elected rather than appointed officers are beginning to replace the officers of the Spanish civil government system in some pueblos. Hopi, Zuni, Laguna, Isleta, and Santa Clara have tribal councils modeled along lines suggested by outside advisers, particularly government employees. These councils are gaining in popularity. A nominating committee prepares a slate of candidates, who are then elected by popular vote of the adult population. In some pueblos women are permitted to vote and to hold offices as well. Since the governor receives a salary, he may devote full time to his work and thus the governorship becomes a position to campaign for. Other members of the council usually receive no salary but are paid on a per diem basis when attending council meetings. As representatives to meetings away from the pueblo, they receive per diem payments as well as costs of travel. The new organizations are vying with the power and authority of the traditional social and ceremonial officers. In the pueblos where elective officers are the rule, a separation of religious and secular functions has been launched, although in none of these pueblos has a complete separation from religious control taken place.

The pueblos which have adopted elective procedures have introduced some new positions. Among the Hopi where a government council has been attempted on the tribal level rather than on the village level, each village provides representatives according to population size. The old governmental system did not provide for "representatives." New titles have also come into pueblo councils, while some traditional ones have been dropped. The Hopi head officer is known as a "chairman." The Rio Grande pueblos have retained the titles of governor and lieutenant governor; but such positions as secretary and treasurer have been added in some pueblos. These pueblos have dropped other offices from the traditional governmental roster, such as *fiscales, sacristan,* and *mayordomos.* The first two, because such officers were associated with the Catholic church and the new government systems, are being restricted to secular affairs. *Mayordomos* as ditch bosses are no longer needed in most pueblos as irrigated farming has declined in favor of wage work as the primary means of earning a livelihood. Another interesting innovation in the performance of specific tasks is the popular American method of setting up committees: an education committee, a dance committee, and the like.

In the traditional Pueblo governmental system there was, in addition to the appointed officers, a Council of Pueblo Officers, distinct from the Council of Ceremonial Priests or Chiefs, which provided a check on the authority of the secular officers. These officers, usually called *principales,* consisted of former governors, lieutenant governors and war captains. In some pueblos the *principales* assisted the town chief in designating the secular officers for the year. When a double chieftainship existed, as among the Tewa and Tiwa, the secular officers were chosen by both dual division chiefs; one of the chiefs designating the governor, the other the lieutenant governor, and then alternating their choices until all of the offices were filled. The next year the order would be reversed, the chief who had named the governor now deferring to the other chief in choosing the governor; then, as before, the two chiefs would alternate in selecting the other officers.

Where elected councils have been adopted, candidates for the various offices are furnished by a nominating committee (compare Pandey for Zuni, 1968:71), or as at Santa Clara, by permitting each of several sociopolitical factions recognized in the pueblo's constitution to provide a slate of candidates. It is interesting to note the persistence of traditional methods of choosing the secular officers even in those pueblos which have shifted to an elective system. In Santa Clara, for example, in the faction which contains the Summer moiety chief, this revered priest is permitted to "choose" the slate of officers. Thus, this faction is continuing the moiety chief's traditional prerogative of choosing the secular officers; in this case, of course, in only providing one of several rosters of candidates. The other factions decide on their candidates by discussion and voting. Another survival of the traditional ways of choosing officers is found in Isleta, where a former cumbersome method of selecting candidates has been carried over to the present. In this pueblo, the voting population, men of twenty-one and above, cast ballots for the governor in early December of each year. The three men receiving the highest number of votes, plus the incumbent governor, become the four candidates for governor. On January first, the pueblo votes again and the candidate receiving the highest number of votes becomes governor; the second highest, president of the council; the third, the vice president of the council. Other officers are chosen by these newly elected officials (Smith 1966:102; Smith manuscript 1967). This method of choosing officers is similar to the one in existence in the pueblo before the adoption of the constitution in 1947. The general voting population has simply replaced a former council of *principales,* that is, a council made up primarily of former governors and lieutenant governors. This council, consisting of twelve men, formerly chose the secular officers along with the town chief in a manner almost exactly like the one now followed by the general voting population (Parsons 1932:251).

TABLE 3
PUEBLO CEREMONIAL ORGANIZATION

Organization	Hopi	Zuni	Keresan
Lineage and clan	Present	Present	Present
Function	Coordinate association and clan activities. Town chief from specific clan.	With aid of council or priests coordinate ceremonial activities. Town chief from specific clan.	Marriage regulation at Zia—clans important in ceremonies.
Dual division organization (Moiety). Nonkinship dual divisions.	None	None	Squash and Turquoise dual divisions.
Function			Dance-drama groups.
Kivas	Several	Several	Two
Function	Associated with dance and Katcina groups.	←	Associated with Squash-Turquoise divisions.
Katcina cult	Tribal-wide	Village-wide	Open to village but not all become members.
Function	To bring moisture (rain or snow).		To bring moisture and well-being.
Medicine association	No specific Association— Individual doctors.	Several associations	Several associations
Function	Individual curers	Individual and communal curing. Exorcism of evil spirits from the village.	Coordinates communal activities. Town chief must be member of.

Jemez	Tewa	Taos	Isleta
Present	Absent	Absent "clan" names for bilateral groups.	Absent
Marriage regulation. Town chief chosen from one or the other of two clans.			
←	Winter and Summer moieties. Population in one or the other. Winter and Summer associations.	Northside and Southside kiva groups.	Winter and Summer moieties.
←	Each moiety association rules for half year. Coordinate communal activities.	Coordinate ceremonial activity.	Moiety associations. coordinate communal activities.
Two	1 large 1 small	3 northside, 3 southside. 1 communal kiva.	1 large house 6 ceremonial structures.
←	Associated with communal (large) and moiety (small) activities.	Associated with ceremonial association activities.	Associated with communal (large) and moiety (small) activities.
←	Organized by moiety but membership restricted.	None	None except Laguna (Keresan) colony.
←	←		
Several associations	Two associations	None—individual curers only.	None—individual curers only.
←	←	Individual cures	Individual and communal curing. Exorcism of evil spirits from the village.

TABLE 3 (*Continued*)

Organization	Hopi	Zuni	Keresan
Hunt association	One association	One association	One association
Function	Prayers for hunting success. Prayers for game fertility.		Prayers for hunting success, game fertility. Doctor hunting accidents or "hunting illness."
Clown associations	No organization. *Ad hoc* clown groups.	Two clown groups.	Two: Koshare Kwirena
Function	Human fertility; comic relief; social control.	⟵	Human fertility; comic relief; social control; assist medicine associations in communal activities.
War association	Present	Present	Extinct but remembered
Function	Offer prayers for success in war. Purify warriors.		
Women's associations	Three ceremonial associations.	One	Extinct
Function (Usually but not always associated with enemy scalps.)	Ceremonial associations for fertility and good health.	Care of enemy scalps; human fertility and good health.	
Locus of ceremonial and sociopolitical control.	Lineage and clan. Each has house, clan fetish and ceremonial property.	Clan heads coordinate ceremonial activities with council of priests.	Medicine associations with council of association heads.
Religious emphasis	Weather control	Weather control; curing.	Weather control; curing; communal works and ceremonies.

Jemez	Tewa	Taos	Isleta
One association	One association	One association	One association
←	Prayers for hunting success and game fertility.	←	←
←	←	Two clown groups.	Two clown groups.
Human fertility; comic relief; social control; associated with Katcina cult.	←	Human fertility; comic relief; social control.	←
Extinct but remembered	Extinct but remembered	Extinct but remembered	Extinct but remembered
Two	One	None	Assistants to town chief. Not an association.
Ceremonial associations for human and plant fertility.	Care of enemy scalps; human fertility and good health.		Care of enemy scalps; general good health.
Council of association heads	Moiety associations —Winter and Summer.	Northside and Southside kiva ceremonial associations.	Moiety and "Corn" ceremonial associations.
←	Weather control; communal works and ceremonies hunting, warfare.	←	Weather control; curing; communal works and ceremonies.

TABLE 4

PUEBLO CEREMONIES

Categories	Types of Ceremonies	When Given
Group I Ceremonies considered sacred and restricted to either members of esoteric associations or to members of the pueblo.	Retreats of ceremonial associations, certain rites of the medicine, clown, war and hunt associations. Katcina performances.* The preparatory rites of Group II and III ceremonies. Native rites connected with birth, puberty, marriage and death, but see Group V ceremonies below.	In a calendric series—except for native life crisis rites.
Group II Semisacred; may be viewed by tourists.	The public aspects of communal ceremonies,† most common is the "tablita" or "corn" dances of the Rio Grande pueblos.	Given on Pueblo Saint (Fiesta) days.
Group III While preparatory aspects are sacred, the public aspect is considered pure entertainment.	The public aspects of village association ceremonies; typical are game animal dances, "war" and eagle dances.	Animal dances were formerly restricted to winter season.
Group IV House or courtyard dances; purely entertainment and recreational.	Round dances; popular Plains Indians as well. Small group dances usually given inside the homes of pueblo residents in the evening.	Evening performances. Winter time especially Christmas—New Year's; season extending to January 6 (King's Day).

196

TABLE 4 (*Continued*)

Categories	Types of Ceremonies	When Given
	Pueblos consider the following borrowed ceremonies and separate from the native categories Groups I through IV. These ceremonies are missing among the Hopi, Hano, Zuni.	
Group V Life crises ceremonies connected with Catholic Church.	Religious observances of Spanish-Catholic derivation involving life crises rites: baptism, confirmation, marriage, death, and burial rites.	Life cycle stages.
Group VI Pageants or dances of Mexican derivation.	Mexican derived ceremonies associated with the Aztec King or "god," Montezuma. Sandaro (soldier) or hobbyhorse dance, the Pecos bull dance of Jemez, the Matacina dance. These dances were probably introduced by Mexican Indians.	Given evening before Saint's Day dance or following the Saint's Day ceremony.

* In the western pueblos Katcina performances would fall into Group II ceremonies open to the public.
† Village communal ceremonies are absent in the western pueblos, Hopi, Hano, Zuni.

TABLE 5
NATIVE GOVERNMENT OFFICIALS

Officers and Government Organizations	Hopi	Zuni	Keresan	Jemez	Tewa	Taos	Isleta
Town or village chief—lifelong in all pueblos.	Kikmonqwi	Pekwin	Tiamunyi, Traikatse	Whivela	Double chieftainship Poetunyo, (Summer) Oyiketunyo (Winter)	Double chieftainship—northside and southside chiefs. Northside chief town chief: Tobiana tunena	Taikabede
Assistants to town chief.	Council of clan chiefs.	Bow or war priests.	War captains	Right arm and left arm assistants.	Each moiety chief has left arm and right arm assistants.	War captains	Right arm and left arm assistants.
Succession to office of town chief.	Succeeded by man chosen to head Bear clan (Horn clan, Walpi).	Succeeded by man chosen to head Dogwood clan.	New town chief selected by Council of Association Chiefs, Clown association and war captains.	Selected by Council of Fathers (Head of ceremonial associations).	Right assistant moves to head, left to right, new left assistant is filled from association membership. Hunt chiefs install town chiefs into office.	Succession by sons approved by council of kiva chiefs.	Like Tewa
Councils	Council of clan chiefs.	Council of ceremonial assoc. chiefs.	→	→	→	Council of kiva chiefs.	None

TABLE 6

SECULAR GOVERNMENT*

Government Organization	Hopi	Zuni	Keresan	Jemez	Tewa	Taos	Isleta
Spanish type government			Present (Laguna excepted.)	Present	Present (Santa Clara and Pojoaque excepted.)	Present	
Council of pueblo officers (Principales).	None		Present (Lagune excepted.)	Present	Present (Santa Clara excepted.)	Present	Present
New councils	A "tribal" council adopted for entire tribe in 1930.	A "tribal" council of 8 members elected by popular vote for 2 year term, 1965.	Laguna Constitution and by-laws adopted 1958.	None	Santa Clara Constitution and by-laws adopted 1935.	None	Constitution and by-laws adopted 1947.

* Major source: Aberle 1948; Smith 1966.

Of the nineteen communities, considering Zuni and Laguna as single communities, only six have adopted elective forms of secular government. Thirteen pueblo villages are still governed in the traditional manner where officers are appointed by a religious hierarchy and remain under the domination of the priestly authority system. Moreover, among the Hopi, including the Tewa of Hano, each major village and its daughter villages still govern themselves in the traditional way.

Ceremonialism

Since moisture is perhaps the most obvious need in the arid Southwest to make crops grow and produce a bountiful harvest, much of Pueblo ceremonialism, particularly among the Western Pueblos, has been characterized as "rain-making" ceremonies. Actually this statement is only partly true. Pueblo ceremonialism is best understood as an aspect of the general Pueblo concept of the interrelatedness and cooperative nature of the universe. Ceremonial activity is the Pueblo's contribution to maintaining a harmonious balance which is believed to be the natural state of affairs. In Pueblo belief, as long as ceremonies are consistently and properly performed, nature will respond by providing the necessities of life. Thus, man and nature cooperate to maintain universal balance. Man alone, however, may upset the balance; he may do so by refusing to engage in ceremonial activity, by harboring ill feelings, by failure to observe minute details of costuming and per-

Blue Bird dance—San Ildefonso Pueblo.

formance. Pueblo Indians engaging in ceremonial activity are careful not to violate these precepts; religious leaders carry the major burden of this responsibility. If drought, disease epidemics, and misfortunes of any kind befall a pueblo, native priests receive the initial blame; but anyone observed to have frustrated the proper performance of a ceremony may become the victim of bitter criticism and punishment.

The following statement by Laura Thompson and Alice Joseph with reference to Hopi ceremonial participation is pertinent here:

> The rules for ceremonial observance have two aspects, the physical and the psychical. If either aspect is neglected or any regulation broken, failure will result. That is, to carry out a rite successfully, the participants must not only follow the prescribed ritual behavior, perform all the proper acts and observe the tabus, but they must also exercise control over their emotions and thoughts. They must keep a "good heart." A "good heart" means that one must not feel fear, anger, sadness, or worry. In other words, one must be inwardly tranquil and of good will (Thompson and Joseph 1944:41).

The welfare of a pueblo rests on the proper, timely and calendric observance and performance of religious ritual. Ruth Benedict has captured the essence of

Pueblo ceremonialism in the following description of Zuni ceremonial concepts and activity:

> The Zuni are a ceremonious people, a people who value sobriety and inoffensiveness above all other virtues. Their interest is centered upon their rich and complex ceremonial life. Their cults of the masked gods, of healing, of the sun, of the sacred fetishes, of war, of the dead, are formal and established bodies of ritual with priestly officials and calendric observances. No field of activity competes with ritual for foremost place in their attention. Probably most grown men among the western Pueblos give to it the greater part of their waking life. It requires the memorizing of an amount of word-perfect ritual that our less trained minds find staggering, and the performance of neatly dovetailed ceremonies that are charted by the calendar and complexly interlock all the different cults and the governing body in endless formal procedure. . . .
>
> This preoccupation with detail is logical enough. Zuni religious practices are believed to be supernaturally powerful in their own right. At every step of the way, if the procedure is correct, the costume of the masked god traditional to the last detail, the offerings unimpeachable, the words of the hours-long prayers letter-perfect, the effect will follow according to man's desires. . . . According to all the tenets of their religion, it is a major matter if one of the eagle feathers of a mask has been taken from the shoulder of the bird instead of from the breast. Every detail has magical efficacy. . . .
>
> If they [the Zuni] are asked the purpose of any religious observance, they have a ready answer. It is for rain. This is of course a more or less conventional answer. But it reflects a deep-seated Zuni attitude. Fertility is above all else the blessing within the bestowal of the gods, and in the desert country of the Zuni plateau, rain is the prime requisite for the growth of crops. . . . Rain, however, is only one of the aspects of fertility for which prayers are constantly made in Zuni. Increase in the gardens and increase in the tribe are thought of together. . . . Their means of promoting human fertility are strangely symbolic and impersonal . . . but fertility is one of the recognized objects of religious observances (Benedict 1934:59–65).

Pueblo ceremonies vary from rather sedate and monotonous dancing of men and women in single file to hilarious and orgiastic rites. Benedict apparently only witnessed the rather calm and repetitive type ceremonies which Pueblo Indians permit outsiders to see. The ecstatic ceremonial rites of the Pueblos (particularly the scalp dances and the antics of the clowns) in former times brought about the censure and suppression of Pueblo religious rites by Spanish and American authorities. At any rate, on the basis of the rather monotonous large group dances of the pueblos, which rarely offend whites, Benedict has typed the Pueblos as "Apollonian." The term is from Nietzsche's characterization of Greek tragedy—the contrast of two opposing values of existence, "Apollonian" and "Dionysian." In Benedict's interpretation, the Dionysian:

> . . . seeks to attain in his most valued moments escape from the boundaries imposed upon him by his five senses, to break through into another order of experience. The desire of the Dionysian, in personal experience or in ritual, is to press through it toward a certain psychological state, to achieve excess. The closest analogy to the emotions he seeks is drunkenness, and he values the illuminations of frenzy. . . . The Apollonian distrusts all this, and has often little idea of the nature of such experiences. He finds means to outlaw them from his conscious life. He "knows but one law, measure in the Hellenic sense." He keeps the middle of the road, stays within the known map, does not meddle with disruptive psychological states . . . (Benedict 1934:79).

Benedict goes on to characterize the "Apollonian" Pueblos as follows:

> The Southwest Pueblos are Apollonian. . . . The known map, the middle of the
> road, to any Apollonian is embodied in the common tradition of his people. To stay
> always within it is to commit himself to precedent, to tradition. Therefore those
> influences that are powerful against tradition are uncongenial and minimized in their
> institutions, and the greatest of these is individualism. It is disruptive, according to
> Apollonian philosophy in the Southwest, even when it refines upon and enlarges the
> tradition itself. That is not to say that the Pueblos prevent this. No culture can
> protect itself from additions and changes. But the process by which these come is
> suspect and cloaked, and institutions that would give individuals a free hand are
> outlawed. . . . [While the Dionysian seeks oblivion and ecstasy in the dances, the
> Pueblo Indians] are bent not at all upon an ecstatic experience, but upon so thorough-
> going an identification with nature that the forces of nature will swing to their
> purposes. This intent dictates the form and spirit of Pueblo dances. There is nothing
> wild about them. It is the cumulative force of the rhythm, the perfection of forty
> men moving as one, that makes them effective (Benedict 1934:79–93).

Despite Benedict's insight into the meanings and concepts of Pueblo
ceremonialism, she obviously never saw nor recognized the obvious Dionysian
aspects of religious expression present in other Zuni ceremonial rites. The initiation
rite for membership into the Onayanakia Order of the Great Fire Fraternity described by Matilda Coxe Stevenson about the turn of the present century is the
epitome of Dionysian behavior:

> The warrior gradually becomes wilder in his gesticulations before the altar, bending
> until he almost kneels before it, which he leaves every now and then to join the
> dancers or to heal the sick. A guest from the pueblo of Sia, who belongs to the Fire
> fraternity of that pueblo, goes to the fireplace and stamps in the fire and literally bathes
> himself in the live coals. He then takes a large coal in his right hand, and after
> rubbing his throat and breast with it he places it in his mouth. Others of the Fire
> fraternity also play with coals, rubbing them over one another's backs. As the night
> wanes, the cries of the theurgists become lounder and wilder, and the dance grows
> faster . . . (Stevenson 1904:495).

Another example of non-Apollonian, Dionysian behavior is the orgiastic
rites of the Newekwe, one of the fraternities of the Zuni Beast God associations.
Again we quote from Stevenson:

> The one who swallows the largest amount of filth with the greatest gusto is most
> commended by the fraternity and the onlookers. A large bowl of urine is handed by a
> Koyemshi, who receives it from a woman on the house top, to a man of the fraternity,
> who, after drinking a portion, pours the remainder over himself by turning the
> bowl over his head. Women run to the edge of the roof and empty bowls of urine over
> the Newekwe and Koyemshi. Each man endeavors to excel his fellows in buffoonery
> and in eating repulsive things such as bits of old blankets or splinters of wood. They
> bite off the heads of living mice and chew them, tear dogs limb from limb, eat the
> intestines and fight over the liver like hungry wolves (Stevenson 1904:437).

This kind of behavior is typically indulged in by the clown associations in
other pueblos. The antics of these groups are not condoned as proper behavior for

the ordinary population and may be regarded from the view of Pueblo society generally as techniques to indicate that the cult groups have license to act in a way the Pueblo population as a whole cannot and should not behave. This type of behavior by these associations is also obviously a social mechanism to "blow off steam." The behavior permitted the general population is highly restricted and circumscribed. These ceremonies permit the pueblo audience to participate vicariously in behavior strictly denied them. The clown associations in all pueblos —east or west—serve the role of maintaining proper behavior, by indulging in behavior no human should engage in and often by ridiculing members of the pueblo who have "fallen out of line" (see Dozier 1954:339–340).

Benedict deemphasized the role of the Pueblo individual and presented an unreal calm and unruffled picture of Pueblo life. Every pueblo had and has its outspoken aggressive individuals and much of the dissension and turmoil in Pueblo life is brought about by such individuals. Yet, these individuals also bring about change and keep Pueblo society and culture in step with the times. During the eighteenth century, a Jose Naranjo of Santa Clara Pueblo was the *capitán mayor* of all the Indian Pueblo warriors. He led Indian troops on successful retaliatory attacks against nomadic Indian enemies. In the latter part of the eighteenth century, Polacca, a Tewa from Hano, served as a highly respected and able interpreter and intermediary between the Hopi and American government officials. Nampeyo (Hano) and Maria Martinez (San Ildefonso) have won acclaim in this century as talented potters, whose influence is firmly established in their respective villages. In 1965, the Governor of Isleta pueblo evicted the Catholic priest from the pueblo because he interferred with Indian customs. These individuals are not atypical Pueblo Indians; they simply indicate that Pueblo individualism is an important ingredient of Pueblo society and culture. In ceremonial organizations and activities, the Pueblo individual may choose to submerge his individuality and he may also oppose nomination or election to a ceremonial office; but there are too many examples of individual deviants to assume that Pueblo culture does not also produce rebels.

World View and Concepts

As we noted earlier, rain-making or weather control ceremonies may be emphasized in the west; but while other concerns receive more attention in the east, petition for rain or moisture is also an important feature of Eastern Pueblo ceremonialism. Another shared series of concepts involve Pueblo ideas of origin, the nature of the universe, and the conceptual ordering and spatial arrangement of the pueblos. There are, of course, detailed differences from pueblo to pueblo. We are not interested in such variations at present, but rather our concern is with the commonalities of Pueblo world view and concepts.

In general form, and even in some of the details, the origin myths of all the pueblos are remarkably similar. All relate emergence from a world underneath the present one. The emergence is reported to be from an opening in the roof of the lower world. An aperture symbolizing the place of emergence is represented by a hole in the floor of some kivas, but not in all Pueblo kivas. It is interesting that despite linguistic differences among the various pueblos, the term for the place of emergence is phonetically similar: *sipap* (Keresan); *sipophene* (Tewa); *sipapu* (Hopi). The origin myths tell of several worlds underneath the earth in which their ancestors lived before ascending into the present one. Once they emerged, the people started to migrate to their present villages. The Western Pueblos, including the Keresans, view the migration as taking place in clans; the Tanoans say they migrated either in dual divisions or the entire pueblo population as a unit. War gods, usually two in number (the Tewa had six but these were associated in pairs) are said to have assisted the people in the emergence. (The war gods are thought to be either younger and older brothers, or they are sometimes said to be twins.) Important events in the myth are repeated four times; often the first three events or trials are ineffective, but on the fourth event or trial, the desired goal or end is achieved. The following excerpt from the San Juan version of the Tewa origin myth (Ortiz 1969) reveals the importance of sequences or events in four:

> The Tewa were living in *Sipofene* beneath Sandy Place Lake far to the north. The world under the lake was like this one, but it was dark. Supernaturals, men and animals lived together at this time and death was unknown. Among the supernaturals were the first mothers of all the Tewa [one for each moiety]. . . .
>
> These mothers asked one of the men present to go forth and explore the way by which the people might leave the lake. Three times the man refused, but on the fourth request he agreed. He went first to the north, but saw only mist and haze; then he went successively to the west, south and east, but again saw only mist and haze. After each of these four ventures he reported back to the corn mothers and people that he had seen nothing; that the world above was still ochu, "green" or "unripe."

Symbolism

The Tewa myth above contains items, events, or conditions occurring in all the myths. One of these is the reference to an original being—the creator of all things, often called "mother." This original being is clearly female (the Tewa have two creators or "corn mothers"). The underworld is also (as in the myth above) generally said to be dark and references to the present world describe it as raw (green, unripe) wet, muddy, but already drying or hardening. Frequently mentioned as characteristic of the place of emergence are: extreme humidity, fog, mist, and often billowing clouds or fog. The Rio Grande Pueblos generally believe the place of emergence to be in the north, the Tanoan believing additionally that the emergence took place from underneath a lake. All these references may be noted in the Tewa myth above. The order in which the cardinal points are given in ritual observance are important. In the above quotation, the typical sequential system is observed counterclockwise: north, west, south, east. For certain rituals, up (zenith) and down (nadir) follow.

Cardinal directions are associated with colors, animals, and mountains. The tables below indicate some color and animal correspondences with the directions and also some differences in the major pueblos:

TABLE 7

CARDINAL DIRECTION—COLOR ASSOCIATIONS*

Cardinal Points	Hopi	Zuni	Keresan	Jemez	Tewa	Isleta	Tiwa Picuris	Taos
North	Yellow	Yellow	Yellow	Yellow	Blue	Black	Black	Blue
West	Blue	Blue	Blue	Blue	Yellow	Yellow	Yellow	Yellow
South	Red	Red	Red	Red	Red	Buff	Blue	Blue
East	White	White	White	White	White	White	White	White
Zenith	Black	All colors	Brown (Laguna-black)	All colors	All colors			
Nadir	All colors	Black	Black	Black	Black			

* Source: Harrington 1916:41–45; Parsons 1939:365–366.

TABLE 8

CARDINAL DIRECTION—MAMMAL AND BIRD ASSOCIATIONS*

| Cardinal Points | Hopi | Zuni | Keresan | Jemez | Tewa | Tiwa | | |
						Isleta	Picuris	Taos
North	Mountain Lion *Oriole*	Mountain Lion *Oriole*	Mountain Lion *Oriole*	Mountain Lion *Oriole*	Mountain Lion *Oriole*	Mountain Lion *Oriole*	Mountain Lion *Oriole*	Mountain Lion *Oriole*
West	Bear *Bluebird*	Bear *Bluebird*	Bear Weasel- (Acoma Laguna) *Bluebird*	Bear *Bluebird*	Bear *Bluebird*	Bear *Bluebird*	Bear *Bluebird*	Bear *Bluebird*
South	Wildcat *Parrot*	Badger *Parrot*	Wildcat *Parrot*	Wildcat *Parrot*	Badger *Parrot* (*Makow*)	Wildcat *Parrot*	Wildcat *Parrot*	Wildcat *Parrot*
East	Wolf *Magpie*	Wolf *Magpie*	Wolf *Magpie*	Wolf *Magpie*	Wolf *Magpie*	Wolf *Magpie*	Wolf *Magpie*	Wolf *Magpie*
Zenith†	*Tanager* (Western?)	Eagle	Eagle	Eagle	Eagle			
Nadir‡	*Mole*	Mole	*Mole*	Mole	*Mole* (*Gopher*)			

* Source: Harrington 1916:41–45; Parsons 1939:365–366.
† No animal association
‡ No bird association

Only five directions are recognized by the Tiwa; the sacred numbers in these pueblos are three and five, with five occurring most frequently. The association of directions with other phenomena is understandably restricted to these five directions in the Tiwa pueblos. Table 7 on Cardinal Direction—Color Associations, shows almost complete correspondence of associations among Hopi, Zuni, the Keresan pueblos, and Jemez, but are set off from the Tanoan pueblos of Tewa and Tiwa by greater internal disagreement but also as a group against the others. It is interesting that social structural differences also exhibit a similar cleavage.

The cardinal direction associations shown in Tables 7 and 8 are made in all the pueblos, but some pueblos have additional associations. Parsons considers Zuni as most thoroughgoing in this respect; even the various animal species have been subdivided by color and direction (Parsons 1939:365). The Tewa, however, must surely vie with the Zuni in the number and complexity of the phenomena associated with directions. Thus, the Tewa have cardinal corn maidens, cardinal birds, cardinal snakes, cardinal shells, cardinal trees, cardinal mountains, cardinal sacred lakes, and cardinal "houses" (Harrington 1916:41–45). Of the latter, "White House" associated with east occurs almost universally among the pueblos. According to the migration legend, after emergence, people lived at White House for a time before taking up residence in their present pueblos. Cardinal mountains and cardinal sacred lakes vary, even in the same language group. This is because mountains and lakes are designated with reference to one's own pueblo as the center and reference point.

Typical in Pueblo thought, in myths and conspicuous in ceremonies and ceremonial concepts are the phenomena of pairing and binary oppositions (Levi-Strauss 1955; 1968:39–74; Parsons 1939:101–102). Pueblo tales tell of "two" war gods, or multiples of two as among the Tewa (above). Other paired mythological beings are: The Corn Girls, the Cloud Boys; and—sometimes sexually opposed or paired—Flute Boy and Girl, Snake Boy and Girl, Hawk Boy and Girl (Hopi). Ortiz (1965:390) provides paired concepts associated with Summer and Winter People among the Tewa:

Winter People	Summer People
Ice Strong People	Summer Strong People
East Side People	West Side People
Ice People	Sun People
Turquoise People	Squash People

Another set among the Tewa (Ortiz 1965:390) illustrates opposition or contrast:

Winter	*Summer*
maleness	femaleness
strength	weakness
hunting	agriculture
food: meat	food: wild and cultivated plants
mountains, shrines, and lakes of the north and east	mountains, shrines, and lakes of the south and west

colors: red [blue?]   colors: yellow and
    and white   black [red?]

The dual division of the Hopi ceremonial year into a season of masked Katcina ceremonies as against a season of non-Katcina ceremonies (approximately February–July; August–January) illustrates binary opposition. The alternation of Pueblo ceremonial rule among the Tewa from the Winter to Summer moiety about the time of the vernal equinox and back again to the Winter moiety at the autumnal equinox is another example. Still other illustrations of paired opposites are the division of foods into "hot" and "cold" categories; animals into predators and nonpredators; ceremonies into sacred and profane, and so on. Pairing and binary contrasts are thus basic in Pueblo thought and ceremonialism, indeed as Leach (1967:3) asserts they may be "intrinsic to the process of human thought." But mediating categories also appear—hence the frequent formation of triads (compare Levi-Strauss 1963:151). Ortiz (1969) notes that the pig and wheat (introduced foods) have both hot and cold qualities and that the carrion-eating birds are neither predators or nonpredators for they eat meat, but do not kill in order to eat. The war captains among the Pueblos have both sacred and secular functions and indeed all village ceremonial associations fit into an intermediary category in both Keresan and Tanoan Pueblo ceremonial organizations.

In ritual events, the repetition or performance of rites in fours is almost pan-Pueblo, but the Tiwa pueblos (Isleta, Picuris and Taos) have three and five as favored numerals. Elsewhere in the pueblos, however, important events must be performed four times before an act, bequest, or ritual is completed, favored, or consummated. Parsons notes that in an Acoma tale, the war chief asks the town chief four times before he brings a foreign spouse into the pueblo. According to the Hopi-Tewa migration legend a delegation of Walpi (Hopi) chiefs invited the Tewa of Tsawareh (the ancestral home of the Hopi-Tewa in New Mexico) three times to come to Hopi, each time they refused, but on the fourth request they consented (Dozier 1954:353).

Another common and interesting phenomenon of the Tewa, but perhaps more widely distributed among the Pueblos, is the association of the ecological environment with the socioceremonial organization. Thus, each Tewa village has concentric ecological zones emanating outwards from the center of the pueblo to the peripheries of the Tewa world. Each zone has four shrines located in approximately the cardinal directions, but in prominent physical locations, mounds, hills, cliffs, and the like. First is a zone encircling the pueblo, second, a zone extending to the edge of the cultivated fields, third a zone including the uncultivated plains and foothills, and finally a fourth zone of the encircling mountains. In the last zone are the directional mountains or peaks bounding the Tewa world, each containing a spring and a shrine. The village and cultivated fields are the domain of the town chiefs or moiety priests, and the village ceremonial association priests have authority in the zones beyond. In somewhat of a different position are the war captains who are in charge of dealing with outsiders. Since the moiety and village association priests are involved with sacerdotal duties they do not engage directly with visitors or secular activities. The war captains are intermediaries between the domain of the sacred and the domain of the profane.

All of the important indigenous social and religious institutions of the Pueblos present today were believed to have been organized before the emergence or while coming into this world. The Katcina cult may be an exception to this statement, for Katcinas are generally considered ancestral spirits, that is, beings who once were mortals and after death became immortal. The metaphysical distinctions or categories of humans are extremely complex among the pueblos and not the same in all the villages. There is variation even in the same language group (Ortiz 1969). There is, however, a distinction between those members of the esoteric cults (associations) and nonassociation people in all of the pueblos. This is a distinction between those who have been initiated and are members of the esoteric organizations and who have been taught and know the Pueblo ritual lore, as against the "commoners" who are not members of these associations and have a restricted knowledge of the rituals, the ceremonies and their meanings.

Pueblo Universes

Settlement in the villages that Pueblos now occupy are believed to have occurred in ancient times. None of the Pueblos put as much emphasis as the Hopi on the order of arrival in the sites these pueblos now occupy. Hopi conceive of the migration as travel by clans and the priority of the arrival of these clans in Hopi country is important in determining the status and the prestige of clan members, particularly in the ranking of clans. But the sequence in which the clans arrived is confused. Eggan provides a clue to the actual Hopi thinking in clan arrival statements:

> The origin legends of the Hopi follow a characteristic pattern. After the emergence of the various clans from the underworld they sent out in various directions, ultimately arriving at one or another of the Hopi villages. During their migrations they met other clans with whom they became associated and lived at various of the ruins which dot the Southwest. The early ethnologists, particularly Fewkes [Fewkes 1900] accepted these legends at their face value and attempted to reconstruct Hopi history in accordance with them. But it soon became apparent that the origin legends of the same clan from different villages showed major contradictions and that even within the same village the stories of associated clans did not always correspond. And later research has suggested that the *order* of arrival of clans at various villages parallels their present ceremonial precedence (Eggan 1950:79, italics in original).

The Pueblo Indian is quite ethnocentric about his pueblo, and considers it the "center" of the universe. Language, appearance, ceremonials, anything that may be compared or evaluated is at its best in one's own pueblo. Other Pueblo Indians, even those of the same language group: speak funny; dance crudely; are without religious devotion; and either look or behave like Mexicans or Anglos. Zuni calls itself the "Middle Place" (Parsons 1935:155); San Juan Pueblo considers itself the "mother village" of the Tewa (Ortiz 1969). Parsons provides other examples of Pueblo ethnocentricism:

> The sense of town solidarity expressed itself again and again in attitudes of conceit or superiority. The Hopi term for "bad" is *kahopi,* "not Hopi." Descendants

of Pecos immigrants to Jemez are still saying that Jemez people "know nothing." An Isletan friend writes: "This pueblo has all different ceremonials; other pueblos or any other pueblos or any other tribe have not much." Santo Domingo will refer to the people of neighboring towns as "no good" or "crazy." They laugh at the way other Keres speak Keresan. They assume that pueblos with customs similar to theirs have borrowed them, never admitting that they themselves have been the borrowers—a common Pueblo attitude. Pottery designs are borrowed from town to to the people of neighboring towns as "no good" or "crazy." They laugh at the bird designs of Sia and Laguna. In Laguna it is asserted that Hopi and Zuni did not know how to get salt from Zuni Salt Lake until Laguna people showed them what to do. . . . White people . . . or other tribes, even the enemy who destroyed whole towns, all seem inferior or ridiculous to the Pueblo patriot (Parsons 1939:7–8).

Politically the Pueblos have never been united and each village or pueblo is an independent unit. Again we quote from Parsons, who emphasized the autonomous character of Pueblo towns:

> The town is the collective unit, not the tribe which may be defined as composed of towns speaking the same language, possessed of the same kinship principles and by and large of the same ceremonial system. With so much in common, a considerable degree of solidarity might be supposed to exist within each of the five tribes. Actually there is but little. Kachina dancers visit other towns, bestowing the blessings of rainfall and abundance; societies may send delegates to a neighboring town to participate in an initiation or installation, and intertown foot or horse races, intertown games, and even intertown working parties occur among Hopi: otherwise I know of no formal intertown cooperation. But visitors or sojourners will be expected to dance or sing for their hosts, or take part in dances performed by their hosts; and there is considerable intertown visiting and trading, particularly in the East, at the fiesta of the patron saint . . . (Parsons 1939:10–11).

Parsons' remark about the absence of intertown cooperation needs qualification. Whenever common oppression was too much to bear or disaster threatened, the Pueblos have united. The Pueblo Indian revolt is an example; another is the threat to losing Spanish grant lands to non-Pueblo squatters in the 1920s. With the aid of white friends, the Pueblos fought the Bill that would have divested them of their rights in the courts and won. The All-Pueblo Council has had a kind of sporadic existence through the years; indeed, the Indians claim that it is the oldest intertribal organization in the United States, having been formed during the Pueblo revolt. However, when common problems are not in evidence, the Pueblos cherish the autonomous character of their home communities and respect the independence of other pueblos. The All-Pueblo Council has, as a result, not emerged as a viable and essential organization for the Pueblos. In the last few years, young educated Pueblo Indians have, however, displayed considerable interest in the organization. An office of the All-Pueblo Council has been set up in Albuquerque, where population figures, health records, and a small library are maintained. A personnel of about four people who perform secretarial duties is supported by regular contributions from the various pueblos. All the pueblos except the Hopi sent representatives to the All-Pueblo Council.

An origin myth which is essentially the same among all pueblos in its basic form, as well as a single world view including the possession of common symbolic concepts, indicates a long history of sharing and pan-Pueblo borrowing. By choice, obviously, the Pueblos have refrained from instituting an overall political organization. The pueblos have cooperated freely in ceremonial life, however, without surrendering political autonomy. In the west, particularly among the Hopi and Laguna pueblos, the emphasis laid on unilineal kinship organizations, households, lineages, and clans, has given the village a loose integration. In the east, association membership and the importance of these organizations in government and religion have given these pueblos greater centralization. The Rio Grande pueblos are actually little city states, having a strong, even despotic, control over their members.

Structural differences between the Western Pueblos and the Rio Grande pueblos are explained by reference to the irrigation hypothesis. Steward (1955:171) has presented a suggestive hypothesis of a clan system developing from preexisting band organizations when certain ecological conditions exist. The Rio Grande pueblos are an example of a stage beyond which political autonomy passes from clan (Keresan pueblos) or kinship control in general (Tanoan pueblos) to nonkin based units that provide highly centralized integration on the village level.

The above account of the Western Pueblos has not restricted itself to these pueblos. All of the Pueblos have shared intimately a common environment and have faced the same kind of problems. As a result, it is not always possible to point out the differences between the pueblos of the west and those of the east. Differences in the structural aspects of their social, political, and ceremonial organizations are apparent, but no clear distinctions are evident in other areas of their culture. This is particularly true in world view and ethical concepts. The following description of the Hopi view of life and its underlying principles may apply equally as well for all the Pueblos:

> The Hopi way of looking at the universe is quite different from our own and accounts for much in Hopi culture and personality which may seem strange to us. It shows that the conception of change in linear, cause-and-effect terms, common among us is absent in the thinking of these people, who see life in terms of inter-related, multi-manifested wholes in the process of metamorphosis, each according to its own mode, rhythm and tempo. Moreover, the Hopi concept of the balanced, correlative interdependence of the manifold aspects of reality excludes an arbitrary over-all dual division, such as that which structures our own thinking and forms the basis for our traditional ethical concept of the competing forces of good and evil. Duality in the Hopi world view exists only insofar as it represents two correlates in a reciprocally balanced universal scheme, and each correlate is conceived as an indispensable part of the whole, neither one being essentially subordinate to the other (Thompson and Joseph 1944:44).

The Western Pueblos received the full brunt of Spanish oppression during the seventeenth century; but after the Revolt of 1680, distance, the waning power of Spain, and the rise of nomadic Indian enemies, these pueblos broke ties with representatives of European culture on the Rio Grande. The Western Pueblos were virtually abandoned by Spanish civil and church authorities during the eighteenth and nineteenth centuries. This was particularly true during the closing periods of the Spanish regime and during the short interim of Mexican control. Native Pueblo ceremonial life might have returned to precontact conditions, but the annexation of Mexico's northern frontier in the nineteenth century by the United States brought in a new people. The newcomers immediately put their energies into quelling the raids of the nomadic Indian tribes, and by the end of the century, these Indians had been pacified and placed on reservations. With the control of the raiding Apaches and Navahos, agents of the United States government and missionaries of various Protestant denominations established relationships with Zuni and Hopi Pueblos and proceeded to convert all the Pueblos to a brand of Christianity and Americanism. Yet, because of their isolation and less intensive contact with representatives of Anglo-American culture, the Western Pueblos have remained more friendly, cooperative and hospitable to whites than the Eastern Pueblos. Euro-American society and culture will eventually overwhelm them; but they will undoubtedly resist assimilation as effectively as their social and cultural relatives along the Rio Grande in New Mexico.

Glossary

ASSOCIATION (societies, sodalities): A group where the basis of membership is determined by voluntary choice or recruitment, not by kinship. Pueblo associations are either moiety organizations or crosscut the entire village in membership. Membership in Pueblo associations is for life, members are recruited and confirmed by an elaborate initiation rite.

BILATERAL: The reckoning of kinship relationships from both the father's and mother's side.

CACIQUE: A word of Arawakan (Caribbean Indians) origin, applied by Spanish officials to indigenous religious leaders. Among the Pueblos the term designates the supreme village or town priest under the native governmental and ceremonial organization. The Pueblo *cacique* is considered the primary authority in all matters—sacred and profane.

CLAN: As used in this study, clans are unilineal descent groups traced through the mother's side. They are exogamous units and among the Western Pueblos they control land, ceremonial associations, and ceremonies. Knowledge of actual consanguineal (blood) ties are unknown—the basis of affiliation is a common clan name.

ENDOGAMOUS: A rule of marriage which enforces its members to marry within the group.

EXOGAMOUS: A rule of marriage which enforces its members to seek marriage partners outside the group.

EXTENDED FAMILY: A situation where membership in a family is extended beyond the limits of a nuclear family.

GENIZARO: Indians who have adopted a Hispanicized way of life in New Mexico, the descendants of Indians who were purchased or captured from nomadic tribes.

HISPANO: The Hispanicized population of New Mexico, which is of mixed Indian-Spanish background.

KATCINA CULT: An association, distinctively Indian, that usually comprises all male members of a pueblo and in some villages female members as well, above ages 6–9. The cult is concerned with supernatural beings somewhat vaguely connected with ancestral spirits and believed to have the power to bring rain. In spectacular ceremonies, male members of the cult impersonate the katcina by donning masks and colorful costumes.

KIVA: Pueblo ceremonial structure used for ceremonies, as a men's workshop and among the Western Pueblos as a man's dormitory. In some pueblos it is wholly or partly underground; it is either circular or rectangular in shape.

LINEAGE: As used in this book, a clan segment whose members can trace relationships from a known common ancestress.

MOIETY: A dual division of the village. In most of the Rio Grande pueblos where moieties exist, an individual takes the moiety of his father, but this affiliation may be changed later for various reasons. In some pueblos if the parents belong to different moieties, their children are assigned alternately to one moiety and then the other. Pueblo moieties are neither endogamous nor exogamous.

NUCLEAR FAMILY: A kinship group consisting of father and mother and their children.

UNILINEAL: The reckoning of kinship relations through a single line of descent only, either through the mother's or father's side.

213

References

ABERLE, S. D., 1948, *The Pueblo Indians of New Mexico: Their Land, Economy, and Civil Organization.* Memoir No. 70, Menasha, Wisc.: American Anthropological Association, Vol. 50, No. 4, Part 2.

ADAIR, JOHN, 1944, *The Navaho and Pueblo Silversmiths.* Norman, Okla.: University of Oklahoma Press.

ADAMS, ELEANOR B., ed., 1954, *Bishop Tamaron's Visitation of New Mexico, 1760.* Historical Society of New Mexico, Publication in History, Vol. 15.

ADAMS, ELEANOR B., and FRAY ANGELICO CHAVEZ, eds., 1956, *The Missions of New Mexico, 1776.* Albuquerque, N.M.: University of New Mexico Press.

AITKEN, BARBARA, 1930, *Temperament in Native American Indian Religion.* Journal of the Royal Anthropological Institute 60:363–87.

ANDERSON, FRANK G., 1955, *The Pueblo Kachina Cult: A Historical Reconstruction.* Southwestern Journal of Anthropology 11:404–419.

ANDERSON, FRANK G., 1956, *Early Documentary Material on the Pueblo Kachina Cult.* Anthropological Quarterly 29:31–44.

ANDERSON, FRANK G., 1960, *Inter-tribal Relations in the Pueblo Kachina Cult.* Fifth International Congress of Anthropological and Ethnological Sciences, Selected Papers, 377–383.

BAHTI, TOM, 1968, *Southwestern Indian Tribes.* Flagstaff, Ariz.: KC Publications.

BAILEY, PAUL, 1948, *Jacob Hamblin, Buckskin Apostle.* Los Angeles: Western Lore Press.

BANCROFT, H. H., 1889, *The Works of H. H. Bancroft, Vol. 17, History of Arizona and New Mexico: 1530–1888.* San Francisco: The History Co.

BANDELIER, ADOLPH F. A., 1890–1892, *Final Report of Investigations Among the Indians of the Southwestern United States.* Cambridge, Mass.: J. Wilson and Sons. 2 vols.

BECK, WARREN A., 1962, *New Mexico, A History of Four Centuries.* Norman, Okla.: University of Oklahoma Press.

BENAVIDES, ALONSO DE, 1630, *The Memorial of Fray Alonso de Benavides.* Translated by Mrs. I. E. Ayer; annotated by F. W. Hodge. Chicago: University of Chicago Press, 1916.

BENEDICT, RUTH, 1934, *Patterns of Culture.* Boston: Houghton Mifflin Company.

BLOOM, L. B., 1931, *A Campaign Against the Moqui Pueblos.* New Mexico Historical Review 6:158–226.

BLOOM, L. B., 1935, *A Trade-Invoice of 1638.* New Mexico Historical Review 10: 242–248.

BLOOM, L. B., 1935–1938, *Bourke on the Southwest.* New Mexico Historical Review 10:271, 322; 11:217–282; 12:41–77; 13:192–238.

BODINE, JOHN J., 1968, *A Tri-Ethnic Trap: The Spanish Americans in Taos.* American Ethnological Society, pp. 162–177. Seattle: University of Washington Press.

BOLTON, H. E., 1916, *The Espejo Expedition, 1582–1583.* In H. E. Bolton, ed.: *Spanish Exploration in the Southwest, 1542–1706,* pp. 161–196. New York: Charles Scribner's Sons.

BRYAN, KIRK, 1929, *Floodwater Farming.* Geographical Review 19:444–456.

BUNZEL, RUTH L., 1932, *Introduction to Zuni Ceremonialism.* Washington, D.C.: Smithsonian Institution, Bureau of American Ethnology, Annual Report No. 47.

BUNZEL, RUTH L., 1929, *The Pueblo Potter: A Study in Creative Imagination in Primitive Art.* Columbia University Contributions to Anthropology, Vol. 8.

CARROLL, H. BAILEY, and J. VILLASAVA HAGGARD, 1942, *Three New Mexico Chronicles: The Exposicion of Don Pedro Bautista Pino, 1912: The Ojeada of Lic. Antonio*

Barreiro, 1832: and the Additions by Jose Augustin de Escudero, 1849. Albuquerque, N.M.: The Qhivera Society.

CHAVEZ, FRAY ANGELICO, 1954, *The Penitentes of New Mexico.* New Mexico Historical Review 29:97–123.

CHAVEZ, FRAY ANGELICO, 1955, *José Gonzales, Genizaro Governor.* New Mexico Historical Review 30:190–194.

CHAVEZ, FRAY ANGELICO, 1967, *Pohe-Yemos Representative and the Revolt of 1680.* New Mexico Historical Review 42:85–126.

CHILDE, V. GORDON, 1950, *The Urban Revolution.* Town Planning Review 21:3–17.

CLELAND, ROBERT GLASS, 1952, *This Reckless Breed of Men: The Trappers and Fur Traders of the Southwest.* New York.

CRANE, LEO, 1928, *Desert Drums: The Pueblo Indians of New Mexico, 1540–1928.* Boston: Little, Brown & Company.

DAVIS, IRVINE, 1963, *Bibliography of Keresan Linguistic Sources.* International Journal of American Linguistics 29:289–293.

DAVIS, IRVINE, 1964, *The Language of Santa Ana Pueblo.* Smithsonian Institution: Bureau of American Ethnology, Bulletin 191, Anthropological Papers, No. 69.

DOZIER, EDWARD P., 1954, *The Hopi-Tewa of Arizona.* University of California Publications in American Archaeology and Ethnology 44:259–376.

DOZIER, EDWARD P., 1955, *Kinship and Linguistic Change Among the Arizona Tewa.* International Journal of American Linguistics, Vol. 21, No. 3, July 1955, pp. 242–257.

DOZIER, EDWARD P., 1956, *Two Examples of Linguistic Acculturation, the Yaqui of Sonora Arizona and Tewa of New Mexico.* Language 32:146–157.

DOZIER, EDWARD P., 1958, *Ethnological Clues for the b. Sources of Rio Grande Population.* In Raymond H. Thompson, ed.: Migrations in New World Culture History. Tucson: University of Arizona Press.

DOZIER, EDWARD P., 1960, *The Pueblos of the Southwestern United States.* Journal of the Royal Anthropological Institute 90:146–160.

DOZIER, EDWARD P., 1960 b., *Comparison of Kereson and Tewa Kinship Systems.* Fifth International Congress of Anthropological and Ethnographical Sciences, Selected Papers 430–436.

DOZIER, EDWARD P., 1961, *Rio Grande Pueblos.* In Edward H. Spicer, ed.: Perspectives in American Indian Culture Change, 94–186. Chicago: University of Chicago Press.

DOZIER, EDWARD P., 1966, *Factionalism at Santa Clara Pueblo.* Ethnology Vol. 15, No. 2, pp. 172–185.

DUMAREST, N., 1919, *Notes on Cochiti, N. M.* Memoirs of the American Anthropological Association, No. 6, Part 3, 1919.

DUNN, DOROTHY, 1968, *American Indian Painting of the Southwest and Plains Areas.* Tucson: University of Arizona Press.

DUTTON, BERTHA, ed., 1963, *Indians of the Southwest.* Santa Fe: Southwestern Association on Indian Affairs, Inc.

DUTTON, BERTHA, 1966, *Prehistoric Migrations into the Galisteo Basin, New Mexico.* Sevilla, Spain: 36 Congreso Internacional de Americanistas, Vol. 1, pp. 287–300.

EGGAN, DOROTHY, 1953, *Personality in Nature, Society and Culture.* New Edition: Clyde Kluckhohn, Harry H. Murray, and David M. Schneider, eds., New York.

EGGAN, FRED, 1950, *Social Organization of the Western Pueblos.* Chicago: University of Chicago Press.

EGGAN, FRED, 1966, *The American Indian, Perspectives for the Study of Social Change.* Chicago: Aldine Publishing Company.

ELLIS, FLORENCE HAWLEY, 1951a, *Patterns of Aggression and the War Cult in the Southwestern Pueblos.* Southwestern Journal of Anthropology 7:177–201.

ELLIS, FLORENCE HAWLEY, 1951b, *Pueblo Social Organization and Southwestern Archaeology.* American Antiquity 17:148–151.

ELLIS, FLORENCE HAWLEY, 1953, *Authoritative Control and the Society System in Jemez Pueblo.* Southwestern Journal of Anthropology 9:385–394.

ELLIS, FLORENCE HAWLEY, 1964, *A Reconstruction of the Basic Jemez Pattern of Social Organization, with Comparisons to Other Tanoan Social Structures.* Albuquerque, N.M.: University of New Mexico Publications in Anthropology, No. 11.

ELLIS, FLORENCE HAWLEY, 1967, *Where Did the Pueblo People Come From?* El Palacio, Autumn.

ESPINOSA, J. M., 1940, *First Expedition of Vargas Into New Mexico, 1692.* Translated, with introduction and notes by J. Manuel Espinosa, Coronado Historical Series, Vol. X. Albuquerque, N.M.: University of New Mexico Press.

FENTON, WILLIAM N., 1957, *Factionalism at Taos Pueblo, New Mexico.* Washington, D.C.: Smithsonian Institution, Bureau of American Ethnology, Bulletin 164.

FEWKES, J. W., 1900, *The Tusayan Migration Myth.* Washington, D.C.: Smithsonian Institution, Bureau of American Ethnology, Annual Report No. 19.

FOSTER, GEORGE M., 1953, *Cofradia and Compadrazgo in Spain and Spanish America.* Southwestern Journal of Anthropology 9:1–28.

FOX, J. R., 1967, *The Keresan Bridge.* London School of Economics Monographs on Social Anthropology, No. 35. The Athlone Press, University of London. New York: Humanities Press, Inc.

FRANCIS, E. K., 1956, *Multiple Inter-group Relations in the Upper Rio Grande Region.* American Sociological Review 21:84–87.

GANAWAY, LOOMIS MORTON, 1944, *New Mexico and the Sectional Controversy: 1846–1861.* Albuquerque, N.M.

GILLIN, JOHN, 1948, *The Ways of Man.* New York: Appleton-Century-Crofts.

GODDARD, PLINY E., 1913, *Indians of the Southwest.* New York: American Museum of Natural History, 2nd ed., 1921.

GOLDFRANK, E. S., 1927, *The Social and Ceremonial Organization of the Cochiti.* Memoirs of the American Anthropological Association, No. 33.

GOLDFRANK, ESTHER, 1945, *Socialization, Personality, and the Structure of the Pueblo Society.* American Anthropologist 47:516–539.

GOLDFRANK, ESTHER, 1952, *The Different Patterns of Blackfoot and Pueblo Adaptation to White Authority.* In Tax, ed., Acculturation in the Americas, Vol. II: Proceedings of the 29th International Congress of Americanists. Chicago: University of Chicago Press.

GREGG, JOSIAH, 1954, *Commerce of the Prairies.* Max Moorhead, ed. Norman, Okla.: University of Oklahoma Press.

GUTHE, C. E., 1925, *Pueblo Pottery Making: A Study at the Village of San Ildefonso.* New Haven: Papers of the Philip's Academy Southwestern Expedition, No. 2.

HACK, J. T., 1942, *The Changing Physical Environment of the Hopi Indians of Arizona.* Cambridge, Mass.: Peabody Museum of American Archaeology and Ethnology Papers, Vol. 36.

HACKETT, CHARLES W., ed., 1937, *Historical Documents Relating to New Mexico, Nueva Vizcaya, and Approaches Thereto, to 1773.* Collected by Adolph F. A. Bandelier and Fanny R. Bandelier. Washington, D.C.: Carnegie Institute of Washington. 3 vols.

HACKETT, C. W., and C. C. SHELBY, 1942, *Revolt of the Pueblo Indians of New Mexico and Otermin's Attempted Reconquest, 1680–1682.* Coronado Historical Series, Vols. 3, 8 and 9. Albuquerque, N.M.: The University of New Mexico Press.

HALE, KENNETH, 1958, *Internal Diversity in Uto-Aztecan, I.* International Journal of American Linguistics 24:101–107.

HALE, KENNETH, 1962, *Jemez and Kiowa Correspondences in Reference to Kiowa-Tanoan.* International Journal of American Linguistics 28:1–5.

HALLENBECK, CLEVE, 1950, *Land of Conquistadores.* Caldwell, Ida. Caxton Printers.

HAMMOND, G. P., 1926, *Don Juan de Onate, and the Founding of New Mexico.* New Mexico Historical Review 1:42–77; 2:156–192.

HAMMOND, G. P., and AGAPITO REY, 1966, *The Rediscovery of New Mexico: 1580–1594.* Coronado Cuarto Centennial Publications (1540–1940), Volume III. Albuquerque, N.M.: The University of New Mexico Press.

HARRINGTON, JOHN P., 1909, *Notes on the Piro Language.* American Anthropologist 11: 563–594.

HARRINGTON, JOHN P., 1910, *On Phonetic and Lexical Resemblances Between Kiowa and Tanoan.* Santa Fe: Papers of the School of American Archaeology, No. 12.

HARRINGTON, JOHN P., 1910, *A Brief Description of the Tewa Language.* American Anthropologist 12:497–504.

HARRINGTON, JOHN P., 1912, *Tewa Relationship Terms.* American Anthropologist n.s. 14 (No. 3):472–498.

HARRINGTON, JOHN P., 1916, *The Ethnogeography of the Tewa Indians.* Twenty-ninth Annual Report (for 1907–1908). Washington, D. C.: Smithsonian Institution, Bureau of American Ethnology.

HAURY, EMIL W., 1956, *Speculations on Prehistoric Settlement Patterns in the Southwest.* In Gordon R. Willey, ed.: Prehistoric Settlement Patterns in the New World. New York: Viking Fund Publications in Anthropology, No. 23, pp. 3–10.

HAURY, EMIL W., 1962, *The Greater American Southwest.* In Robert J. Braidwood, ed.: Courses Towards Urban Life, pp. 106–131. New York: Wenner-Gren Foundation for Anthropological Research, Inc.

HAWLEY, FLORENCE, 1937, *Pueblo Social Organization As A Lead to Pueblo History.* American Anthropologist 39:504–522.

HAWLEY, FLORENCE (ELLIS), 1948, *The Keresan Holy Rollers: An Adaptation to American Individualism.* Social Forces 26 (No. 3):273–280.

HAWLEY, FLORENCE, 1950a, *Big Kivas, Little Kivas and Moiety Houses in Historical Reconstruction.* Southwestern Journal of Anthropology.

HAWLEY, FLORENCE, 1950b, *Keresan Patterns of Kinship and Social Organization.* American Anthropologist 52:499–512.

HAWLEY, FLORENCE, and DONOVAN SENTER, 1946, *Group-Designed Behavior Patterns in Two Acculturating Groups.* Southwestern Journal of Anthropology 2:133–151.

HILL, W. W., No date, Unpublished manuscript on Santa Clara Pueblo.

HODGE, F. W., 1906, *Pueblo Indian Clans.* American Anthropologist 9:345–352.

HODGE, F. W., 1907, *The Narrative of the Expedition of Coronado by Pedro de Castaneda.* In F. W. Hodge, and T. H. Lewis, eds.: Spanish Explorers in the Southern United States, 1528–1543, pp. 275–387. New York: Charles Scribner's Sons.

HODGE, F. W., ed., 1912, *Handbook of American Indians North of Mexico.* Washington, D.C.: Bureau of American Ethnology, Bulletin 30, Parts 1 and 2.

HODGE, F. W., C. P. HAMMOND, and AGAPITO REY, 1945, *Revised Memorial of Alonzo de Benevides, 1634.* "Coronado Historical Series," Vol. IV. Albuquerque, N.M.: University of New Mexico Press.

HOEBEL, E. ADAMSON, 1962, *The Authority Systems of the Pueblos of the Southwestern United States,* pp. 555–563. Akten Des 34. International Amerikenisten Kongress, Wien, 18–25. July 1960, Verlag Ferdinand Berger, Horn.

HOIJER, HARRY, 1946, *Introduction* by Harry Hoijer and others, *Linguistic Structures of Native America.* No. 6, pp. 9–29. New York: Viking Fund Publications in Anthropology.

HOIJER, HARRY, and EDWARD P. DOZIER, 1949, *The Phonemes of Tewa, Santa Clara Dialect.* International Journal of American Linguistics 15:139–144.

HOLMES, JACK E., 1967, *Politics in New Mexico.* Albuquerque, N.M.: The University of New Mexico Press.

JENNINGS, JESSE D., 1956, *The American Southwest: A Problem in Cultural Isolation.* In Robert Waucope, ed. Seminars in Cultural Isolation, 1955, pp. 59–127. Salt Lake City: Memoirs of the Society of American Archaeology, No. 11.

JENNINGS, JESSE D. 1968, *Prehistory of North America.* New York: McGraw-Hill Book Co.

JONES, OAKAH L., 1966, *Pueblo Warriors.* Norman, Okla.: University of Oklahoma Press.

KELLEY, J. C., 1952, *Factors Involved in the Abandonment of Certain Peripheral Southwestern Settlements.* American Anthropologist 54:356–387.

KELLY, WILLIAM H., ed., 1954, *Indian Affairs and the Indian Reorganization Act—The Twenty Year Record*. Tucson: University of Arizona.

KIRCHOFF, PAUL, 1954, *Gatherers and Farmers in the Greater Southwest: A Problem in Classification*. American Anthropologist 56:529–550.

KLUCKHOHN, FLORENCE, and FRED L. STRODTBECK, 1961, *Variations in Value Orientations*. Evanston, Ill.: Row, Peterson & Company.

KROEBER, ALFRED L., 1917, *Zuni Kin and Clan*. New York: Anthropological Papers of the American Museum of Natural History, Vol. 18, Part 2.

KROEBER, ALFRED L., 1928, *Native Culture of the Southwest*. University of California Publications in American Archaeology and Ethnology 23:375–398.

KUBLER, GEORGE, 1940, *The Religious Architecture of New Mexico in the Colonial Period and Since the American Occupation*. Colorado Springs, Colo.: The Taylor Museum.

KURATH, GERTRUDE, 1949, *Mexican Moriscas*. Journal of American Folklore 62:87–106.

KURATH, GERTRUDE P., 1957, *The Origin of the Pueblo Indian Matachines*. El Palacio 64:259–264.

LA FARGE, OLIVER, 1956, *Assimilation—The Indian View*. New Mexico Quarterly 26:5–15.

LA FARGE, OLIVER, 1959, *Santa Fe: The Autobiography of a Southwestern Town*. Norman, Okla.: University of Oklahoma Press.

LANGE, CHARLES, 1952, *The Feast Day at Zia Pueblo, New Mexico*. Texas Journal of Science 4:19–26.

LANGE, CHARLES, 1953, *The Role of Economics in Cochiti Pueblo Culture Change*. American Anthropologist 55:674–694.

LANGE, CHARLES, 1957, *Corn Dances of the Rio Grande Pueblo Indians*. The Texas Journal of Science 9:59–74.

LANGE, CHARLES, 1959, *Cochiti: A New Mexico Pueblo Past and Present*. Austin, Tex.: University of Texas Press.

LASKI, VERA, 1959, *Seeking Life*. Philadelphia: Memoirs of the American Folklore Society, Vol. 50.

LEACH, EDMUND R., 1967, *Genesis as Myth*. In John Middleton, ed.: Myth and Cosmos, pp. 1–13. Garden City, N. Y.: The Natural History Press. Reprinted from *Discovery*, May 1962.

LEIGHTON, DOROTHEA, and JOHN ADAIR, 1966, *People of the Middle Place: A Study of the Zuni Indians*. New Haven, Conn.: Human Relations Area Files, Inc.

LEVI-STRAUSS, C., 1955, *The Structural Study of Myth*. In Sebeok, T. A., ed.: Myth: A Symposium. Bloomington, Ind.: University of Indiana Press.

LEVI-STRAUSS, C. 1963, *Do Dual Organizations Exist?* In Structural Anthropology, pp. 132–163. New York: Basic Books, Inc.

LEVI-STRAUSS, C., 1968, *The Savage Mind*. Chicago: The University of Chicago Press, Third Impression.

LINTON, RALPH, ed., 1940, *Acculturation in Seven American Indian Tribes*. New York.

MARTIN, PAUL, W. A. LONGACRE, and JAMES N. HILL, 1967, *Chapters in the Prehistory of Eastern Arizona, III*. Fieldiana: Anthropology, Vol. 57.

McNICKLE, D'ARCY, 1957, *Indian and European: Indian-White Relations from Discovery to 1887*. The Annals 311:1–11.

MARRIOTT, ALICE, 1948, *Maria the Potter of San Ildefonso*. Norman, Okla.: University of Oklahoma Press.

MEADERS, MARGARET, 1963, *The Indian Situation in New Mexico*. Bureau of Business Research. Albuquerque, N.M.: The University of New Mexico.

MERA, H. P., 1934, *A Survey of the Biscuit Ware Area in Northern New Mexico*. Santa Fe: Laboratory of Anthropology Technical Series, Bulletin 6.

MERA, H. P., 1940, *Population Changes in the Rio Grande Glaze-Paint Area*. Santa Fe: Laboratory of Anthropology Technical Series, Bulletin 9.

MERIAM and ASSOCIATES, 1928, *The Problem of Indian Administration*. Baltimore: The Johns Hopkins Press.

MICKEY, BARBARA, 1956, *Acoma Kinship Terms*. Southwestern Journal of Anthropology 12:249–256.

MILLER, WICK R., 1959, *A Note on Kiowa Linguistic Affiliations*. American Anthropologist 61:102–105.

MILLER, WICK R., 1959–1960, *Spanish Loanwords in Acoma*. I, II: International Journal of American Linguistics 25:147–153; 26:41–49.

MOSKOWITZ, IRA, and JOHN COLLIER, 1949, *Patterns and Ceremonials of the Indians of the Southwest*. New York: E. P. Dutton Co., Inc.

MURDOCK, GEORGE P., 1960, *Social Structure in Southeast Asia*. Viking Fund Publications in Anthropology, No. 29. Chicago: Quadrangle Books.

NAVAREZ VALVERDE, FRAY JOSE, 1937, *Notes Upon Moqui and Other Recent Ones Upon New Mexico*. In C. W. Hackett, ed.: Historical Documents Relating to New Mexico, Vizcaya, and Approaches Thereto, to 1773, Vol. 3, pp. 385–387. Washington, D.C.: Carnegie Institution.

NEWMAN, STANLEY S., 1958, *Zuni Dictionary*. Bloomington, Ind.: Publications of the Research Center in Anthropology, Folklore, and Linguistics, No. 6, Part 2.

NEWMAN, STANLEY S., 1964, *A Comparison of Zuni and Californian Penutian*. International Journal of American Linguistics 30 (No. 1):1–13.

NEWMAN, STANLEY S., 1954, *A Practical Zuni Orthography in Zuni Law: A Field of Values*. In Watson Smith, and John M. Roberts, eds.: Papers of the Peabody Museum of American Archaeology and Ethnology, pp. 163–170. Harvard University, Vol. 43, No. 1.

O'BRYAN, DERIC, 1952, *The Abandonment of the Northern Pueblos in the Thirteenth Century*. In Sol Tax, ed.: The Indian Tribes of Aboriginal America. Chicago: Selected Papers of the Twenty-ninth International Congress of Americanists.

ORTIZ, ALFONSO, 1963, *A Processual Analysis of a Social Movement in the Rio Grande Pueblos*. A paper submitted to the faculty of the Department of Anthropology in Candidacy for the degree of Master of Arts, University of Chicago.

ORTIZ, ALFONSO, 1965, *Dual Organization as an Operational Concept in the Pueblo Southwest*. Pittsburgh, Pa.: Ethnology, 4 (No. 4):389–396.

ORTIZ, ALFONSO, 1969, *The World of the Tewa Indians*. Chicago: University of Chicago Press.

PANDEY, TRILOKI NATH, 1968, *Tribal Council Elections in a Southwestern Pueblo*. Pittsburgh, Pa.: Ethnology, Vol. 7, No. 1.

PARSONS, E. C., 1923, *Laguna Genealogies*. New York: Anthropological Papers of the American Museum of Natural History, Vol. 19, Part 5.

PARSONS, E. C., 1924, *Tewa Kin, Clan, and Moiety*. American Anthropologist, n.s. 26: 333–339.

PARSONS, E. C., 1925, *The Pueblo of Jemez*. Andover, Mass.: Phillips Academy.

PARSONS, E. C., 1929, *The Social Organization of the Tewa of New Mexico*. Menasha, Wisc.: Memoirs of the American Anthropological Association, No. 36.

PARSONS, E. C., 1932, *The Kinship Nomenclature of the Pueblo Indians*. American Anthropologist 36:377–389.

PARSONS, E. C., 1932, *Isleta*. Washington, D.C.: Forty-seventh Annual Report of the Bureau of American Ethnology.

PARSONS, E. C., 1936, *Taos Pueblo*. Menasha, Wisc.: General Series in Anthropology, No. 2.

PARSONS, E. C., 1939, *Pueblo Indian Religion*, 2 Vols. Chicago: University of Chicago Press.

POWELL, J. W., 1891, *Indian Linguistic Families of America North of Mexico*. Bureau of American Ethnology Annual Report No. 7.

RAUP, RUTH M., 1959, *The Indian Health Program From 1800 to 1955*. Washington, D.C.: Division of Indian Health, U. S. Department of Health, Education, and Welfare.

READ, BENJAMIN M., 1912, *Illustrated History of New Mexico*. Santa Fe: Santa Fe New

Mexican Printing Co.

REED, ERIK K., 1944, *Aspects of Acculturation in the Southwest.* Acta Americana 2:62–69.

REED, ERIK, 1949, *Sources of Upper Rio Grande Culture and Population.* El Palacio 56:163–184.

REED, ERIK, 1956, *Types of Village-Plan Layouts in the Southwest.* In Gordon R. Willey, ed.: Prehistoric Settlement Patterns in the New World, pp. 11–17. New York: Viking Fund Publications in Anthropology, No. 23.

REMEU DE ARMAS, ANTONIO, 1944, *Historia de la Prevision Social en Espana Confradiasgremios Hermandades.* Montepios (Madrid).

SALPOINTE, J. B., 1898, *Soldiers of the Cross.* Banning, Calif.

SAPIR, EDWARD, 1913–1915, *Southern Paiute and Nahuatl: A Study in Uto–Aztecan.* Journal de la Societe des Americanistes de Paris 10:379–425; 11:443–488, and American Anthropologist 17:98–120, 306–328.

SCHNEIDER, DAVID M., and JOHN M. ROBERTS, 1956, *Zuni Kin Terms.* University of Nebraska: Laboratory of Anthropology, Notebook No. 3.

SCHOLES, FRANCE V., 1930, *The Supply Service of the New Mexico Missions in the Seventeenth Century.* New Mexico Historical Review 5:93–115, 186–198.

SCHOLES, FRANCE V., 1935, *Civil Government and Society in the Seventeenth Century.* New Mexico Historical Review 10:71–111.

SCHOLES, FRANCE V., 1942, *Troublous Times in New Mexico, 1659–1670.* Historical Society of New Mexico, Publications in History: Vol. 2.

SCHROEDER, ALBERT H., and DAN S. MATSON, 1965, *A Colony on the Move, Caspar Castano de Sosa's Journal 1590–1591.* Santa Fe: The School of American Research.

SCHWARTZ, D. W., 1957, *Climate Change and Culture History in the Grand Canyon Region.* American Antiquity 22:372–377.

SIEGEL, BERNARD J., *Anthropological Analysis of Shared Respect: Contributions to a Study of Revolution.* Southwestern Journal of Anthropology 5:351–368.

SIEGEL, BERNARD J., and ALAN R. BEALS, 1960, *Pervasive Factionalism.* American Anthropologist 62:394–417.

SIMMONS, MARC, 1964, *Tlascalans in the Spanish Borderlands.* New Mexico Historical Review 39:109–110.

SMITH, ANNE M., 1966, *New Mexico Indians: Economic, Educational, and Social Problems.* Santa Fe: Museum of New Mexico.

SMITH, M. ESTELLE, 1967 MS, *Power and Politics: More Factionalism at Isleta Pueblo.* Paper presented at the Annual Meeting of the American Anthropological Association, Washington, D. C., November 1967.

SMITH, WATSON, and LOUIE EWING, 1952, *Kiva Mural Decorations at Awatoui and Kwaika-a.* Cambridge, Mass.: Papers of the Peabody Museum of American Archaeology and Ethnology, Harvard University, Vol. 37.

SPENCER, ROBERT, 1947, *Spanish Loanwords in Keresan.* Southwestern Journal of Anthropology 3:130–146.

SPICER, EDWARD H., 1940, *Pascua, A Yaqui Village in Arizona.* Chicago: The University of Chicago Press.

SPICER, EDWARD H., 1954, *Spanish-Indian Acculturation in the Southwest.* American Anthropologist 56:663–678.

SPICER, EDWARD H., 1961, *Yaqui.* In Edward H. Spicer, ed.: Perspectives in American Indian Culture Change, pp. 7–93. Chicago: University of Chicago Press.

SPICER, EDWARD H., 1961, *Perspectives in American Indian Culture Change.* Chicago: University of Chicago Press.

SPICER, EDWARD H., 1962, *Cycles of Conquest.* Tucson: University of Arizona Press.

SPIER, LESLIE, 1928, *Havasupai Ethnology.* New York: American Museum of Natural History Anthropological Papers, Vol. 25, Part 2.

SPIER, LESLIE, 1929, *Problems Arising from the Cultural Position of the Havasupai.* American Anthropologist 31:213–222.

STEWARD, JULIAN H., 1937, *Ecological Aspects of Southwestern Society.* Anthropos 32:87–104.

STEWARD, JULIAN H., 1938, *Basin-Plateau Aboriginal Sociopolitical Groups.* Washington, D. C.: Bureau of American Ethnology, Bulletin 120.

STEWARD, JULIAN H., 1955, *Theory of Culture Change: The Methodology of Multilinear Evolution.* Urbana, Ill.: University of Illinois Press.

STEVENSON, M. C., 1904, *The Zuni Indians.* Washington, D. C.: 23rd Annual Report of the Bureau of American Ethnology.

STRONG, WILLIAM DUNCAN, 1927, *An Analysis of Southwestern Society.* American Anthropologist 29:1–61.

SWADESH, FRANCES LEON, 1966, *Hispanic Americans of the Ute Frontier from the Chama Valley to the San Juan Basin 1694–1960.* Boulder: Ph.D. Thesis, Graduate School, Department of Anthropology, University of Colorado.

SWADESH, FRANCES LEON, 1968, *The Alianza Movement: Catalyst for Social Change in New Mexico.* American Ethnological Society, pp. 162–177. Seattle: University of Washington Press.

TANNER, CLARA LEE, 1957, *Southwest Indian Painting.* Tucson: University of Arizona Press.

TANNER, CLARA LEE, 1968, *Southwest Indian Craft Arts.* Tucson: University of Arizona Press.

THOMAS, A. B., 1932, *Forgotten Frontiers: A Study of the Spanish Indian Policy of Don Juan Bautista de Anza Governor of New Mexico, 1777–1787.* Norman, Okla.

THOMPSON, LAURA, and ALICE JOSEPH, 1944, *The Hopi Way.* Haskell Institute, N. S. Indian Service. Laurever, Kan.

TITIEV, MISCHA, 1944, *Old Oraibi, A Study of the Hopi Indians of the Third Mesa.* Cambridge, Mass.: Papers of the Peabody Museum of American Archaeology and Ethnology, Vol. 32, No. 1.

TRAGER, GEORGE L., 1942, *The Comparative Phonology of the Tiwa Languages.* Studies in Linguistics 1:1–10.

TRAGER, GEORGE L., 1943, *Kinship and Status Terms of the Tiwa Language.* American Anthropologist 45:557–571.

TRAGER, GEORGE L., 1944, *Spanish and English Loanwords in Taos.* International Journal of American Linguistics 10:144–158.

TRAGER, GEORGE L., and EDITH CROWELL TRAGER, 1959, *Kiowa and Tanoan.* American Anthropologist 61:1078–1083.

TRAGER, GEORGE L., 1962, *Annotated Glossary of Isleta Terms.* In Esther Goldfrank, ed.: Isleta Paintings, pp. 295–298. Washington, D. C.: Smithsonian Institution, Bureau of American Linguistics 10:144–158.

TRAGER, GEORGE L., 1967, *The Tanoan Settlement of the Rio-Grande Area: A Possible Chronology.* In D. H. Hymes, ed.: Studies in Southwestern Ethnolinguistics, pp. 335–350. The Hague, Paris: Mouton and Company.

TWITCHELL, RALPH E., 1909, *History of the Military Occupation of the Territory of New Mexico from 1846 to 1851.* Denver: Smith-Brooks Co.

TWITCHELL, RALPH E., 1914, *The Spanish Archives of New Mexico,* 2 Vols. Cedar Rapids, Mich.

TWITCHELL, RALPH E., 1963, *Old Santa Fe.* Chicago: The Rio Grande Press, Inc.

UNITED STATES, United States vs. Joseph, 94 U. S. 619; United States vs. Sandoval, 231 U. S. 28; Trujillo vs. Garley, D. Ct., New Mexico, 1948.

UNITED STATES DEPARTMENT OF AGRICULTURE, SOIL CONSERVATION SERVICE, 1939, *Tewa Basin Study: The Spanish American Villages, Vol. II.* Albuquerque, N.M.: Economic Surveys Division.

UNITED STATES, RAUP, RUTH M., 1959, *The Indian Health Program from 1800–1955.* U. S. Department of Health, Education, and Welfare: Public Health Service.

UNITED STATES DEPARTMENT OF THE INTERIOR, 1894, *Moqui Pueblos of Arizona and*

Pueblos of New Mexico. Washington, D. C.: Report on Indians Taxed and Not Taxed in the United States at the Eleventh Census, 1890.

VICTOR, FRANCES E., 1871, *The River of the West: Life and Adventure in the Rocky Mountains and Oregon.* Hartford, Conn.

VOEGELIN, CARL F., and FLORENCE M. VOEGELIN, 1957, *Hopi Domains: A Lexical Approach to the Problem of Selection.* Indiana University Publications in Anthropology and Linguistics, No. 14.

VOGT, E. Z., 1955, *A Study of the Southwestern Fiesta System as Exemplified by the Laguna Fiesta.* American Anthropologist 57:820–839.

WALLACE, ANTHONY F. C., 1956, *Revitalization Movements.* American Anthropologist 58:264–281.

WENDORF, FRED, 1954, *A Reconstruction of Northern Rio Grande Prehistory.* American Anthropologist 56:200–227.

WENDORF, FRED, and ERIK REED, 1955, *An Alternative Reconstruction of Northern Rio Grande Prehistory.* El Palacio 62:131–173.

WETHERINGTON, RONALD, 1968, *Excavations at Pot Creek Pueblo at Fort Burgwin Research Center.* Taos, N.M.: Fort Burgwin Research Publication No. 6.

WHITE, L. A., 1932, *The Acoma Indians.* Washington, D. C.: Smithsonian Institution, Forty Seventh Annual Report for 1929–1930: Bureau of American Ethnology, pp. 17–192.

WHITE, L. A., 1932, *The Pueblo of San Felipe.* Menasha, Wisc.: Memoirs of the American Anthropological Association, No. 38.

WHITE, L. A., 1935, *The Pueblo of Santo Domingo, New Mexico.* Menasha, Wisc.: Memoirs of the American Anthropological Association, No. 43.

WHITE, L. A., 1942, *The Pueblo of Santa Ana, New Mexico.* Menasha, Wisc.: Memoirs of the American Anthropological Association, No. 60.

WHITE, L. A., 1962, *The Pueblo of Sia, New Mexico.* Washington, D. C.: Smithsonian Institution, Bureau of American Ethnology Bulletin 184.

WHITE, L. A., 1964, *The World of the Keresan Pueblo Indians.* In Stanley Diamond, ed.: Primitive Views of the World. New York: Columbia University Press.

WHITMAN, WILLIAM, 1940, *The San Ildefonso of New Mexico.* In Ralph Linton, ed.: Acculturation in Seven American Indian Tribes, pp. 390–460. New York: Appleton-Century-Crofts.

WHITMAN, WILLIAM, 1947, *The Pueblo Indians of San Ildefonso; A Changing Culture.* New York: Columbia University Press.

WHORF, B. L., 1946, *The Hopi Language, Toreva Dialect.* In Harry Hoijer, *et al.*, eds.: Linguistic Structure of Native America, pp. 158–183. New York: Viking Fund Publications in Anthropology, No. 6.

WHORF, B. L., and G. L. TRAGER, 1937, *The Relationship of Uto-Aztecan and Tanoan.* American Anthropologist 39:609–624.

WILLEY, GORDON R., 1966, *An Introduction to America Archaeology, Vol. 1: North and Middle America.* Englewood Cliffs, N. J.: Prentice Hall, Inc.

WINSHIP, G. P., 1896, *The Coronado Expedition, 1540–1542: Fourteenth Annual Report.* Washington, D. C.: Smithsonian Institution, Bureau of American Ethnology.

WISSLER, CLARK, 1917, *The American Indian.* New York: Oxford University Press.

WITTFOGEL, K. A., 1957, *Oriental Despotism: A Comparative Study of Total Power.* New Haven, Conn.

WITTFOGEL, K. A., and E. S. GOLDFRANK, 1943, *Some Aspects of Pueblo Mythology and Society.* Journal of American Folklore 56:17–30.

WOODBURY, RICHARD B., 1961, *Climatic Changes and Prehistoric Agriculture in the Southwestern United States.* Annals of the New York Academy of Sciences, Article 1. 95:705–709.

WOODWARD, DOROTHY, 1935, *The Penitentes of New Mexico.* Doctoral Dissertation, Yale University.

YEGERLEHNER, JOHN, 1959, *Arizona Tewa I and II.* International Journal of American Linguistics 25:1–7, 75–80.

Orthographic Note and Bibliography

Transcriptions of native terms are approximated by the use of English sound symbols. For technical studies of the various Pueblo languages see the following and other studies of the scholars listed:

Hopi

WHORF, B. L., 1946, *The Hopi Language, Toreva Dialect*. In Harry Hoijer *et al.*, eds.: Linguistic Structure of Native America, pp. 158–83. New York: Viking Fund Publications in Anthropology No. 6.

VOEGELIN, CARL F., and FLORENCE M. VOEGELIN, 1957, *Hopi Domains: A Lexical Approach to the Problem of Selection*. Indiana University Publications in Anthropology and Linguistics No. 14.

Hano

YEGERLEHNER, JOHN, 1959, *Arizona Tewa I and II*. International Journal of American Linguistics 25:1–7, 75–80.

Zuni

NEWMAN, STANLEY S., 1954b, *A Practical Zuñi Orthography*. In Watson Smith, and John M. Roberts, eds.: Zuñi Law: A Field of Values, pp. 163–170. Papers of the Peabody Museum of American Archaeology and Ethnology, Harvard University, Vol. 43, No. 1.

———, 1958, *Zuñi Dictionary*. Bloomington, Ind.: Publications of the Research Center in Anthropology, Folklore and Linguistics, No. 6, Part 2.

Keresan

DAVIS, IRVINE, 1963, *Bibliography of Keresan Linguistic Sources*. International Journal of American Linguistics 29:289–93.

———, 1964, *The Language of Santa Ana Pueblo*. Washington, D. C.: Smithsonian Institution, Bureau of American Ethnology, Bull. 191. Anthropological Papers, No. 69.

MILLER, WICK R., 1959–60, *Spanish Loanwords in Acoma: I, II*. International Journal of American Linguistics 25:147–53; 26:41–49.

Jemez

HALE, KENNETH, 1958, *Internal Diversity in Uto-Aztecan: I*. International Journal of American Linguistics 24:101–7.

———, *Jemez and Kiowa Correspondences in reference to Kiowa-Tanoan*. International Journal of American Linguistics 28:1–5.

Tewa

HARRINGTON, JOHN P., 1910b., *A Brief Description of the Tewa Language*. American Anthropologist 12:497–504.

HOIJER, HARRY, and EDWARD P. DOZIER, 1949, *The Phonemes of Tewa, Santa Clara Dialect*. International Journal of American Linguistics 15:139–144.

Tiwa

TRAGER, GEORGE L., 1942, *The Comparative Phonology of the Tiwa Languages*. Studies in Linguistics 1:1–10.

———, 1946, *An Outline of Taos Grammar*. In Harry Hoijer, *et al.*, eds.: Linguistic Structure of Native America, pp. 184–221. New York: Viking Fund Publications in Anthrolopogy, No. 6.

———, 1962, *Annotated Glossary of Isleta Terms*. In Esther Goldfrank, ed.: Isleta Paintings, pp. 295–98. Washington, D. C.: Smithsonian Institution, Bureau of American Ethnology, Bull. 181.

Recommended Reading

BAHTI, TOM, 1968, *Southwestern Indian Tribes*. Flagstaff Ariz.: KC Publications.
A brief but excellent survey of all Southwestern Indian tribes including all the Pueblos. Superb color photographs of Pueblo villages and Pueblo arts and crafts.

BUNZEL, RUTH L., 1932, *Introduction to Zuni Ceremonialism*. Bureau of American Ethnology Annual Report No. 47.
A description and brilliant analysis of Zuni ceremonial life.

DOZIER, EDWARD P., 1966, *Hano, A Tewa Indian Community in Arizona*. New York: Holt, Rinehart and Winston.
An account of the total lifeway of a single Tewa speaking community in Arizona.

EGGAN, FRED, 1950, *Social Organization of the Western Pueblos*. Chicago: University of Chicago Press.
A penerating and illuminating analysis of the social organization of Hopi, Hano, Zuni, Acoma, and Laguna. Eggan also provides a comparative survey of the Eastern or Rio Grande Pueblos.

LANGE, CHARLES, 1958, *Cochiti: A New Mexico Pueblo Past and Present*. Austin, Tex.: University of Texas Press.
An exemplary study of a Rio Grande Keresan Pueblo in the context of its past and present.

LEIGHTON, DOROTHEA C., and JOHN ADAIR, 1966, *People of the Middle Place: A Study of the Zuni Indians*.
A succinct presentation of the results of psychological tests on Zuni children and a brief, but good account of Zuni social and ceremonial organization. The book is one of the series of tribal monographs reporting on the project on Indian Education, Personality, and Administration undertaken jointly by the University of Chicago and the U. S. Office of Indian Affairs.

PARSONS, E. C., 1939, *Pueblo Indian Religion*. Chicago: University of Chicago Press.
An encyclopedic two-volume work covering all aspects of Pueblo Indian religion, social organization, and the changes brought about by contacts with other people and cultures.

THOMPSON, LAURA, and ALICE JOSEPH, 1944, *The Hopi Way*. Chicago: University of Chicago Press.
A summary of the results of psychological tests on Hopi children made by a research team. Excellent synthesis and analysis and a superb account of Hopi socialization techniques, and Hopi social and ceremonial organization. This book like the one by Leighton and Adair on Zuni (above) reports on the project on Indian Education, Personality and Administration sponsored by the University of Chicago and the U. S. Office of Indian Affairs.

TITIEV, MISCHA, 1944, *Old Oraibi: A Study of the Hopi Indians of Third Mesa*. Cambridge, Mass.: Papers of the Peabody Museum of American Archaeology and Ethnology, Vol. 22, pp. 1–277.
A study of the social and ceremonial organization of the Hopi Indians of Third Mesa and an excellent analysis of the disintegration of "Old Oraibi" over factional disputes.